CHINESE AMERICAN MOTHERING

Chinese American Mothering

Toy Len Goon's Legacy and the Myth of the Model Minority

Andrea Louie

NEW YORK UNIVERSITY PRESS
New York

NEW YORK UNIVERSITY PRESS
New York
www.nyupress.org

Please contact the Library of Congress for Cataloging-in-Publication data.

ISBN: 9781479859900 (hardback)
ISBN: 9781479855568 (paperback)
ISBN: 9781479848225 (library ebook)
ISBN: 9781479857753 (consumer ebook)

This book is printed on acid-free paper, and its binding materials are chosen for strength and durability. We strive to use environmentally responsible suppliers and materials to the greatest extent possible in publishing our books.

The manufacturer's authorized representative in the EU for product safety is Mare Nostrum Group B.V., Mauritskade 21D, 1091 GC Amsterdam, The Netherlands.
Email: gpsr@mare-nostrum.co.uk.

Manufactured in the United States of America

10 9 8 7 6 5 4 3 2 1

Also available as an ebook

For my grandmother, Toy Len Goon, and all those who are part of her legacy

CONTENTS

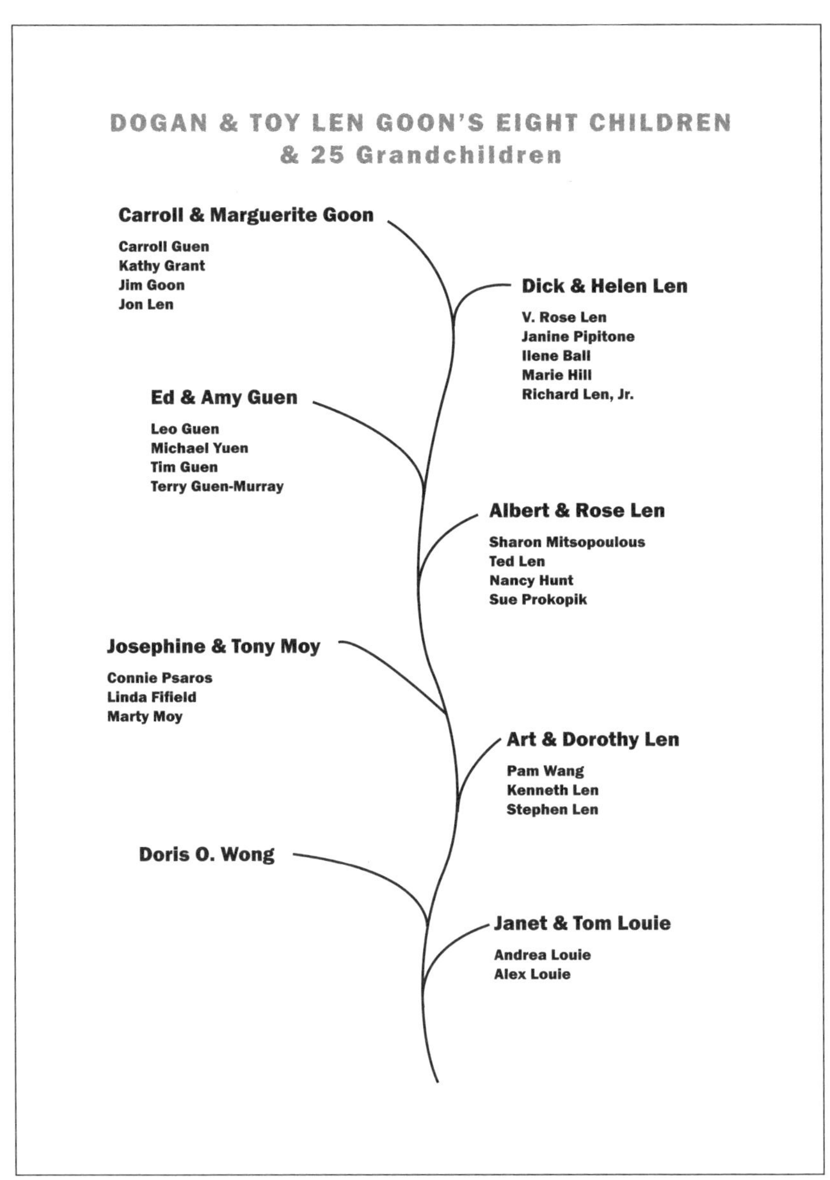

Figure 1.1. Family tree of Dogan and Toy Len Goon, their eight children and spouses, and their twenty-five grandchildren. Created by Terry Guen in Adobe InDesign.

Introduction

An Ethnography of the Model Minority Myth

Grainy black-and-white images of a newsreel showing Toy Len Goon, a fifty-seven-year-old Chinese American woman, hair in a bun, working in her laundry and talking with her children, are accompanied by an announcer's dramatic voiceover:

> A Chinese laundry in Portland Maine, and that magical universal word "mother."
>
> Mrs. Toy Len Goon, a widow, Chinese-born, carrying on in her husband's place bringing up eight children to be fine American citizens. . . .
>
> Her eldest is a doctor, one son is in the Navy, another is an MIT graduate, still another is studying law. . . .
>
> All were encouraged to go to college. . . .
>
> Today she is honored by the National Golden Rule Foundation as American Mother for 1952. . . .
>
> With daughters Doris and Janet, she modestly takes her place in the limelight, giving her eight children all the credit for her success.[1]

In May 1952, a modest widow in Portland, Maine, temporarily closed her hand laundry and boarded a train with her two youngest daughters to travel to Washington, DC, to meet First Lady Bess Truman. It was one of the few times her daughters had seen her without the work apron she always wore over her housedresses. She was dressed in a new outfit she had picked out and purchased with the help of Clara Soule, the Americanization teacher who had nominated her for the Mother of the Year award and who accompanied them on their trip. Indeed, it was one of the few times the family had traveled out of state. Between running the laundry and running the household, Toy Len Goon was rarely able to take time off, especially after her husband, Dogan, had his leg amputated due to gangrene and was later hospitalized due to blood pressure and cardiac issues; he passed away when the youngest was only six.

Her selection as Mother of the Year became the subject of national and international media coverage, and she received commendations at local, national, and international levels. It also became the subject of family lore and a central part of family identity for her children and their descendants, including myself as one of her granddaughters. To many, Toy Len Goon exemplifies the American Dream. A poor girl from rural China emigrates to the United States as a young woman to join her husband, Dogan. As the story was told in the media, under her guidance, her hardworking children became successful professionals—a doctor, lawyer, chemist, businessman, engineer, and office manager. As her children reflected on their upbringings during interviews I conducted for this book, they emphasized how she had refused Mother's Aid, a federal aid program for widows with dependent children, which she believed would have provided temporary financial support at the expense of keeping the family together and retaining ownership of her home.

Toy Len Goon was honored as US Mother of the Year by various communities. Local merchants and associations in Portland showered her with awards and commendations; parades were thrown in her honor in Boston and New York Chinatowns; she was hosted at the White House and introduced to Congress; and she met with the Taiwanese ambassador to the United States. However, she and her children were unaware that the latter event had been orchestrated by Representative Robert Hale of Maine in a strategic move to bring attention to the possibilities for the success of Chinese families in the United States at a time when the nation's democratic values were being called into question. They were also unaware of how her story would become significant in the context of the United States' Cold War relations with both mainland China and Taiwan in ways that invoked her identities as a woman, a mother, an American, and a Chinese immigrant. Perhaps most significantly, she was highlighted as a woman who had risen out of poverty and had produced successful Americanized children due to opportunities provided by US democracy. The narratives invoked in the context of Cold War diplomacy took advantage of the powerful symbolism of her story to communicate messages about Chinese American women and families as the center of a new form of domesticity in the United States, characterized by upward mobility and assimilation in the context of US meritocracy.[2]

Drawing upon immigration records, interviews, and secondary sources, this book tells an expanded version of Toy Len Goon's life story, focusing on the multiple ways it has been told. It traces the larger historical contexts that frame her migration to the United States, her selection as Mother of the Year, and the role that her story had in bolstering the model minority myth. It also examines what her life history and the memory-making around it represent for both her descendants and public memory. It addresses themes of migration, gender, racialization, Americanization, and "success" through the evolving lens of the model minority myth, as situated in and around a Chinese American institution—a family-run hand laundry.

In the remainder of this introduction, I provide an overview of my research and discuss its theoretical contributions. I then delve further into the methodologies and how they are intertwined with my positionality not only as one of Toy Len Goon's grandchildren, but also as an anthropologist researching a story steeped in multiple histories and memories about my own family. I end with a brief discussion of the historical context for this story, including the rise of the model minority myth during the Cold War.

Overview of Research

The book begins with a discussion of Dogan Goon's migration story in the context of Chinese Exclusion and the bureaucracy he navigated to bring over Toy Len Goon as his wife. I continue with an overview of Toy Len Goon's childhood in China and her migration story as told from her perspective, a period that overlaps with Dogan's migration, and then discuss their marriage and the formation of their family in the United States, ending with Dogan's death in 1941. I then focus on the transnational connections to their home communities in China that Dogan and Toy Len maintained despite the Cold War, which cut them off from their homeland. Using a spatial analysis of the Chinese laundry as a metaphor for their relationship to the broader community, I discuss the division of labor within the laundry based on gender and age, and how the mixed use of space within the laundry reflected the relationships between the Goon family and the broader Chinese and non-Chinese communities in Portland, Maine, and beyond. I then examine Toy Len Goon's Mother of the Year award and the Cold War context of the 1950s that shaped her selection, focusing on media coverage and the various ways that her story was told in the media, in exhibits, in popular writing, and by herself and her descendants. As an anthropologist and as one of Toy Len Goon's grandchildren, I put multiple renderings of Toy Len Goon's story into dialogue and reshape them into a more fully fleshed-out version, replacing flattened-out renditions presented in the media and propaganda. My hope is to add nuance and complexity to uncritical, decontextualized, and sentimentalized versions of her story. By situating her story in the broader historical and political context of exclusion and marginalization of Chinese Americans, while also highlighting how she was able to persevere within those constraints, I aim to do fuller justice to her life and accomplishments. I consider how ideas about assimilation and integration that her children and grandchildren grew up with in the context of the Cold War United States affected their understanding of their family story. In this sense, this book is an ethnography of a particular symbolic moment, contextualized within its broader cultural and historical interpretations, as well as the multiple legacies of that moment.

Thus, while this story is about my family, it is also about so much more. Toy Len Goon's achievements were extraordinary, and her story continues to impact later generations. But it is not a singular narrative. It has been told in many ways—by academics, the media, and politicians, but also by her children and grandchildren. Toy Len Goon herself narrated her life story in different ways, at different times, to different people. The central, public narrative—one of Americanization, assimilation, being rewarded for good behavior and hard work—is certainly compelling.

In providing an ethnographic account of the construction of the model minority myth as exemplified by her selection as Mother of the Year, I trace the social repercussions of the event through an anthropological lens that brings into conversation the multiple narratives surrounding her story and its insertion into the public imagination. I examine the work these narratives perform as they are reimagined by both the family and the broader public through the lenses of current ideas of Chinese American exceptionalism and of continued discrimination and xenophobia. I focus on how her family continues to engage with the concept of the model minority as ideas regarding the racial positioning of Asian Americans and cultural citizenship shift, examining immigration, upward mobility, and welfare as central themes.

Media coverage portrayed Toy Len Goon as a symbol of the integration of patriotic, compliant, and successful Chinese Americans into US society—a model minority. But her story complicates narratives of assimilation, Americanization, and Chinese American belonging in the nation. The public discourses surrounding her story flatten out the complex relationships she had with both her Chinese homeland and the United States, and do not capture the multiple new relationships that she and her family forged as they situated themselves in Woodfords Corner as one of the few Chinese families in Portland, Maine. In addition, they render the nuances of her and her children's stories invisible in the shadow of the rags to riches story portrayed in the media. My analysis elucidates these alternative perspectives and places them in dialogue with these other narratives to illustrate how histories are not static archives of the past but are reinterpreted by later generations through new lenses. Toy Len Goon's story provides an opportunity to analyze changing ideas of race, gender, and belonging that emerged with the rise of the model minority myth during the Cold War from the perspective of a family whose story was used to buttress this myth.

The retelling of Toy Len Goon's story also highlights the shifting dynamics between state discourses, policies, and propaganda regarding ideas of citizenship, Americanness, and belonging, and how they are understood by later generations. From the Cold War origins of her story, which was spread nationally and internationally by the media and politicians, to the early 2020s, when I conducted my interviews, the model minority myth continues to be intertwined with attitudes regarding "good" and "bad" immigrants, the United States' relationship to the People's Republic of China, and the shifting racial positioning of Chinese Americans. The regime of immigration regulation that made the question of Dogan Goon's legality in the United States the subject of state scrutiny is a clear precursor to the systems of immigrant surveillance and regulation used today. Yet Toy Len Goon's descendants interpret the family legacy and its implications for contemporary issues of immigration, work, and upward mobility in varying ways.

Celebrations of Toy Len Goon's story often focus on the opportunities she had by virtue of her migration to the United States—a rags to riches story. They highlight her resourcefulness and work ethic, giving her well-deserved credit for her ability to overcome hardships and for the successes of her children. However, while it is important to recognize that migrants do exercise agency as they navigate life in new lands, it is essential to consider the role of the state, in addition to economic, environmental, and social factors, in shaping migrants' life possibilities.

By the state, I refer not only to the previously discussed Cold War politics between the Chinese and US governments that would eventually motivate the US media and politicians to characterize the Goon family as "good minorities," but also to how US state policies and procedures regulated Chinese migrants as citizens or alien citizens, determining who could enter and stay in the United States in the first place. Thus, while official state-sponsored celebrations were held in Washington, DC, following Toy Len Goon's selection as Mother of the Year, it is important not to forget that in enacting Exclusion, the state had devoted vast resources for creating and enforcing many of the barriers that her selection as US Mother of the Year implicitly celebrated her as having overcome. These include anti-Chinese racism and discrimination, and the legislation that reflected these ideas and created the conditions of economic and occupational marginalization experienced by Chinese migrants.

Theoretical Contributions

In this book I make four key but integrated theoretical contributions. The first is to the literature on the model minority myth, from its Cold War origins focusing on the exceptionalism, upward mobility, and good behavior of Chinese American and Japanese Americans, to the more recent focus on hyper-educated students, primarily from post-1965 immigrant families, who aim to attend elite educational institutions.[3] I discuss how generation, socioeconomic background, and the historical context of one's family's migration to the United States can shape varied engagement with the model minority myth, even for Asian Americans who grew up during the same period. In showing how the myth has changed over time, I touch upon how the racial positioning of Chinese Americans has shifted over generations in relation to whites and non-whites, including other Asian American groups.

The second is the focus on Toy Len Goon's telling of her own story as a female emigrant from a modest background, highlighting her mother's role in her pre-migration life, to center women's perspectives and agency in the context of transnational migration from China. This body of work has most often focused on male sojourners. Using a transnational framework for understanding her continued connections to China and the Chinese American community not only builds on the rich historical literature on transnational migration from China, but also disrupts the narratives of assimilation and Americanization that were central to renderings of her story in the media.

The third is methodological, looking at a particular intersection of anthropological and historical analysis through the lens of narrative, history, and memory. In other words, while the historical facts surrounding Dogan and Toy Len Goon's immigration are important, so are the ways that they and their descendants talk about their family's immigration history and experiences in the United States. In examining documents and narratives that reflect multiple perspectives on Toy Len Goon and her legacy, I reconsider ideas of legitimacy and bias in both written and oral sources, and how placing these sources in dialogue with one another can produce alternative narratives.

The fourth is in grounding this work in the Chinese laundry as a Chinese immigrant institution, which also serves as a metaphor in the book for understanding spatial flows, gender, and power. My spatial analysis of the Goon laundry, which brings in concepts from cultural anthropology and geography to expand on Henry Yu's discussion of Paul Siu's classic ethnography *The Chinese Laundryman* provides a framework within which to understand the Goon family's economic and social positioning, and ideas of difference and assimilation, in relation to the predominantly white community in which they lived and worked.[4] Thinking about space also provides insight into the gendered work responsibilities within the family, how the spatial layout of the building in which they both lived and worked reflected these relationships, and how Toy Len Goon's roles intersected across these spaces, which obfuscated her non-domestic work in the eyes of the public. These perspectives are deeply informed by my positionality.

Positionality and Methodologies

I had been thinking about writing about my grandmother for quite some time, but initially worried about how others would perceive the legitimacy of exploring a family story as an academic project. How could I tell her life story in a way that both employs my training as an anthropologist and is enhanced by my access to insights on her story as a family member? How could I employ my own positionality as someone so close to the story, who feels accountable to both my academic peers and family members invested in telling the story in particular ways, to create a robust multivocal portrayal of my grandmother?

My anthropological training enables me to situate discourses within the contexts in which they are produced, to examine how they shift, how people interpret and act upon them, and to bring sometimes disparate perspectives into dialogue, while also remaining vigilant regarding issues of bias and positionality. Ethnographic methods involve gathering multiple sources and perspectives to create an in-depth, nuanced, and comprehensive picture of an ethnographic site or moment, while ethnographic analysis and writing employ multivocal perspectives and thick description to analyze data and present a thorough and contextualized overview to readers.[5] Cultural anthropologists routinely, but also with great thought and care, include their own voices in the scholarship they create, in recognition that all knowledge is situated in specific experiences, perspectives, and power relations, and that the reader should be made aware of these positions. Thus, rather than trying to remain "unbiased," I employ my multiple subjectivities to provide context for how people's views may have been shaped.

As such, what at first glance appears to be the story of one individual and her family enables the exploration of much more complex issues. As Tiya Miles notes in her history of a Cherokee chief and his marriage to his African descendant slave, "The family can thus be read as a barometer for the society, tracing and reflecting the atmospherics of social life and social change."[6] The idea of a female-headed, assimilated Chinese American family was appealing to the US public and strategically useful to policy makers at the time. But while this book may in many ways seem like a microhistory or biography of Toy Len Goon, I approach it from an anthropological perspective and situate it within a broader historical and familial context that makes it relevant to a set of larger issues and questions.

Throughout my research, I have realized that despite sharing a similar grand narrative regarding Toy Len Goon's hard work, sacrifices, and accomplishments, each of her children and grandchildren related to her somewhat differently based on birth order, gender, and other factors that shaped how they engaged with her on a day-to-day basis and throughout their life course. Many of their recollections were framed within political and social values that they held regarding self-reliance and their perceptions of family values. These ideas could be interpreted in various ways, but often included rhetoric about pulling oneself up by one's bootstraps, and the role of Chinese cultural and familial values in achieving success, which resonated with ideas about Chinese Americans as model minorities. Their varying recollections illustrate how historical events and associated memories can be created and recalled in ways that allow for the perception of shared memories and for variability in the content of those memories, as well as the significance assigned to them. In expanding beyond the version of Toy Len Goon's story that I grew up with, I do not erase the original narrative that I share with my cousins, aunts, and uncles. Rather, the alternative readings that I will build on, around, and through it reinvigorate the story, provide openings for further dialogue about her life, and facilitate the exploration of different interpretations and perspectives.

As Tiya Miles asserts, "Historical scholarship is not simply the objective collection and presentation of facts."[7] In writing a history of a Cherokee slave master husband and the slave who became his wife, she had to grapple with the multiple contexts and perspectives that shaped both sides of the narrative, as well as with her own positionality as a Black woman descended from enslaved people. She concludes, "To capture the multiplicity and contradictory nature of this past, I would have to tell at least two stories—sketch two histories, enter two worlds, enlist two purposes . . . at once."[8]

Her assertion that "historical narratives are shaped, not found" helps set the stage for my telling of Toy Len Goon's story in a fashion that juxtaposes multiple perspectives—of media and politicians in the context of the Cold War, of her children and grandchildren, and of folk and academic historians.[9] While I do not equally privilege these various perspectives—keeping in mind the methods and rigor that go into producing academic histories, and understanding that the stories told by her descendants are filtered through memories and do not necessarily aim for rigor—I believe that it is important to acknowledge that they each represent historical narrative forms, each with their own biases and purposes, and each informed by their own process of knowledge production.

Indeed, my positionality has enabled me to write her story in a way that nobody else can, giving me access to multiple sources that I bring together and analyze through an anthropological lens. I consider how histories are written and rewritten, how memories are created and acted upon, and how these processes play into the construction of narratives of family and identity in the global context of Chinese migrations, an approach I used in my previous monographs.[10]

As the project evolved, I grappled with what its scope would be, what sources I would use, and how I would incorporate both traditional and nontraditional, academic and non-academic sources and perspectives. I have concluded that the multiple subjectivities I occupy are not in conflict with one another, and in fact that occupying them enhances the integrity of the scholarship. In addition to secondary academic sources, I use traditional primary sources such as immigration documents as well as family memory books and interviews with family members. I also draw heavily on two multivocal and multilayered sources created within the family that I discuss further in the following sections. One is an interview I conducted with my grandmother in 1992, when I was in my mid-twenties and she was one hundred years old. The second is the detailed unpublished biography of my grandmother that my aunt Amy Guen wrote based on the notes she took at my grandmother's request during multiple conversations over many years after she entrusted her with telling her life story.

Interview with Toy Len Goon

In 1992 I participated in a roots searching program in which participants learned about Chinese immigration history from the Pearl River Delta in preparation for conducting family histories and visiting our ancestral villages.[11] I had chosen to visit my paternal ancestral village, but was inspired to also interview Toy Len Goon, my maternal grandmother.[12] On June 16, 1992, with the help of my mother and her sister Doris, both of whom spoke my grandmother's dialect of Toisanese (Hoisanwa), and a portable cassette recorder, I asked my grandmother questions about her youth, her migration to the United States, her marriage to my grandfather, her work in the laundry, and becoming Mother of the Year. Her mind was still sharp at the age of one hundred, as she recollected the details of her past in a combination of Toisanese and English in a manner that illustrated her charismatic personality and wit. She passed away the following spring, in May 1993. It wasn't until nearly ten years later, in 2003, that I fully realized the significance of having recorded her discussing her experiences in her own words. At a family reunion held in Portland, Maine, at the Maine Historical Society, I did a PowerPoint presentation detailing her life story, placing it within the broader historical context of Chinese emigration and Exclusion.[13] I ended the presentation with a sound clip from the interview, not fully realizing the power of hearing her voice ten years after her death. Despite the poor quality of the digital audio transferred from a cassette tape and the technical glitch that delayed its play, nearly everyone in the room who remembered her began to tear up upon hearing the sound of her voice.

While the interview might be seen as her telling her story in her own voice, it is important to consider that her narrative was mediated. My mother and aunt, who were translating, served as one filter, as they did not translate everything she said and inserted their own comments and reactions. After having the interview recording translated by Genevieve Leung, a linguist specializing in the dialect my grandmother spoke, I was able to think about the interview as a dynamic, nuanced text with multiple possible readings.[14] Genevieve used her expertise to point out instances where my grandmother asserted her agency and to reveal what was said during the parts that my mother and aunt did not translate.

Amy Guen's Biography of Toy Len Goon

Amy Chin Guen was an invaluable resource for this project. I spent many hours with her, conducting numerous interviews and discussing the extensive materials she would produce from her living room "archive." The wife of Toy Len Goon's third son, Edward, Amy wrote a comprehensive biography from the notes she had taken over the years based on conversations she had with Toy Len Goon. This biography has gone through various iterations, awaiting further edits and the addition of more details about Dogan Goon's life per Edward, who felt that his father should be featured more positively and prominently in the story, before it could be shared more broadly. Edward passed away in 2011, but I use the biography with Amy's permission. The most recent version, from 2019, includes a table of contents and Chinese characters for all proper names, which Amy added to the word-processed version with the help of her son Leo. Their aim was to standardize the names by using the original Chinese characters so that later generations would be able to reference them. I draw on Amy Guen's biography, putting it in dialogue with interviews with her and the surviving Goon siblings, archival research, media coverage, and secondary sources.

Amy had not planned to become Toy Len Goon's unofficial biographer. She had a special connection with Toy Len, speculating that this was because they spoke the same village dialect of Toisanese (Hoisanwa [H]).[15] She was part of the family, yet not one of Toy Len's own children, which possibly made Toy Len more willing to share details of her life that she might not have revealed to her own children. Amy and her sisters Helen and Rose (née Chin) had married three of the Goon brothers (Edward, Richard, and Albert, respectively). Though they had been born in Boston Chinatown, they had been sent back to their ancestral village in Toisan to live with their father's first wife after their mother died in childbirth and their father later passed away. As Amy writes in her biography of Toy Len Goon, after Amy and her siblings and some of the Goon brothers traveled to China in 1984, Toy Len viewed the slides that Carroll, her oldest son, had taken of the Hong How (Hong Hau) village, which seemed to spur memories of her younger years. She then asked Amy to begin writing down her recollections of her childhood. Prior to that time, Toy Len Goon did not believe her experiences in China to be of particular significance, but seeing the slides made her want to tell the story of her upbringing, focusing on how her mother had managed to create opportunities for her and her siblings as they were being brought up without resources.[16] Amy writes, "From then on whenever she felt she had a wave of thoughts, she could be annoyed that I could not find a piece of paper and a pen immediately, lest she lose her train of thought. I ended up with many scraps of incoherent pieces of valuable information which I made attempts to unscramble, and pieced the abbreviated phrases and sentences together."[17] Amy surmised that had Toy Len Goon still been alive, she would have wondered why Amy had taken until 2006 to finally write up her notes to produce her biography.[18]

Amy possesses a seemingly infallible memory. In 2018, at the age of ninety-five, when I first interviewed her about Toy Len Goon, she was able to recall in detail many of the conversations she had with her over the years, as well as the details gleaned from archival research that she and Edward had done, and from her own interactions with Toy Len Goon.[19] The biography is thorough and methodical, including a prologue and acknowledgments, and a note on the spelling and pronunciation of Chinese names. A social worker by profession, in chronicling Toy Len Goon's history, Amy viewed herself as a historian and was very concerned about getting the facts right without inserting her own opinion. She had the Chinese-language version of the biography fact-checked by her sister Rose. Helen had classmates in China who had married into the Goon village, and she asked them to corroborate what Toy Len Goon had shared. Toy Len would sometimes revise or correct what she had told Amy, often asking Amy's sisters Helen or Rose to write down the corrected information and pass it on to Amy.[20]

I used Amy Guen's carefully crafted biography not only as a valuable research source, but also as one of the narratives that I bring into conversation in this book. Given her relationship to Toy Len Goon as a confidante with whom she could speak fluently in her native dialect and who could relate to village life in the region where they both grew up, her rendering of Toy Len Goon's life story in the book and in her interviews with me adds a depth of descriptive detail and a perspective that perhaps no one else could provide. Amy's ability to remember details of her interactions with Toy Len Goon and her keen eye for observation, combined with her understanding of Toy Len's pre-migration context, adds an essential continuity and context to Toy Len's story. Though filtered through her own memories and narration, her perspective helps to create a counterpoint to one-dimensional media accounts of Toy Len Goon's selection as Mother of the Year. After all, as histories are narrated, they become curated versions of the past that are reinterpreted in new contexts and with new lenses.

Interviews with Other Family Members

To investigate the legacy of Toy Len Goon's award for her descendants, I conducted interviews with my aunts, uncles, and cousins. Like me, my cousins had grown up knowing of her award and its legacy, but not necessarily understanding the full picture. While my original idea had been to travel to the Boston area to conduct interviews with cousins there, my plans were thwarted by the COVID-19 pandemic, which led to a shutdown of the United States in March 2020.[21] So, in the spring of 2021, I turned to Zoom, FaceTime, and my phone to conduct these interviews. Because some are retired and others were working from home due to the pandemic, it was easier for me to schedule interviews with them. I did not have the challenge that most interviewers have of establishing rapport, though I had not seen many in years or interacted with them in a substantial way as an adult, particularly since I am one of the youngest cousins. Perhaps because we had not talked in so long, or because of the social isolation caused by the pandemic, or most likely because they had so much to say about Toy Len Goon, some of my interviews lasted four hours. I also spoke to a couple of my cousins' children who reached out to me after hearing about my research.[22]

The interviews covered several topics, including their memories of our grandmother, what her being selected as Mother of the Year meant to them, how they viewed our grandmother's legacy and its effect on their own identities as individuals and parents, the significance of family food and traditions, and the impact of anti-Asian hate. I also asked them whether they had heard of the model minority idea, and when possible shared common critiques leveled by scholars in Asian American studies. These include how the idea homogenizes Asian Americans as a group, how it attributes "Asian" success to shared cultural or religious values that do not cut across this diverse group, how the myth's focus on the exceptionalism of Asian Americans allows them to be used as a racial wedge between whites and Black/Latinx people, who are subsequently deemed less successful in comparison, and how the myth puts pressure on Asian Americans to be successful along these narrow definitions.

Interviewing my cousins created an iterative process as I shared information from my research with them during the interviews. I came to recognize that though they believe that they share the same set of memories of their interactions with our grandmother, they each hold pieces of knowledge and fragments of memory based on their specific interactions with her. They created new narratives by "recovering" and piecing together memories, artifacts, and stories. Their understanding of family history shifted over time as they formed their own families and reflected on both their parents' and the next generation's success. Though many felt that they were distanced from knowledge about family history and Chinese traditions, they found other ways to connect to their heritage—for example, through cooking her recipes for both Chinese and American food as a way of honoring her memory and crafting relationships to the family legacy.

Historical Setting: An Ethnography of a Historical Moment

As one of Toy Len Goon's twenty-five grandchildren, I grew up hearing from senior family members about the hard work and sacrifices she and her children made as a parable for the importance of hard work as a key to upward mobility and overcoming adversity. I remember going as a young girl to visit my grandmother at her house on Chatham Street in Lynn, Massachusetts. She lived on the meticulously kept second floor of an old three-story house owned by my Uncle Richard, who had moved to Lynn to open a television and electronics shop after completing his degree in physics at Rensselaer Polytechnic Institute. I have only vague memories of the creaky floors and a slightly musty odor. I recall how happy she always was to see us, how she would putter about in her characteristic "uniform," a housedress and apron, and the softness of her skin when she would take my hand. I remember that my mother would often bring her food, such as a bag of oranges, and we would always return home with some of what we brought, plus more that my grandmother had added. Those gestures became significant to me, as I was not able to communicate with her much due to her limited English and my lack of ability to speak Toisanese. However, I enjoyed hearing her laughing and conversing in a mix of Toisanese and English with my parents. Later, she moved with my Aunt Doris to Crown Pointe Condominiums in Swampscott, Massachusetts, a gated complex of brick buildings high up on a hill consisting of spacious luxury units. Her awards were prominently displayed on the condo's living room wall, including the official commendation from the Golden Rule Foundation, as well as awards from local Portland organizations, the Taiwanese government, and various Chinatown-based organizations. When we would go to visit her, she would tell me, in Toisanese-inflected English, "You smart girl, study hard, get a good grades, make lotta money." I later found out that she would say similar things to all her grandchildren.

Like her other grandchildren, I grew up with the proud knowledge that she had been selected as US Mother of the Year in 1952, but without a sense of the full context or significance of the award. We were told that she had grown up in poverty in a rural Chinese village and had migrated to the United States as a young woman to join her husband, Dogan Goon, who was already running a hand laundry in Portland, Maine. They had eight children together. After Dogan died in 1941, Toy Len Goon continued to run the laundry with the help of her oldest son, Carroll, who dropped out of high school for two years, later resuming his studies with the encouragement of Principal Wiggins and going on to become a doctor. After school, the other children helped with the ironing, washing, and household duties in the building where they both lived and worked. Though she never received formal education and was unable to read in either Chinese or English, her children give her credit for instilling in them a work ethic and a respect for the importance of education. They remember her as efficient, hardworking, self-sacrificing, and attentive to the individual needs of her many children. They respected her and followed her lead and that of the older siblings in doing their part in the laundry and around the house without much prodding from her. She kept a large broomstick on a high shelf for disciplining her children but recalled that she had only had to use it once on one of the older boys for it to have its intended effect of keeping the children on their best behavior. But they also remember her taking the time to talk to her children individually if they were having difficulties and gathering around the radio to listen to President Franklin D. Roosevelt's "fireside chats" together, despite her busy schedule. They credited her with cultivating strong moral values and work ethics. Her grandchildren grew up with the constant reminder of how fortunate they were to benefit from the comfortable lifestyle that their now middle-class parents were able to give them and were encouraged to study hard so that they could carry the tradition of family success.

Though Toy Len Goon was fully deserving of her honor, her selection as Mother of the Year occurred at a time when public perceptions of Chinese Americans were shifting from "definitively non-white and excluded" to "assimilated, upwardly mobile, politically non-threatening, and definitively non-black."[23] The end of Asiatic Exclusion in 1952 with the passing of the McCarran-Walter Act occurred, not coincidentally, during the Cold War, a period when the United States endeavored to portray itself as a racially liberal democracy that was suited to be the leader of the free world.[24] Though Toy Len Goon had migrated prior to this period, additional legislation had enabled Chinese women to migrate in the 1940s, resulting in a marked increase in Chinese women admitted to the United States between 1945 and 1965. Women comprised 70 percent of Chinese migrants during that period, with 65 percent coming as wives of Chinese men with US citizenship.[25]

The creation of Chinese American families made it possible for some to re-envision the American family in a more inclusive, multiethnic context.[26] Newly positive views of Asian American women enabled them to be seen as a central part of families, associated with a safe, domestic realm. According to Chiou-Ling Yeh, "This transformation likely conferred on Chinese American women the ability to be wives and mothers and provided an opportunity for Goon to receive recognition."[27]

Chinese and Japanese Americans also were becoming more racially acceptable, as strategic examples of safe, assimilable minorities, who would later be held up against African Americans as model minorities who were less radically different, less outspoken, and therefore less dangerous.[28] Models of diversity promulgated by anthropologists such as Franz Boas and Ruth Benedict paved the way for new conceptions of tolerance that explained differences between populations not in terms of immutable racial characteristics but instead in terms of malleable cultural traits that could allow immigrants to adapt to US society.[29] However, the appearance of inclusion did not mean that Chinese Americans would achieve complete acceptance and integration. Lacking the right to naturalize, they remained subject to racism and discrimination. As Mae Ngai observes, "Japanese and Chinese American citizenship experienced numerous shifts according to shifting exigencies of United States foreign policy in East Asia."[30]

As much as Toy Len Goon's story was used to promote the idea of the integration of Chinese Americans into American society, the idea was also employed in an international context for the containment of communism.[31] Chinese Americans were viewed as a proxy for China, which after Mao Zedong's rise to power in 1949 was perceived by the United States to be a communist threat to US global hegemony.[32] With the start of the Korean War, the United States was eager to gain recognition in Asia as a democratic superpower.[33] Toy Len Goon's example could be used to "emphasize the superiority of US democracy over communism."[34] Her story was deployed as part of a "cultural cold war" through which the United States aimed to refute the Soviet Union's accusations that the United States treated its minority populations poorly and was therefore not a true liberal democracy.[35] Taiwan also interpreted her selection as an opportunity to signal the United States' support for Nationalist China over communist China.

Toy Len Goon's achievement of providing for and keeping her family together could be held up as a minority success story that emphasized the liberties and upward mobility that US democracy afforded her. Propagandists asserted that her mainland Chinese counterparts were oppressed by the new communist leadership and that their families were being torn apart.[36] Toy Len Goon's story supported the narrative put forth by propagandists that US democracy allowed for individuals from minority backgrounds to ascend the ladder of upward mobility through sheer hard work and their own merit, ostensibly proving that there were no racial barriers affecting people's success or failure. This focus on individual achievement helped lay the foundation for the model minority myth and for Asian American exceptionalism.

Mother of the Year Award

The American Mothers Committee was founded in 1931 as part of Eleanor Roosevelt's program that included the creation of a Mother's Day to honor the role of mothers and draw attention to the needs of "dependent mothers and needy children."[37] The committee aimed to garner support for poor mothers and children in an effort to move away from the commercial aspects of Mother's Day and instead encourage Americans to help these needy mothers.[38] In its efforts to re-envision the role of mothers, the committee asserted its vision of what an "ideal mother" should look like, encompassing not only household duties, but also responsibilities in raising children and possessing particular "feminine and moral qualities such as courage, moral strength, patience, affection, kindness, and understanding."[39] The AMC encouraged mothers to become involved in both national and international affairs, thus extending the role of motherhood to a global scale.[40]

The committee was sponsored by the J. C. Penney Golden Rule Foundation. Earlier roots can be found in celebrations organized following the Civil War as a "day of love and friendship across battle lines" to help heal battle wounds.[41] The first national Mother of the Year award, presented in 1935 by Sarah Delano Roosevelt, mother of Franklin D. Roosevelt, at the Waldorf Astoria in New York, was given to an exemplary mother who would "provide an inspiration to the nation that would represent a mother's unconditional love, inner strength, and courage."[42] Toy Len Goon's selection as Maine Mother of the Year and later American Mother of the Year in 1952 was unprecedented, as a Chinese immigrant woman had never been chosen for this honor. Prior to Toy Len Goon, Emma Clarissa Clement, a Black woman, had been given the honor in 1946, and Elizabeth Bender Roe Cloud, who was half Chippewa, had been selected in 1950.[43] But though she was deserving of this award, how did Toy Len Goon come to be selected for this honor, presumably from among all the US mothers in 1952? Yeh argues that

> the selection of non-white women as ideal mothers illustrated the AMC's effort to strengthen the international reputation of the United States. Government agencies used the mass media to create a Cold War consensus. This would encourage individuals and civic organizations to develop and support the image of a multicultural society and presumably defuse foreign criticism of racial inequality.[44]

Thus, the choice of a Chinese woman as Mother of the Year at this historical moment had been far from accidental. The groundwork had been laid in the preceding decades through the efforts of both Chinese American activists and mainstream institutions and media to highlight the formation of Chinese American nuclear families and celebrate the virtues of assimilated Chinese women as mothers and keepers of domesticity.[45] These positive images stood in stark contrast to prior portrayals of Chinese Americans as unassimilable male laborers who threatened the jobs of white workers, and of immoral female prostitutes, both of whom were legally excluded from entry into the United States. In the 1930s, public figures such as Mom Chung, a Chinese American doctor who took US servicemen under her wing, and Song Mei-Ling, the cultured and modern wife of Taiwanese leader Chiang Kai-shek, helped create positive perceptions of Chinese women in the United States.[46]

The Model Minority Myth

The model minority myth permeates both public and scholarly discourses on Asian Americans. The apparent disproportionate success of Asian Americans in their academic and career endeavors has been explained by cultural essentialist models that credit Confucianism or other Asian values for instilling a work ethic and a focus on education.[47] Other explanations focus on environmental and structural factors that create the conditions for success or combine the two models.[48] While many people, including some Asian Americans, buy into the idea that Asian Americans are model minorities, academics who study the model minority myth have consistently observed that these ideas of Asian American exceptionalism are harmful in a number of ways, both to Asian Americans and to those they are compared against.[49] The misconceptions that Asian Americans have lower crime rates, higher educational success rates, and greater career success are often used by policy makers to shame other minority groups who, they argue, have not similarly lifted themselves up by their bootstraps. In other words, the image of Asian American success can be used to deny the existence of both racism and structural factors as barriers to minority success. These assumptions do not necessarily help Asian Americans either, as they rely on inaccurate information and obscure the broad spectrum of differences between Asian Americans of various ethnic and socioeconomic backgrounds. For example, education and income statistics usually do not differentiate between refugees who arrived in the United States fleeing turmoil in their own countries, and post-1965 voluntary immigrants, who arrived under occupational preference categories.[50] They do not consider household size and number of workers that factor into the calculation of household income. And the educational and occupational success of some Asian Americans is clearly not evidence of the end of racism.

Ultimately, Toy Len Goon's story gives us a way to think about what it means for Chinese Americans to be considered American (or Chinese American) and how they see themselves as such. The positioning of Chinese and other Asian Americans between Black and white has been deliberately shaped by state policies and other discourses circulating in the media and popular culture portraying them as model minorities. More recently, academics, activists, and some in the media have worked to dispel the model minority myth. However, less attention has been paid to how Asian Americans come to view themselves in relation to evolving versions of the model minority myth, and how this intersects with how they see themselves as Americans. Some scholars examine how a confluence of factors, including selective immigration demographics, cultural and social value placed on education, and the strategies that families and communities implement to achieve these educational goals, produces children who appear to be fulfilling the model minority myth.[51] Those scholars who focus on the very real implications of the model minority myth emphasize the lengths that people go in trying to achieve it, or at least appearing to do so.[52] More than just a myth that needs to be dispelled, my study of the Goon family across generations shows that the model minority has become an ever-changing and multifaceted set of ideas that are interpreted in different ways at different moments during the life course by individuals in relation to their life experiences.

A Note to Readers

I have often wondered what my grandmother would think of this book. I think she would be happy that I tried to highlight her perspectives in telling her story. She would have been overjoyed to hear how much her children and grandchildren admired her and were influenced by her legacy. But she may have been less interested in my spatial analysis of the laundry, the political context for her award, and its implications for the model minority myth.

I know that individual readers will engage with this book for varying reasons and in different ways. Toy Len Goon's descendants will be curious about the immigration stories of Dogan and Toy Len Goon and the festivities surrounding her award. Because it involves the analysis of material traditionally covered by historians and sociologists within an anthropological framework, scholars from those disciplines may each focus on specific parts of the book, but also find that I approach these topics with methodologies and perspectives that they might not have employed themselves. Those interested in gender and migration history might find interest in the woman-centered migration story and the Cold War's impact on transnational connections between Chinese migrants and their homelands. Sociologists might consider the questions of assimilation raised by my discussion of Paul Siu's work and my use of sociological literature discussing the model minority myth and pressure to achieve for the second generation, particularly the children of post-1965 immigrants. However, I caution against a comparison between this population and the Goon family, whose immigration occurred much earlier and was shaped by their lack of education and working-class roots. Anthropologists might focus on local and transnational kinship ties, gender roles, and the role of the state in shaping Chinese migrant experiences. They may also be interested in theoretical questions of space and power in the context of the Chinese laundry, particularly in relation to questions of economic precarity, assimilation, and community, and how the family story is remembered, narrated, and enacted through cooking, the preservation of material culture, or particular values. Scholars of Asian American studies and education might engage with how the model minority myth plays out for the family who was used to help create it. However, this book is meant to be read as a whole, and I hope that this book's mix of perspectives will encourage readers to engage with topics of their own interest and think more interdisciplinarily, albeit through an anthropological lens.

1

Chinese Migrants and the State

Dogan Goon's Emigration Story

Toy Len Goon's journey to the United States started before she set foot on US soil with her husband, Dogan, in 1921. I discuss her pre-emigration life in China, her marriage to Dogan, and her life in the United States in the next chapter. However, her story can't be understood outside the context of transnational migration from Dogan and Toy Len's home county of Toisan (C) (Taishan [M], Hoisan [H]) in Guangdong Province, China, to the United States and other locales abroad.[1] Though there are many things that distinguish Toy Len Goon's life from that of other Chinese women who emigrated to the United States, her experiences were also shaped by larger patterns of labor migration of Chinese men from Toisan to the United States, and the US state regimes of migrant regulation and exclusion that developed to regulate this migration.

This chapter details this historical context of labor migration, regulation, and exclusion, discussing why so many men from Toisan traveled abroad. It then focuses more specifically on how Dogan Goon's experiences as a regulated migrant in the United States fit within these broader patterns, particularly in relation to the legality of his entrance into the United States, his interview and subsequent arrest by a Chinese inspector, and his hearing with the Chinese commissioner, all of which set the stage for him to apply for legal permission to return to China and bring back a bride. Dogan's experiences reflect the regulation of migrant lives by state bureaucracies, a theme that continues in chapter 4, in which I discuss the challenges that Toy Len and Dogan Goon faced in continuing the transnational connections to family members in China throughout the Cold War.

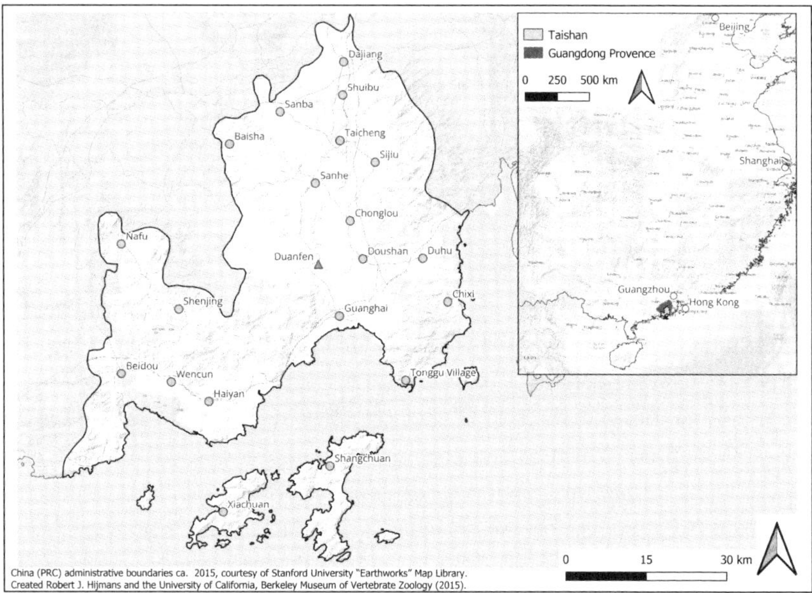

Figure 1.1. Map of Taishan (M) (Toisan [C]) County with the city of Duanfen marked. Created by Jeffrey J. Burnett in QGIS.

Toisan: Home of the Overseas Chinese

But first it is important to set the stage for why so many Toisanese traveled abroad, forming transnational households and communities. Toisan County is in Guangdong Province in southern China, not far from Macao. Toisan prides itself as being the home of the overseas Chinese, citing the generations-old pattern of emigration from the region that has resulted in its population abroad numbering more than its population at home in China. But what spurred them to go abroad? Though picturesque, with rolling hills and farmland dotted with small villages, Toisan historically did not have enough arable land to feed its population.[2] In combination with Qing government policies that cleared the Guangdong coastline and a series of natural disasters, many Toisanese were left to eke out a marginal existence. During the nineteenth century, many Toisanese men migrated abroad, some as merchants, others as coolies. Migration to North America began in significant numbers in the mid-nineteenth century, with most emigrants, at least 80 percent, coming from the 9,000-square-kilometer Sze-Yup (C) (Si Yi [M]) area, which included Toisan.[3]

I experienced the Toisanese landscape for the first time while participating in the "In Search of Roots" program in 1992 and again as a researcher in 1995, as the group visited ancestral villages in the area to carry out the "rootings" of participants.[4] Even after nearly twenty years of the Open Door Policy and economic reform that spurred drastic changes in China's urban areas, the landscape of Toisan looked as if it had not changed much over the last century. Despite some power lines, an occasional commercially produced umbrella, or a Coca-Cola can holding incense, it was not difficult to imagine the Toisan that their ancestors had left. As we drove to or walked through the villages, we saw fields being plowed using water buffalos, stacks of drying rice stalks, outhouses precariously perched over the edge of ponds, unpaved and sometimes impassable roads, and old houses that made the villages seem anachronistic, despite the fact that massive social, economic, and environmental changes had occurred in the villages during the various communist reforms enacted by Chairman Mao.[5] In some villages, the group would be shown a house or a school constructed with newer materials, and various motor vehicles could be seen and heard puttering around the countryside. To the untrained eye, Toisan appeared to not have "developed" over the years and most villages remained poor, even by Chinese standards. This was in large part because the environmental conditions in Toisan meant that there has never been sufficient arable land to support its population. Over half of the land in Toisan—56 percent—was too hilly or mountainous to farm, and only 34.9 percent of the land was farmable.[6] Rice farmers had to plant twice per year (the third and sixth lunar month) and harvest in the sixth and tenth months.[7] In addition, the soil quality was extremely poor. However, despite the poor soil conditions, Toisanese farmers were able to eke out a living by producing several crops, including "rice, taro, and sweet potatoes, and crops includ[ing] 24 kinds of vegetables, 12 kinds of melons, and 24 different fruits, as well as chicken, ducks, geese and pigs."[8]

In 1995, at the tail end of my dissertation research in Guangzhou, I visited Toisan with historian Madeline Hsu. Madeline had conducted her dissertation research on Toisan's transnational ties to its overseas community during the Chinese Exclusion Era (1882–1943), which eventually became her groundbreaking first book, *Dreaming of Gold, Dreaming of Home: Transnationalism and Migration Between the United States and South China, 1882–1943*. Together, we visited emigrant villages in Toisan, including returned overseas Chinese houses and watchtowers (*diao lou* [M]) featuring a blend of turn-of-the-century Chinese and Western architecture. We spoke with local officials from the Office of Overseas Chinese Affairs and the Returned Overseas Chinese Union (Qiao Lian), and with some local villagers.

Supporting Relatives at Home

We also visited Hong How village, where Toy Len and Dogan Goon's relatives were living. They were the descendants of Dogan's brother. Dogan's brother Doo Wong had died as a child. Dogan's mother subsequently adopted a son to continue that branch of the lineage, a common practice in a society in which lineage membership determined access to resources and connections to others that provided social, material, and spiritual support. Toy Len had been brought into the Goon family to care for this adopted son and the daughter that Dogan's first wife had left behind. That son had a son named Jeong Nguen, who in turn had three sons. One of the sons had married a woman who had migrated from the countryside from a northern province, possibly to work in one of the small industries that had been established in the village. However, it appeared that many young people had moved out of the village to look for work opportunities elsewhere.

During my visit to the village, I visited Dogan's ancestral house in the company of Jeong Nguen, and I paid my respects at the altar, accidentally cutting my finger using a knife they gave me to open a bag of candy I had purchased as an offering. We then visited the new house built in 1992 with money that Toy Len Goon and her sons had remitted to China. Jeong Nguen had written to Toy Len after some of Toy Len's children and their wives, including Amy Guen, had visited the village in 1984 and re-established contact with them.[9] He told her that nobody would marry his sons if they did not own property. Toy Len requested that each of her five sons contribute funds for her to send back to China for the purchase of the home. With the help of A Xiu Ong, a cousin living in Hong Kong who was building his own house in the village, the family built a new house.

Toy Len had bought a pickup truck for Jeong Nguen's oldest son, and that was used to haul materials for both Xiu Ong and Jeong Nguen's houses. The house was completed the year before Toy Len died.[10]

The newly constructed house, which the two older sons and their wives shared, had high ceilings and was brightly lit, having been constructed with tile and newer materials in a style characteristic of recent construction in the region. It prominently featured a portrait of Toy Len Goon, with the words "Generous Mother" underneath, in recognition of her funding the home. Amy Guen and other relatives saw the house during a visit in 1999.

These social systems and migration patterns developed out of institutionalized discriminatory immigration restrictions such as the Page Law and the Chinese Exclusion Laws that prevented women from migrating to the United States.[11] Chinese Exclusion thus powerfully shaped the possibilities for Chinese migrants within US society. So, while Toy Len Goon's story is remarkable in many ways, her journey to the United States as the wife of a Chinese immigrant who entered the United States illegally and worked as a laundryman, one of the few occupations available to Chinese, is also clearly part of a broader picture shaped by the Exclusion Laws and the racialized ideas about Chinese immigrants that undergirded them.

While some Chinese migrants were able to eventually bring over wives and establish families in the United States during the Exclusion Era (1882–1943), this would have been possible only if the woman married a man who was a US citizen. To obtain US citizenship, the man would have to have been the son of a citizen or would have had to be in the United States prior to the establishment of Chinese Exclusion. Many Chinese men obtained citizenship as paper sons, purchasing the identity papers of another Chinese man who was a US citizen or being admitted based on a claim to citizenship. Alternatively, he could have been from one of the non-excluded classes (merchant or student), or a US war veteran.

State Recordkeeping: Researching Dogan and Toy Len's Immigration Files

If things had gone just a little bit differently, Dogan Goon would have been sent back to China and Toy Len Goon would not have been able to come at all. His experiences navigating the US immigration system were shaped by the large bureaucratic structure created around Chinese Exclusion that was designed to distinguish legal from illegal entries. Like many other Chinese immigrants, Dogan Goon lived a marginalized life as a laundryman in the United States, and his legality was tested under the regime of Chinese Exclusion. As historian Lucy Salyer notes, what might have appeared to be specific individual interactions between Chinese immigrants wanting to enter the United States and US government inspectors were shaped by the governmental bureaucratic system and Chinese immigrant community organizations. The development of this complex "bureaucratic maze" illustrates the extent of the reach of the state into Chinese immigrant lives.[12]

Because Dogan passed away in 1941, when the eldest of the Goon siblings was seventeen and the youngest six, not much is known about his early life. Much of what is known is told from the perspective of Amy Guen, as related to her in her conversations with Toy Len, and from fragmented recollections of Dogan's children. Amy's husband and Toy Len Goon's third son, Edward Guen, had been persistent in applying for copies of documents relating to Dogan's immigration, military service, and time in the Veterans Administration hospital to document his parents' migration histories. He was able to obtain records from the VA hospital and gathered some other documents, most likely those saved by Toy Len Goon, but was never able to find Dogan's complete immigration record. In the process of researching this book, I located Dogan Goon's immigration file in the National Archives in Boston using the number from Dogan's certificate of identity that my cousin Terry Guen, daughter of Edward and Amy, had scanned from documents preserved by her parents.[13]

Not a Paper Son in the Usual Sense

How did Dogan end up in the United States in the first place, and how did he obtain US citizenship, which enabled him to go back to China to marry Toy Len? In the 1992 interview I conducted with my grandmother, she was insistent that he had been born in San Francisco, but that his mother had taken him back to China at the age of four when his father died. He then returned to the United States at the age of nineteen

Figure 1.2. Dogan Goon in US Army uniform, ca. 1918. Courtesy of Maine Historical Society.

and fought in World War I. She related this story in her Toisanese-accented English: "My husband born in San Francisco. Four years old no father. Mother take him go to China. Nineteen years old, he come back United States. Go to Army. World War I. Have picture here."[14] Both my mother and Aunt Doris, who were translating, seemed a bit dubious about this story. However, Toy Len remained steadfast in her rendering of events, repeating it once more, and quickly changed the subject.[15]

However, she was very much aware that he had grown up in China. According to Amy Chin Guen, Toy Len had told her that when Dogan brought her back to his village to marry her, Dogan's seventh uncle (Ngen Shieu) had shared with her that Dogan was "bright, disliked formal schooling, and liked pleasure seeking activities."[16] He advised Toy Len that she would need to "bear much of their burden." Dogan's mother had told her that Dogan did not like school and referred to him as "my gambler son."[17] She told Toy Len "not to expect too much."[18]

We now know that Dogan had lived in the United States as an undocumented migrant after having entered the United States via Montreal. He had taken the transcontinental Canadian railway from Vancouver in 1915. Amy Guen elaborated further in response to my follow-up question in May 2024. She said that she had spoken to the children of Goon clan members who had remembered their parents talking about Dogan's arrival in the United States via Canada. He had come from China to Canada and was brought from Canada to Maine via Boston by a smuggler. Upon his arrival in Maine, he connected with other Goon clan members and started to work at a hand laundry located at 640 Forest Avenue in Portland, Maine.[19] He also studied English by attending language classes for Chinese men on Sundays.[20] In 1917 he was interviewed by an immigration inspector and subsequently summoned to a hearing, during which he gave a detailed account of his childhood in San Francisco and Boston, answering the commissioner's questions without a translator. Because of Dogan's undocumented entry into the United States, he had no immigration record on file that could be used to cross-check his claims. For the purposes of this chapter, I focus on Dogan's interactions with the regime of Chinese Exclusion, and the bureaucratic afterlife of the commissioner's decision, which made Dogan Goon legible as a resident of the United States and legitimized his claims of citizenship, enabling him to initiate paperwork to return to China and bring Toy Len back to the United States with him.[21]

Interview with Inspector McCabe

Dogan Goon was interviewed by Chinese inspector John McCabe at his laundry at 640 Forest Avenue on August 16, 1917, with T. W. G. Wallace interpreting. He was determined to be a Chinese alien illegally residing in the United States. Bail was set for $1,500, and he was brought before US Commissioner Arthur Chapman for a hearing in Portland on October 26, 1917. Most of the paperwork in Dogan Goon's immigration file pertains to that hearing, in addition to the paperwork relating to the charge of being in the United States illegally, his application for a certificate of identity to return to China to marry, and the documents associated with his arrival in Boston after bringing Toy Len to the United States as his wife as a returning citizen. In the following sections I detail his interview, arrest, and hearing in more depth.

The transcript begins with Inspector McCabe introducing himself: "I am a Chinese Inspector. I want to ask you some questions as to your right to be and remain in the United States. Anything you say should be voluntary on your part as it may be used for or against you later."[22] The interview continues with the inspector asking basic questions such as name, age, date of birth, siblings, and marital status. Most questions focus on his parents' names and whereabouts. Dogan claims that he had last seen his father in San Francisco when he was only eight years old. However, he claims to not know his father's name. He identifies his mother as Ng Shee and says that she died when he was fifteen years old. However, we know that his mother died after Toy Len had married Dogan by proxy, as Toy Len had arranged her funeral. The inspector asks where he was living when his mother died, and Dogan replies, "Boston." The line of questioning continues with inquiries about where Dogan lived and worked in Boston. He claims he arrived in Boston when he was eight years old and had been brought there by some Goon clansmen. He lived in Boston for a short time before moving to Springfield and New York, claiming to have worked at a restaurant in Chinatown while in New York. He claims he had moved to the laundry at 640 Forest Avenue three years prior to the interrogation but had lived prior to that in Chin Kum's Chinese store in Lawrence, Massachusetts. The inspector also asks where he had been living twelve years before "in K.S. 31 when the Chinese Inspectors made a census of the Chinese."[23] Dogan replies that he had been living in Boston but could not remember the name of the street. Toward the end of the interview, the inspector inquires, "Is there any person now in the US that knows anything about your birth in the US?," to which Dogan replies, "I do not know of any?" To the inspector's question about whether he knows anything about San Francisco, Dogan replies, "No sir, I do not." When asked whether he has any papers documenting his right to be in the United States, Dogan says he does not. Finally, when the inspector asks him whether he understands English, Dogan replies in English, "No, I talk not much." The inspector asks where he learned English, and Dogan replies, "No, I never 'stand; I can't talk too much." Once again, the inspector asks, "Did you know how to talk English when you first went to Lawrence?" and Dogan responds, "I don't understand you."[24]

At the end of the statement, Dogan's distinguishing marks were noted: "Scar right cheek bone; scar center right cheek about 1–1/4" about the first mentioned scar; scar near left corner mouth; scar right arm just above wrist."[25]

As Anna Pegler-Gordon argues, the US federal government enacted race-based policies restricting immigration, employing "visual systems of observation and documentation" including "photographic identity documentation and visual medical inspection."[26] While the notes on Dogan's scars may seem an oddly specific way to end an interview transcript, medical inspections along with photographs were standard procedure for verifying Chinese immigrant identities.

The interview is circuitous and repetitive. The inspector's repeated questions regarding Dogan's parents and inquiries about where he lived and worked at particular times were aimed at establishing a case regarding his legality in the United States. If he could identify any inconsistencies or catch Dogan making a claim that could later be verified as false, then it would be hard for Dogan to make a case regarding his legal presence in the United States before the commissioner.[27] Dogan attempted to dodge the inspector's line of questioning with repeated claims of not remembering, interspersed with specific names and places of employment. Because he responded that he did not remember where he was living during the Chinese census, it would be difficult to verify whether he had been recorded. The inspector's repeated inquiries regarding whether Dogan knew English and where he learned after Dogan said that he did not speak it well were a curious line of questioning. Perhaps he believed that Dogan's English should have been better if he had lived in the United States all his life, as he had claimed.

Arrest

Dogan's arraignment was announced in the *Portland Evening Express* on August 17, 1917, as follows:

> Goon Do Gun, Chinaman, was charged with being illegally in this country late Thursday afternoon; arraigned before US Commissioner Chapman, and the case was continued August 24 bail being fixed at $500.[28]

In Dogan Goon's immigration file, we see a document with his photo and case number summarizing his case. The text reads,

> No. 2513–126-C Goon Do Gun.—Arrested at #640 Forest Ave., Portland, ME, August 16, 1917, for unlawful residence.
> Hearings: October 26, 1917
> Commissioner: Arthur Chapman.
> Bail: $1500.
> Atty for Government:
> Atty for Defendant:
> Discharged October 26, 1917, as native

In his photo, Dogan is wide-eyed and unsmiling, with a haircut that spikes up on top, with the sides shaved shorter. He is wearing a collared shirt with a tie and suit jacket. The photo was taken by the Hansen Studio, located at number 12 Monument Square in Portland. A letter dated November 7, 1917, from the commissioner to the studio asks that a bill be sent by the studio so that the expense could be charged to his office. On August 21, the office of the commissioner had written to the US marshal in Portland to ask whether Dogan had been photographed as the office had not yet received them. The marshal, John S. Wilson, responded on August 22 that he had not been instructed to have Dogan photographed, also noting, "All of the four Chinamen arrested last week have been released on bail."[29] As Anna Pegler-Gordon notes, the careful documentation of immigrants, in which photography played a central role, would become key to regulating them.[30] However, the process did not become standardized until the 1930s, and previously had been "uneven," as there was not yet a standard system for tracking immigrants from different countries. The correspondence surrounding the photographing of Dogan illustrated the lack of systematized procedures for photographing undocumented migrants.

Hearing with Commissioner Chapman

One wonders what the inspector and commissioner thought when two months later, on October 26, 1917, Dogan testified at his hearing in English, with only occasional help from an interpreter. He is first questioned by John B. Kehoe, counsel for the defendant, about his name, address, business, and the names and whereabouts of his family. Dogan's responses were like those he provided in his initial interview with the Chinese inspector. However, while he had claimed in the previous interview that he did not know anything about San Francisco, he tells the commissioner that he lived at 42 Waverly Place with his father, who was a tailor who made Chinese clothes. Though during his initial interview, he claimed that he could not remember who took him to Boston, this time he identified "a company cousin" named Goon Lum. He mentions several addresses where he stayed in Boston, including a laundry at 6 Lowell Street, where he stayed for three and a half years, and rooms run by his company on 26 Oxford Street. He also discussed living and working at a laundry on Common Street in Lawrence, Massachusetts, and later in Lowell. He describes working in New York at a restaurant on 125th Street named Yin Wun Low, and later working at a tea store in Springfield, Massachusetts, before ending up in Woodfords Corner in Portland, Maine. Several questions focused on how he got from San Francisco to Boston, and Dogan responded with surprising specificity, saying that he got a car on Clay Street and took a ferry to Oakland, where he boarded a train to Boston. The level of detail in Dogan's testimony regarding where he lived and worked after coming to Boston seemed convincing. When asked whether he knew anyone who could verify that he had lived in San Francisco, he pointed to Chin Bow, whom he identified as his company cousin.

As Salyer notes, because most Chinese immigrants lacked documents to prove that they were not in one of the excluded groups, hearings instead relied on interviews of witnesses, particularly for those saying they had been born in the United States. Officials usually assumed "the testimony to be fraudulent," that "Chinese felt no obligation to tell the truth," and that "San Francisco is full of old men, that will, for $5, identify ANY Chinaman as his son."[31]

Questioning was then turned over to the Assistant US District Attorney Elmer Perry for cross-examination. While some of the questions overlapped with previous lines of inquiry by Kehoe, others were oddly specific but also unclear. Kehoe asks Dogan, "How old were you when your parents told you when you were born and where you were born?" Dogan replies, "I am seven year, six year, everything, I can't tell you, I can't talk English, see?" Kehoe continues, "You mean between six and seven years, you think?" and Dogan replies, "Six or seven or five year." Kehoe again asks, "Wait just a minute. How old, if you can remember, when your parents told you where you were born?" Dogan responds, "My father, my mother, Chin Bow tell me all the time." At this point, the commissioner intervenes, saying, "I think that what he intended to convey was they told him when he was four years old, five years old, and six years old."[32]

The questions Kehoe persistently asks are difficult to answer. Few people would be able to precisely recall how old they were when their parents told them when and where they were born. However, Dogan sticks to his answer, giving a ballpark range of five, six, or seven, until the commissioner steps in to clarify what he thinks Dogan intended to say. It is well known that the immigration officials would ask Chinese trying to enter the country difficult or misleading questions to try to determine whether they were telling the truth. The inspectors refined their craft as time went on, causing "confusion, fear, and anger at the questions that seemed arbitrary and designed only to trick them."[33]

Salyer relates the recollections of immigrants of their interrogations:

> "I couldn't understand why they asked such questions," said Mr. Poon of his interrogation in 1927. "They asked about everything and anything. . . .

They even asked me where the rice bin was kept. Can you imagine?" Mrs. Chin, arriving at Angel Island in 1913, remembered that "I was interrogated one day for several hours. They asked me so much, I broke out in a sweat. Sometimes they would try to trip you: 'Your husband said such-and-such and now you say this?' But the answer was out already and it was too late to take it back, so I couldn't say anything about it. If they said you were wrong, then it was up to them whether to land you or not."[34]

It's unclear why Kehoe continued to press Dogan for more precise responses. However, Dogan's experience seemed consistent with the repeated questioning that had become the modus operandi of the inspectors.

Kehoe then begins a new line of questioning regarding where Dogan lived while in San Francisco. Dogan says he was born at 42 Waverly Place. Kehoe then asks him the streets near Waverly Place, and Dogan names Clay and Washington Streets, which indeed border Waverly Place. Kehoe next asks him whether there were any stores on Waverly Street. This line of questioning was marked by numerous misunderstandings. Through the Chinese interpreter, Dogan says that the buildings are "Mook Low," which the interpreter says are "frame buildings." The commissioner restates the original question regarding whether there are any shops on Waverly, to which Dogan replies, "Yes, you tell me, I know; I can't tell you. I don't know English what you mean. I don't know what you mean."[35]

The questioning continues, but the commissioner and Perry are unable to get any firm responses from Dogan. They ask whether there are tea stores on Waverly Place, and Dogan replies that there are only Chinese people's homes on that street. Was Dogan being purposefully evasive so that they could not cross-check his responses? Or was he truly having difficulty understanding their questions, given his limited English? Why didn't they use a translator for all the questions and allow him to respond in Chinese and have his answers translated back to English? Was Dogan's decision to speak English during the hearing made in consultation with his lawyer, and was it their intention to demonstrate that he could effectively communicate in English, as might be expected of someone who has lived in the United States all his life?

Dogan is also asked what he did during the eight years he lived in San Francisco, and whether he attended school. Once again, the commissioner intervenes, noting, "Perhaps that is a rather hard question for him to understand, just what he did then, but you go in your own way; that is all right." But Perry continues, asking, "Were you outside on the streets more or less in San Francisco near your home?" When Dogan expresses his confusion to this question and the rephrased follow-up question, the commissioner once again steps in to ask whether there were other Chinese boys at Waverly Place and whether or not they and Dogan went to school, to which Dogan replies, "The United States government no let Chinese go to school; I no go."[36]

Questioning then turns back to the geography of Waverly Place and nearby streets, then to where he lived in Boston for eight and a half years. At one point, Kehoe tells the commissioner that there was no prior statement about Dogan having lived at Oxford Street for eight and a half years. The commissioner tells him, "Of course you can go into that as far as you like on cross examination, to see if he is consistent in what he said."[37]

Many questions originally asked during the interview with Inspector McCabe are repeated, including where he had lived in Boston, Lawrence, Lowell, and Springfield, and how old he was when his mother went back to China. He is also asked whether there were any other women at Waverly Place, particularly white women.

Then Kehoe asks, "Were you registered?" and Dogan replies, "Yes, I registered, yes." Kehoe notes that while he does not need to see the card, Dogan will have to make sure to carry it with him.[38]

Next, Chin Bow is asked how he knows Dogan. Chin Bow says he worked for Dogan's father in a tailor shop at Waverly Place before moving to Lawrence, Massachusetts. When asked whether he had seen Dogan in San Francisco, he replies that he did. Chin Bow is then cross-examined by Perry. Chin Bow is asked for his certificate of residence, which he produces, and the information is recorded. Perry asks additional questions regarding on what occasions Dogan and Chin Bow met in Massachusetts.

When he is done questioning Dogan, Perry asks for a continuance "in order that the government may have an opportunity to look up the witness who has testified here."[39] The commissioner replies that it would

13

Commissioner: Any further questions, Mr. Kehoe?

Mr. Kehoe: Nothing, Your Honor. Just one question. Were you registered?

A Yes, I registered, yes.

Q Have you got your card with you? A Yes, I got card here.

Mr. Kehoe: Do you want to see the card?

Commissioner: Do you want to offer that in evidence?

Mr. Kehoe: No, I don't care to; he will have to have that with him, I mean under the registration law.

Mr. Kehoe, of witness: Are you ready to go to war for America? A Sure.

Q Will you fight? A Yes.

Figure 1.3. Excerpt from the transcript of Dogan Goon's hearing.

not be "customary" to look up witnesses, but wants to know whether there has been an opportunity for Dogan's claims of living in specific places to be verified. McCabe replies, "The government has had a chance but would not be bothered doing it because we didn't know but what probably he would come into court and claim he was a student, landed at such and such a date, at the hearing."[40] At this point, Joseph E. F. Connolly (Dogan's lawyer) speaks at length, explaining to the commissioner that he had planned to call McCabe and Sullivan to testify:

> To show that the man I represent has told him a story which was told here on the stand, to show the consistency of the story, and was going to argue to Your Honor that the manner and means under which that statement was taken was calculated and was used by the department for testing the truth, and if any contrary statement was made, I propose to have it come from the mouth of Mr. McCabe as part of our case, and in doing it I thought perhaps we could use the testimony of Mr. McCabe to avoid calling other people to corroborate the testimony of my man as to place of residence and things of that kind.[41]

He argues that it would not be fair for the case to be continued at another time. Perry withdraws his request, and Inspector McCabe, translator

T. W. G. Wallace, and J. G. Sullivan are sworn in as government witnesses. McCabe reads the transcript of the testimony taken on August 16, 1917, at the laundry at 640 Forest Avenue. The commissioner asks whether Dogan had refused to respond in English and whether Dogan had asked for an interpreter, and McCabe says that he cannot remember. Perry states that the government rests, and Kehoe has no rebuttals. The commissioner then says, "The decision in this case is NOT GUILTY OF THE OFFENCE AS CHARGED."[42]

As illustrated by the extensive discussion of Dogan's hearing, a large amount of time and resources were put into the case of just one Chinese migrant, reflecting the massive bureaucracy that had been created around Chinese exclusion. At many points, the questioning was repetitive and Dogan was pressed on issues that would have been difficult for him to address. While it was certain that they were trying to catch Dogan in a lie or contradiction, they only had the original interview conducted by Inspector McCabe, and their assessment of his responses to the new questions they asked at the hearing to assess. Still, Dogan had come prepared with a story regarding his father's profession that was consistent with Chin Bow's testimony about having worked for Dogan's father and having seen Dogan as a young child. The fact that Dogan appeared to "remember" many details he claimed to not know about just a couple of months earlier during the initial interview was never directly questioned.

Chinese Immigrants and the State

During the Exclusion Era, a comprehensive and thorough state apparatus was developed to regulate Chinese migrants, based on interrogation and recordkeeping, including both photography and interviews to determine the legality of entry and rights to citizenship.[43] Migrant lives were shaped within the context of not only formalized state policies governing the entry and departure of migrants, but also access to citizenship status, and the racialized ideas that underlay these policies, which determined the terms of inclusion or exclusion from the nation. While the transcripts of Dogan Goon's initial interview by the Chinese inspector and his later hearing seem to pit Dogan Goon as an alleged illegal alien against the state prosecutor, the hearing was just one part of a much larger system governing Chinese immigrants as described by Salyer:

> When Chinese decided to come to the United States, they had to wind their way through the bureaucratic maze that had been established in piecemeal and incremental fashion by Congress over many years. The administration of the laws was fragmented and divided among several different federal offices under the control of the secretary of the treasury, the secretary of state, and the Department of Justice. The collector of customs at each port, supervised by the secretary of the treasury, assumed the primary duty of deciding whether to admit or exclude Chinese coming to the United States. Other federal officials played supporting roles. United States consuls in China inspected the documents of Chinese claiming to be exempt from exclusion and attached their endorsement if all seemed in order. When Congress enacted the Geary Act in 1892, requiring Chinese legally residing in the United States to register with the government, it gave the task of issuing registration certificates to the collector of internal revenue in each district. Finally, the United States attorneys represented the government in all litigation involving Chinese exclusion.[44]

It is unclear what led the commissioner to rule in Dogan's favor. Nevertheless, Dogan's hearing shows the power of the US state's immigration apparatus not only to regulate the entry and exit of Chinese immigrants, but also to determine their legality or illegality, in ways that followed set judicial procedures but still relied heavily on the interpretation and judgment of commissioners.[45] While it is well known that the state has historically played and continues to play a central role in migrant lives, the example of Dogan Goon shows how through a combination of chance and subjective rulings by officials, Chinese immigrants were largely at the mercy of the system. But at times they could also exercise agency in the strategies they chose for arguing their cases within the system. The US government would later engage in Cold War politics with communist China and the Soviet Union that would drive a temporary wedge between Chinese immigrants in the United States and their families back in China. This deeply affected the Goon family and other Chinese immigrants who had followed a return migration pattern in previous generations and continued to send remittances to China.

However, in establishing who could legally stay in the United States as a citizen and who was forced to return to China, the US government had already developed a comprehensive system that determined on which side of the Pacific Chinese immigrants (or would-be immigrants) would end up.

Paper Trail to Citizenship

Based on his immigration file, we know that on March 21, 1921, Dogan, with the help of lawyer Joseph E. F. Connolly, wrote to the Department of Labor at Long Wharf in Boston, to inquire about obtaining a passport "for the purpose of going to China where he intends to marry a Chinese woman and to return to this Country."[46] Connolly shares that Dogan had been accused of being in the United States unlawfully and had been discharged by Arthur Chapman on August 16, 1917, and inquires how he should proceed in helping his client. On April 1, 1921, Connolly filed form 430, "Application of Alleged American Citizen of the Chinese Race for Preinvestigation of Status," in triplicate to the commissioner of immigration in Boston. He includes a certified copy of the Complaint, Warrant, Docket Entry, and Testimony and Judgment of the United States v. Do Gun Goon. Connolly emphasizes that Dogan wants to "set sail on May 18" and asks to be notified if Dogan needs to appear in person.

The preprinted form states in English and Chinese that the applicant intends to leave the United States temporarily, departing and returning through the "Chinese Port of Entry of Seattle, Washington." It also states that he is prepared to appear with documentary proof of his status as a US citizen "under the provisions of Rule 16 of the Chinese Regulations." It is signed by Dogan in Chinese and in English, and includes his photo affixed to the left of the text. The form was stamped "Received April 2, 1921 Immigration Service, Chinese Division, Boston, MA" with the handwritten number 2500/3557. Scrawled at an upward angle, covering both part of Dogan's photo and the text to its right, was the signature of "W. Callaghan, Insp.," indicating his approval.[47]

Connolly follows up with another letter on April 18, and receives a response on April 27 noting that "owing to the pressure of business before this office due to the very large number of applicants for admission at this port under the Chinese Exclusion Law, it will be impossible to take up any cases of applicants for return certificates at this time." They note that they hope to be able to process the application within three weeks. A few weeks later, Connolly receives a letter from the assistant commissioner H. K. Skeffington (written on May 10) requesting that Dogan appear at 287 Marginal Street, East Boston, on May 12 at 9:00 a.m. However, at Connolly's request, the examination was rescheduled for May 16, as he had been ill and out of the office and did not receive the notice about the May 12 appointment in time. Dogan is finally interviewed for his "return certificate as a native" by Inspector W. D. Callaghan of the US Department of Labor Immigration Service office, with Dek Foon listed as Chinese interpreter, on May 16, 1921. A summary at the top shows that the documents related to Dogan's trial with Commissioner Arthur Chapman had been reviewed and that Chapman's ruling that Dogan "has a lawful right to be and remain in the United States" was noted. The photograph on Dogan's discharge certificate was determined to be "a good likeness of the applicant." Furthermore, it was noted that Wallace, who had been the interpreter for Dogan's hearing and was now an inspector, verified that Dogan was the same person who had appeared at the hearing.

Under sworn testimony, Dogan is asked about his name(s), age, occupation, and address. He reports that his name is Goon Do Gun, that he is not married (and therefore has no married name), and that he is twenty-nine years old, works as a laundryman, and lives at 640 First Avenue in Portland, Maine.[48] When asked why he has visited their office, he responds, "I want to go to China." He is asked where he was born and what his father's name was, to which Dogan responds that he had been born in San Francisco, that his father's name was Goon Gin Way, and that his father had died in San Francisco. When asked whether he has brothers and sisters, he says that he does not. He reports that he plans to depart from the port of Boston and that his address in China is going to be the Hung Dock Lung Company in Hong Kong. When asked whether he had "further statements to make," he responds, "I want to go to China and get married and bring my wife back with me." However, when asked whom he intended to marry, he replies, "I don't know yet," even though his marriage to Toy Len had already been arranged. He is then asked whether he has registered for military service, and he informs them that he had been in the Army for eight months and has an honorable discharge certificate but had left it at home. Dogan's signature follows, and the words "Recommend Favorable Action" are typewritten at the very bottom of the page. Another copy of form 430 is noted as being a "duplicate," with Commissioner Skeffington's signature at the bottom. It was dated May 16, 1921.[49]

The commissioner's decision on Dogan's case had created documentation for him to establish legal residence in the United States through obtaining his return certificate/certificate of identity, which he navigated with the help of a white lawyer, Joseph E. F. Connolly. Once the commissioner made his ruling, that evidence became the basis for Dogan's claim as a US citizen within the state apparatus governing Chinese migrants in the United States. A system designed to verify or weed out Chinese migrants not eligible for citizenship could also, seemingly quite arbitrarily, verify them as legal. This model rested on faith in the bureaucratic system, which seemed on the surface to be comprehensive, organized, and official.

As Mae Ngai has observed,

> The courts' discharge papers in these cases *created* documentation of native-birth citizenship when none had previously existed. Chinese immigrants thus invented a system of illegal entry built entirely upon a paper trail derived from the state's efforts to enforce exclusion. In many instances, documentation supporting the identity of two or three generations of American citizens—including certificates of identity and citizenship, passports, and an ongoing registry of names of children born in China to American citizens—rested on a slender reed of evidence, an oral claim.[50]

Dogan's case for US citizenship was indeed based on a "slender reed of evidence, an oral claim" that he had been born in San Francisco. In my analysis of his hearing with Commissioner Chapman, it became clear that there were inconsistencies between his interview with the Chinese inspector and his testimony in front of the commissioner, and there was doubt about the veracity of his claims. Ngai discusses how increasingly complex interrogation processes and detailed records about villages and family members were created as part of authorities' efforts to identify fraudulent entries.[51] However, in Dogan's case, the record focuses on his claimed experiences as a boy in San Francisco and as a young man living in Boston and New York. The records in his growing file were used to check the consistency in Dogan's claims when he applied for his certificate of return to China, and when he reentered the United States with Toy Len as his bride. It built upon itself as Dogan repeated his testimony throughout various interviews required for obtaining the necessary documentation to return to China and to allow his reentry into Canada and then the United States. Later, he was able to use this same paper trail to apply for his certificate of identity. If we view his record without this context, it seems that the Chinese Bureau was just making busywork for itself, with its numerous and detailed forms and interviews. However, Ngai explains that immigration officials were caught in their own system, such that

> the logic of enforcing exclusion compelled immigration officials to enforce an upward spiral of evidentiary requirements upon Chinese immigrants, but at the same time the authorities mistrusted the entire register of documents they had created. Captives of their bureaucratic procedures, immigration officials were indignant that they were mocked by imposters—the service frequently remarked that each woman residing in the United States before the 1906 earthquake would have had to have giving birth to one hundred sons to account for all the native born citizens and despaired they could ever solve the problem of paper immigration.[52]

The papers in Dogan's file also illustrate the lengths to which Dogan went and the resources he enlisted in traveling back to China to marry Toy Len Chin. While family legend states that he decided to return on the advice of Sing Bon, who, while on a return visit to China, had met Toy Len Goon, who had already been married to Dogan by proxy, the process of returning to China was drawn out and complicated, showing that he was not just acting on a whim.

Dogan was given the duplicate copy to give to the immigration officer at the port of departure as a form of identification, who gave him the original in exchange. It's not clear whether he was able to board the ship on May 18 as he had originally planned (no record was found of his passage to China). Based on Amy's biography and Dogan and Toy

Len's testimony for the Veterans Administration, we know that he wed Toy Len Goon in a custom marriage ceremony in Toisan on July 15, 1921. They then went to Toisan City to borrow two hundred taels (Chinese silver currency) for passage to the United States from Dogan's cousin. The cousin agreed, with the stipulation that Toy Len be responsible for the repayment of the loan, which would need to be remitted in more valuable Hong Kong dollars. The couple stayed overnight in Toisan City in the Goon clan residence before taking a boat to Hong Kong, and a ship to Vancouver. From there, they took the Trans Canadian Railroad to Montreal, where they transferred to the Boston and Maine line, ending their journey at the East Boston immigration station.[53]

They arrived in Boston on December 7, 1921, having landed at the Port of Montreal on December 6, 1921. Form 400-A (number 1085) of the US Department of Labor Immigration Service was a "Descriptive List of Chinese person proceeding in transit through Canada through port of entry for Chinese to undergo examination for admission to US." Dogan's name, age, and marital status are indicated, as well as his arrival in Vancouver on November 28, 1921, via the ship *Empress of Asia*, with a destination of Portland, Maine. His birthplace was listed as San Francisco and his "Last Place of Residence" as "Tong Hau Toi Shan China." His physical characteristics were also noted: His height of 5 feet, 6 ½ inches, a mole on the left side of his face, and a pit on the right side of his face. Form 430 was referenced and "CPOS 13642" was written in the space next to "Head Tax." The form, signed by US Immigrant Inspector Harry N. Phillips, states in typewritten text,

> I have made a strict examination for, and noted, the physical peculiarities of the Chinese person whose description and photograph appear hereon, and am satisfied that the applicant is admissible under Immigration Law; the person having been certified as free from disease by a Public Health Surgeon stationed at this port. I have permitted landing under bond in order that this person may proceed to the port mentioned above to undergo examination under the Chinese-Exclusion Laws.[54]

Dogan and Toy Len Goon arrived at the port of Boston on December 7, 1921. The Department of Labor Immigration Service record identifies his case number as 2500/3557 and his ship name as *Empress of Asia*. He is also identified as a returning citizen. When asked his name, he identifies himself as Goon Do Gun, with a married name of Goon Yow Hung. His address is listed as 640 Forest Avenue. He is also asked how many times he has been married and to provide additional details about his marriages. He reports, "Once; I married C.R. 10-16-15, to Chin Shee, 26 years old, natural feet, from the Gom Tun village." When asked whether he has any children, he replies, "no." He is asked whether he has "taken any money, letters, or anything else from the United States to any one in China on this trip, if so, to whom?" Dogan replies that he "took $30 and a letter from Chin King Sing to his mother in the Chung Chai village." When asked whether he visited any houses in China, he says that he visited Chin King Sing's home and has also brought a letter and money for Chin Chung Lok for his mother, who lives in the village of Har Cai. He is also asked whether he had been introduced to any son, daughter, or wife, to which he replies, "no." Finally, he is asked whether he attended any weddings, and he replies that he attended the "Goon Yuen wedding in Her Young village."

A note on the top of page 2 reads, "Witness should be advised that his statements in reply to these questions will be used should he testify at any future time as to the relationship claimed to exist between an applicant for admission and a Chinese resident of the United States." He curiously does not list his first marriage or the daughter from his first marriage, whom Toy Len Goon had been brought in to care for after her proxy marriage to Dogan. Below this statement, he is asked whether he is "accompanied by anyone, if so, by whom?" to which he replies, "My wife."

The document was signed by Dogan in Chinese as the applicant, followed by Callaghan as inspector, and finally by the interpreter in English. The final two lines read,

> Q Do you desire a certificate of identity: A Yes.
> Satisfied as to identity; applicant admitted and guarantee returned.

On March 26, 1922, Dogan finally received his certificate of identity. By going through the process of applying for a "return certificate as a native," going to China, and being re-interviewed upon return to the

United States, he became an official citizen-subject in the eyes of the US government.[55]

Dogan's file was not altered again until July 1939, when it was forwarded to the Central Office and eventually forwarded together with Toy Len's file (under the name "Goon Chan Shee Al. Wife") in September 1939 to the commissioner of immigration and naturalization in Washington, DC. Here, Dogan's file ends, but we know that these documents were used by the Veterans Administration to verify the custom marriage of Dogan and Toy Len so that she could be eligible for his veteran's pension.

Creating Immigrant Identities Through Bureaucracy

For her book title, Salyer borrows the words of a Chinese prisoner on Angel Island who carved a poem into the walls of the barracks calling the Exclusion Laws "harsh as tigers."[56] She notes that those in charge of enforcing the law found that task to be difficult, observing,

> If the law was a tiger, as the Chinese poet claimed, administrative officials thought its teeth dull and full of gaps. Though apparently contradictory, both perspectives were grounded in reality; the law was both harsh and difficult to enforce. The law's severity stemmed in part from its discriminatory nature. By 1891 the Chinese were the only group of immigrants to be specifically excluded from the United States. American officials made it even more difficult for Chinese to enter through their stringent enforcement of the law. Yet officials did not find their task as America's gatekeepers simple or easy. Through protest, evasion, and, especially, persistent litigation, Chinese often thwarted the exclusion policy.[57]

The paperwork in Dogan's file creates a bureaucratic map of Dogan's interactions with the US government, specifically the state apparatus for regulating Chinese immigrants: from his initial apprehension as a suspected illegal alien (1917), to the commissioner's hearing in which he was deemed to be in the country legally (1917), to the paperwork he submitted for a certificate of identity to ensure that he would be able to reenter the United States after traveling back to China to marry Toy

Len Goon (1921), to the interrogation he submitted to upon return to the United States with Toy Len Goon as his wife (1921). Dogan did not legally "exist" as a person in the United States prior to this paper trail. Until he was caught by Chinese Inspector McCabe, he was largely invisible to the continually developing state bureaucracy. His identity as a legal US citizen was in essence produced through the interviews, trials, and verifications found in the file. And the same processes could have easily led to his being determined to be a non-citizen. Dogan Goon does appear in the 1920 census, enumerated on January 21, 1920, by Katherine Palmer.[58] He is listed at 640 Forest Avenue under the name Goon, Dogun, as head of household, and as a Chinese male, age twenty-seven. His marital status was single, and the record indicated he could read, write, and speak English. His father's place of birth was listed as California, and his mother's as China. His occupation was "laundryman," working on his own account (indicated with the abbreviation OA).

In addition to his immigration file that I obtained from the National Archives, I also received a wealth of documents related to Dogan and Toy Len Goon from Terry Guen, who scanned the materials that her parents had collected. These included a transcript of Dogan's immigration hearing and documents related to his military service, including his discharge papers, which had been requested by Edward Guen on November 3, 1992, with a response on December 8, 1992.[59] Also included in the batch of scanned documents were an operator's license for a 1935 Studebaker sedan; medical records from Togus, Maine; Toy Len Goon's naturalization certificate; and a letter of congratulations by Edward Kennedy and the governor of Massachusetts. While these documents existed and were preserved within a comprehensive regulatory system, they can also be seen as tracings of family migration histories. Participants in the "In Search of Roots" program that I took part in and later studied for my dissertation research also discovered the value of exclusion files for understanding the immigration experiences of previous generations, even if they only reflected the paper son version of their family story marked by Chinese Exclusion.[60]

Beyond the official media coverage and family stories and memories, there are few records of Toy Len and Dogan Goon, and even fewer in their own words. Though the documents are part of the state's immigration apparatus, they also provide insight into their experiences as immigrants interacting with the state. We see transcriptions of interviews in which we view renderings of their own responses to questions, albeit often through a translator. We see their signatures, their photographs. The fact that there are very few other records in their "voices" means that even the transcribed testimonials they gave while being questioned by authorities become valuable in their own right.

Retelling Dogan's Story

There have been a few theories as to why Dogan Goon was determined by US Commissioner Chapman to be residing in the United States legally. According to Gary Libby in an interview for an online exhibit,

> The interesting thing is that he was a laundryman here in Portland, an illegal alien at a time that there were Chinese Exclusion Acts that prevented Chinese people from being able to come to the country. He was arrested by the Chinese inspectors and prosecuted, and the trial was in 1917 just before America was about to get involved in World War I. But he told a great story, which was "I am an American citizen." I was born in San Francisco. And the wonderful thing about that was that when the San Francisco earthquake happened in 1906 San Francisco City Hall was destroyed along with all the vital records. So, there was no way to prove or disprove that he was born in San Francisco. It was a lie. All of this was just made up. But when he was having his trial, the judge listened to that and then asked Dogan Goon a question, if America goes to war, would you fight? And Dogan was a brilliant man. He knew the answer to that question. He said, Yes I would. And the judge, over the objection of the US government who didn't believe Dogan Goon's story at all, decided that he was going to find that he was a natural born US citizen. And Dogan got citizenship papers which eventually allowed him to go back to China to marry Toy Len Goon.[61]

Gary believes that Dogan's reply helped sway the commissioner, even though the claims he was making regarding having been born in San Francisco were likely false.

Interestingly, many in the family believed that Dogan's citizenship came from having served in World War I, rather than his desire to become a citizen leading him to enlist in the military. According to a memory book created by the family,

> He was brought before a commissioner of the district of Maine and charged by the inspector as being "unlawfully" in the US. Dogan had to post a $1,500 bond. Dogan also had two witnesses who posted sureties of $1,500 each. The US Inspector could not convince the commissioner that Dogan was unlawfully in the US. At the end of the hearing, the commissioner asked Dogan, "Are you ready to go to war for America?" Dogan answered, "Sure." "Will you fight?" "Yes." In 1918, Dogan was drafted into the US Army. On discharge in 1919, Dogan received his US citizenship. With this, Dogan was able later in 1921 to return to China and marry Toy Len Chin.[62]

Notably, as Gary Libby describes, Dogan was able to obtain US citizenship because of the commissioner finding Dogan not guilty for being in the United States illegally, not because of his service in the US Army. Either way, the family realized that had it not been for the commissioner's leniency, Dogan would not have been able to remain in the United States and bring Toy Len Goon over using the privilege of citizenship, and the family would not have had the opportunity to live in the United States. Dogan's status as an undocumented immigrant to the United States has also been interpreted in a variety of ways by family members whose views on the subject are shaped by their specific political understandings of migration in the current moment. Though Toy Len had insisted when I interviewed her in 1992 that Dogan had been born in the United States, she knew that this was not the case. She had heard about his childhood in China from his mother and others in his village. Toy Len had told Amy that Dogan's mother had advised her not to expect too much from Dogan, whom she referred to as her "gambler son." Dogan's mother told Toy Len that Dogan had not liked school, gambled too much, and had been spoiled by her after the death of her older son during childhood. He was also considered to be untrustworthy by others in the village.[63]

Amy Guen surmised that since I had asked her in English, Toy Len had given the response she had rehearsed in English for immigration officials, implying that if the question had been in Chinese and not the language of state bureaucracy, she would have revealed the true story.[64] It was common for Chinese immigrants to stick to the stories that they told immigration inspectors while being interrogated out of fear of being outed as paper sons. Even decades later, when a confession program was implemented that enabled "paper sons" to reveal their true identities, most families chose to keep their paper names due to unclear benefits and potential risks involved in confessing.[65] What was perhaps more impressive is that at the age of almost 101, Toy Len Goon was able to remember the details of that story.

Was Dogan a war veteran and citizen (and thus a hero) or an undocumented immigrant? He was remembered as a war veteran and citizen rather than a suspected undocumented immigrant. Even prior to Toy Len Goon's selection as Mother of the Year, the local news media had run several stories praising Dogan for his patriotism and skills as a father. A 1940 article in the *Portland Press Herald* entitled "Ambition and Pride Keynotes of Character Local Chinese Family: Professional Careers Planned for Chinese Father of Eight" mentions that Dogan was "trained for war service" and focuses on the children's career goals and how while the family still retains some Chinese traditions such as eating one Chinese meal a day, they "are raising a family of eight sturdy and very much Americanized boys and girls, all of whom were born in this city."[66] Correspondence from the selection committee for the Maine Mother of the Year award and later media coverage also emphasized that he was a veteran, with no mention of the earlier uncertainty of his legal status in the United States.

Within family memories, the question of Dogan's legality took a back seat to the fortunate circumstances that allowed him to gain citizenship, marry Toy Len, and bring her to the United States. His hearing before the commissioner nevertheless speaks to Dogan's involvement in Chinese social networks that enabled him to produce Chin Bow as his witness and somehow learn the details about Waverly Place that he used in his testimony, even if it was not believed by the prosecuting attorney. Dogan's connection to other Chinese immigrants and immigrant organizations represents an alternative narrative to his invisibility to the US state, which treated him as a presumed illegal body that needed to be regulated. As Salyer and others have discussed, the Chinese Consolidated Benevolent Association and other Chinese networks were sources of protection for immigrants.[67]

Dogan went from being an illegal alien to a war veteran, while being celebrated for his role as a father and patriot. Yet, despite this overarching narrative of success, the life stories of both Dogan and Toy Len were shaped and restricted by the state in the form of immigration law, state bureaucracy, and the Cold War between the United States and China, as well as conditional and contingent forms of acceptance predicated on judgments of legality within the US legal system, and also shaped selectively within public narratives.

2

Toy Len Goon's Migration Story

Pre–Mother of the Year Award

While the previous chapter traces Dogan's arrival to the United States and his interactions with the bureaucracy of Chinese Exclusion, this chapter takes place during the same time period, focusing on Toy Len's early life in China as a foster child, her arranged marriages, and her emigration to the United States. It then merges with Dogan's timeline as she raises a family with him and continues by documenting how she navigated life after his passing. Amy Guen's biography of Toy Len Goon and the interview I conducted with my grandmother in 1992 when she was one hundred years old are key sources for this chapter and reflect how she told her own story. This chapter also discusses the community's concern for Toy Len and her family after Dogan's death and attempted interventions by the local community.

Toy Len Goon was born in 1891 on the fourteenth day of the eighth lunar Chinese month in a small village called Kam Chun (柑村) in Toisan County, Duanfen Township (端芬鎮), in Guangdong Province, China.[1] She was born near the Sheng Juck (上澤圩) marketplace. Her parents, named Chin Wah Fue and Ng Leong Ho, lived in a mud brick house that was the fourth from the village front walk and made their living as tenant farmers, renting the land they worked.[2] As a young girl, she helped her family raise pigs and grow vegetables.[3] She was the fifth child in the family, with two older brothers, two older sisters, and one younger sister. At the age of ten, in a fostering arrangement made by her mother, Toy Len was sent to a more well-to-do family in nearby Ping Jew village to be raised. Toy Len's mother felt she had no choice but to send her daughter to another family to work, as her own family could not provide for all their children. In relating these events to me, Amy Guen, wife of Toy Len Goon's son Edward, praised Toy Len's mother for having the foresight and intelligence to make such an arrangement for her daughter. She also speculated that Toy Len had been chosen from among her other sisters to have the opportunity to be raised in a more cultured and financially stable family due to the potential her mother saw in her. It was not uncommon in the region to send daughters to work for and be raised by other families, a practice that Amy said was referred to as *yeung neui* (*yang nu* [M]) by locals, literally "adopted daughter."[4]

Toy Len's mother made sure that Toy Len's future remained under her control and that she was not relinquishing her daughter to the foster family. She made it clear that she would be the one to choose Toy Len's husband and that the foster family would not have her marry into the family. Leong Ho had met the foster parents, Chin Tsiang Yee and Ng Toy Fung, at Sheng Juck marketplace, where the family had a grocery business. Toy Len's mother arranged for her to live with them to help with the children and housework in exchange for taking care of her basic needs. In the Chin household, Toy Len cared for a seven-year-old boy named Stanley, who was away at school the majority of the time, and an infant girl. According to Amy, the Chin family's higher social and cultural capital provided her with knowledge of social skills of a class standing that her parents likely would not have been able to teach her. In reminiscing about her childhood, Toy Len often spoke with Amy Guen of how her foster family wanted to adopt her. The Chin family became very attached to Toy Len and viewed her as a daughter, not as someone with lower status. And Toy Len was very fond of them. However, her mother remained clear that Toy Len would remain part of her natal family, and was not willing to have her daughter be adopted by the Chin family. Stanley and his sister eventually migrated to the Boston area, where he ran a restaurant called Chin's Village in Wellesley, Massachusetts. When I visited Amy Guen in May 2024, she made sure to show me the clipping of Stanley's obituary as soon as I walked in the door. She had saved the obituary in a photo album, on the same page as a photo of Toy Len Goon, Stanley, and Stanley's sister gathered at Toy Len's home with her sons Edward and Richard and some of their children. Amy wanted to convey that after all of these years, Stanley still considered Toy Len to be his sister, as evidenced by her name being included in his obituary as one of his surviving siblings. She emphasized once again that the foster family found Toy Len Goon to be "so sweet and intelligent" that they asked her mother if they could adopt her, but her mother refused, as she wanted to determine whom she would marry.[5]

Toy Len Goon often talked with Amy about her mother's decision to place her with the foster family and the close relationship she developed with them. She lived with them from the age of ten until she was twenty. Indeed, one of the main reasons she wanted Amy to document her life story was so that she could share the impact that her mother's decision had on her early life. Toy Len's aunt, her mother's younger sister, had met Toy Len just prior to her departure to live with her foster parents. The aunt hoped that Toy Len could meet her sister-in-law, whose son had migrated to the United States. When Toy Len turned twenty-one, the son, who was eleven years her senior, returned to the village to marry Toy Len, with her parents' blessing. In fact, she had been betrothed to him since she was ten years old, unbeknownst to her foster family. Her foster family generously provided the items traditionally given to the bride during marriage as if she were their own daughter, as they knew that Toy Len's own parents could not afford them. These included a dowry, sets of clothing, and ritual pastries.[6] Per tradition, the dowry included three types of clothing for the various seasons—silk for summer, wool for winter, and cotton for all year round. Toy Len's trousseau included three outfits she sewed using a very fine-quality mud silk, produced in that region of China.[7]

Toy Len's husband returned to the United States to work soon after their marriage, sending remittances and writing letters home for important holidays and festivities. However, he died of lung disease a few years later. Per tradition, Toy Len was told to adopt a son to continue the male lineage.[8] However, her mother embarked on finding an alternative arrangement for her daughter in which she could be supported by a new husband and his family. Toy Len told her mother that she wanted to stay in her deceased husband's village, but her mother insisted that she remarry.[9] During this period, her mother also brought her to see a fortune teller, who said that Toy Len would have a very difficult life until around age sixty.[10]

Toy Len's mother had a friend named Mo Nuey who knew Dogan's family and had heard that Dogan's mother was quite ill. Dogan was in the United States, and Mo Nuey knew that Dogan's mother was hoping to find a daughter-in-law whom she could bring into the family to help

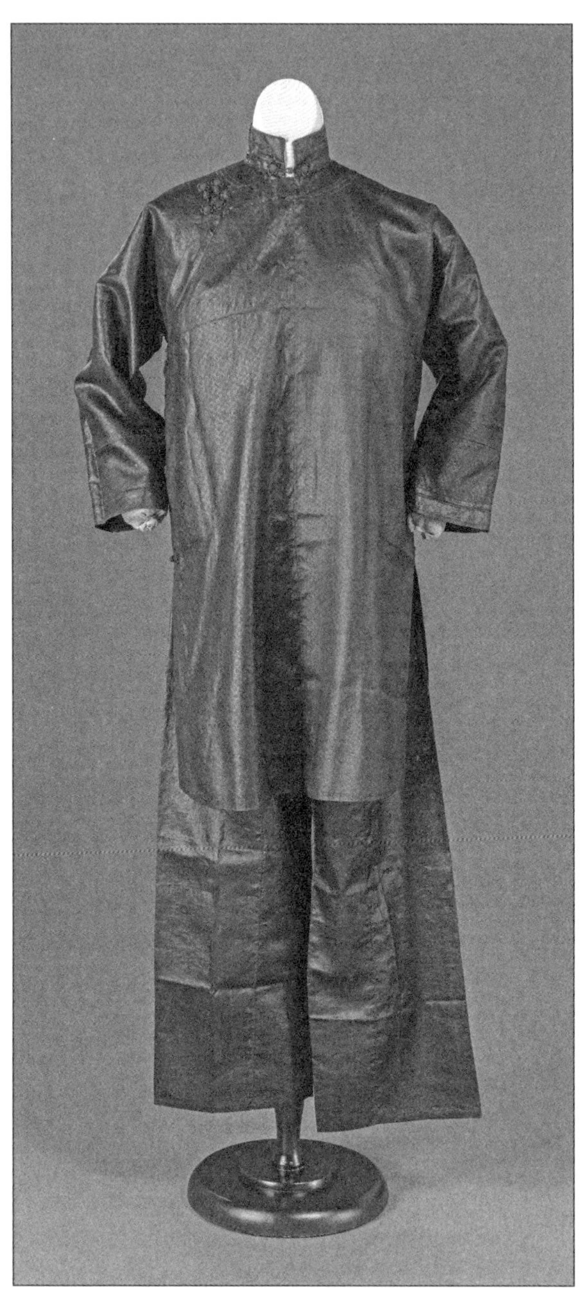

Figure 2.1. Toy Len Goon's mud silk tunic and pants, Guangdong, ca. 1920. Courtesy of Maine Historical Society.

care for her and to run the household. After the introduction by their mutual friend, Toy Len's mother went to meet with Dogan's mother to find out more about their circumstances. She learned that Dogan had been previously married at the age of eighteen, but his wife left the family after giving birth to a daughter, Hung Gee. Also living in the household was a young boy, Doo Nguey, who had been adopted by Dogan's mother after his older brother had died, to continue the family line.[11] Toy Len's mother was willing to consider having Toy Len marry into the family, provided that she would not have to work in the fields. Dogan's mother "boasted that her family had not had to wear farmer's rain gear for several generations."[12] Toy Len's mother determined the Goon family to be a prosperous clan with good *feng shui*, as indicated by the fact that they had so many sons (Dogan's father was the ninth of ten sons).[13]

At the urging of her mother, Toy Len moved from her now-deceased first husband's Moy village to Dogan Goon's village. Dogan's mother then selected "an auspicious day" for the ceremony in which they were married by proxy. "In front of the altar in the living room, a rooster took the place of Dogan to stand beside her, bowing to the ancestors."[14]

Her daily work was arduous—cooking two meals per day, washing clothes, getting water from the well, and processing the six bushels of rice received from a tenant farmer.[15] A mere four months later, her mother-in-law died from a lung ailment. Toy Len arranged a lavish funeral for her, befitting her status as a relatively prosperous widow, selling the family's last rice paddy for five hundred taels to finance the funeral. She was praised by the other villagers for this filial act. Dogan's childhood friend who now lived in Boston, named Sing Bon Goon, had been visiting the village at the time, and heard them talk about Toy Len's good character. Sing Bon had implored Dogan to marry Toy Len and bring her to the United States as the wife of a citizen, even offering to make the personal sacrifice of temporarily leaving behind his gambling business in Boston to move to Portland for six months to run Dogan's laundry. He was reported to have said, "A good wife is worth more than any amount in gold," and "A citizenship should not be wasted."[16] Sing Bon's son repeated his father's words to Amy and Edward Guen when they saw one another at an event in 1983. Sing Bon himself had told Ed and Amy in 1952 that helping Dogan marry Toy Len was one of his greatest personal achievements, and that he also "took pride in Toy Len's achievement as American Mother of the Year."[17]

The value that Sing Bon attributed to US citizenship reflected the patterns of overseas migration that had become a way of life in Toisan. However, Sing Bon's desire for Dogan to bring his wife from China to the United States was a departure from the generations-old practice of men returning to China to marry and having the wife and children remain in China.

Toy Len Goon's Arrival in the United States

In my 1992 interview with her, my grandmother's recollections about coming over to the United States and arriving in Boston in 1921 remained vivid. When asked about the ship name, she recalled that they called the ship Wong Yen Hong. At the time of the interview, my mother, Aunt Doris, and I assumed that this was the official name of the ship. However, when she listened to the audiotaped interview I did with Toy Len Goon in 1992 as part of the filming of a segment of the PBS documentary *Asian Americans* in 2019, Amy remarked that Wong Yen Hong translated to "yellow smokestack ship," a colloquial term that Chinese immigrants called the ships.[18] Having never before been on a ship and possibly not knowing that ships had names or why it might be important to know the ship's name, Toy Len Goon likely did not consider seeking out the ship's official name. A passenger list obtained by a search of Dogan's name in Ancestry.com shows that they arrived on the *Empress of China* on November 28, 1921, from Hong Kong to Vancouver. Dogan was listed as Goon Do Gan and Toy Len was listed as Goon, Chan Shee (indicating that her own surname was Chan [Chin] and that she was married). Dogan was listed as passenger number 11, ticket number 980. Toy Len was listed as a female; age: twenty-six; married; country of birth: China; race: China; occupation: housewife; religious denomination: Buddhism.[19]

During my 1992 interview with her, she recalled being interrogated upon arriving at the Boston immigration station. She was shown photos of Chinese men by the immigration inspector and was asked by a white Chinese-speaking interpreter which one was her husband. After correctly identifying Dogan, she was released to temporary housing in Boston, where she lived for ten days, remarking in Chinese to my mother and aunt that "the fish was terrible."[20] Amy notes in her biography of Toy Len that Dogan brought her food from Chinatown daily, and she shared her meals with the others.

Toy Len Goon's immigration file, which I obtained through an A-file record search request through the US Customs and Immigration Service, details the interrogation process.[21] The transcript of "In the Matter of Goon Chan Shee 'Wife of a Citizen'" contained in her file shows that a Board of Special Inquiry was held in East Boston on December 16, 1921. Present were Inspectors J. H. Jensen, who served as chairman and secretary, W. P. Callaghan, and J. E. Fitzgerald. The file notes, "Applicant does not hold the usual identification paper generally presented by applicant and has no papers to present." The document includes her description, noting her height ("5–0 1/2 with shoes"), occupation (housewife) and distinguishing marks. The testimony, done through translator Moy Don Shing, begins by asking her age, date of birth, and birthplace.[22] To this, she replies that she is twenty-six years old; born the eighth month, fifteenth day, in "Gam Toon" village. She did not know the year, but this may have been because she followed the Chinese calendar. Subsequent questions asked whom she was married to and when the wedding took place, including specifics such as how she was transported from her village to Dogan's village, what time of day she was carried to his village on the sedan chair, what the weather was like, and what she was wearing. She reported that she had been transported around dusk, and that she wore a red topcoat. She was asked whether she had a marriage feast and was in possession of a marriage certificate. She lacked any paper documentation for her marriage, as she has been "married under the old custom."[23]

The set of questions that followed related to her family members, whether Dogan had met them, and details about Dogan's age, family, and birthplace. The interrogation then went into detail regarding Dogan's village, including its size, location, the direction it faced, market days, and who lived in the neighboring houses. She was then asked how they traveled from the village to Hong Kong, how they traveled to the United States, and whom else she knew in the United States. Finally, she was shown a photograph of Dogan and asked, "Of whom is this a photograph?" The transcript notes that she had correctly identified Goon Do Gun from form 430 in Boston file 2500/3557. When asked why

Figure 2.2. Photo of Dogan and Toy Len Goon, 1922. Courtesy of Linda Fifield.

she was not in possession of identification papers, she replied that her husband "had no chance to make out an affidavit for me" but that he had been born in the United States and was a US citizen. At the bottom of the paper, we see an *x* next to the "Applicant Signature" with the words "her" and "mark" on either side. As Toy Len Goon was unable to write in English or Chinese, that mark served as her signature. Later, in preparation for her application for US citizenship in 1968, she would practice writing her name in English and was able to sign the relevant documents, including her certificate of naturalization.[24]

Life in Portland

Toy Len told Amy that upon her release, Dogan called Sing Bon, who had been working in the laundry in his absence, to notify him of their arrival in Portland. By the time they arrived in Portland, Sing Bon had already departed for Boston.[25] She recalled that the streets in Portland were unpaved, and that milk was delivered by horse-drawn carriage, and during my interview with her she imitated the "ga-lup, ga-lup, ga-lup" noise of the horse hooves. Toy Len told Amy that just after arriving in Portland, Dogan had sent her to the grocery store to buy food. He explained that it was on the same street as the laundry, two corners down, and sent her on her way. She headed there on her own, not speaking a word of English. Amy said that Toy Len took this as a sign that Dogan was confident in her ability to learn quickly and accomplish the necessary tasks.[26] Toy Len also told Amy that upon her arrival in Portland, Dogan bought a sewing machine and told Toy Len to make herself American-style housedresses and aprons.[27]

According to Amy's biography, Toy Len wasted no time learning from Dogan how to run the laundry, working sixteen-hour days so that she could earn money to pay back the debt they owed to Dogan's cousin.[28] Five months later, their first son, Carroll, was born. She had been pregnant for her whole passage to the United States from China and detainment. She maintained her rigorous work schedule while also caring for Carroll and sewing and mending clothes to save money, always conscious of the debt she owed. She carefully managed the budget, giving Dogan an allotment to spend on the games he played with other laundrymen in the area. She would ensure that Dogan sent money back to his two children in China and the people watching over their ancestral home for Chinese New Year and other important dates on the lunar calendar. In addition, she would take money from the cash register and keep it in a brown paper envelope under their bed, between the mattress and the wire grate of the bed frame underneath.[29] She saved enough money for a $500 down payment toward the purchase of the building on 615 Forest Avenue they had been renting. The building cost $5,000, and the down payment was 10 percent, with monthly payments of $50.[30] The family had been living in substandard housing above their laundry in two different rental locations, the first, at 640 Forest Avenue, with only one toilet in the basement and one wash basin on the second floor where they lived, and the second that they had to vacate before it was slated to be demolished.[31]

615 Forest Avenue

The story of Toy Len Goon saving money behind Dogan's back has taken on mythic proportions in family folklore. As Amy relates the story in her biography, Toy Len was able to borrow money and sort out the legalities of the purchase of the house without Dogan knowing about the money she had secretly put aside. She consulted with a family friend, a real estate broker named Norton Lamb, regarding how to get a mortgage for the property. Lamb advised her to apply for a loan from the bank, under the assumption that Dogan's status as a veteran would increase their chances of the mortgage being approved. For the down payment, she pretended to borrow $200 from a friend, Git Hing (Helen) Wong, to whom she had actually given a portion of the savings from under the mattress. She then sent Dogan to Chinatown to borrow another $200 from Bon Man Bak, the head of the Goon clan. She took $100 out of the cash register in front of Dogan to make up the rest.[32]

In addition to documenting the story in the biography, Amy related this story to me a number of times in my interviews with her. She knew that Toy Len had been proud of having purchased the laundry building and admired the foresight and ingenuity that Toy Len must have had to be able to orchestrate that transaction, particularly given her level of English proficiency and limited knowledge of US financial procedures. For Amy and the rest of the family, the tale is used to emphasize Toy Len's resourcefulness, while at the same time raising the uncomfortable topic of Dogan's lack of responsibility in not saving money or investing in property. Buying 615 Forest Avenue proved to be a very strategic move on Toy Len's part, helping to establish the financial stability of the household and business. Located in Woodfords Corner, the Goon family was able to settle in and establish a steady clientele of laundry customers.

When I interviewed my cousins, some asked why she had to hide money from our grandfather instead of saving it systematically and with his knowledge in a bank account. I was not clear about this until I saw the fully translated version of my interview with my grandmother. Toy Len Goon talks about how she had been saving money in a bank account for her children, but had discovered, with the help of a friend/relative who could read the statement, that Dogan had withdrawn the money she had saved for her children from the bank, most likely to gamble. From the 1992 interview with Doris and Janet translating, later fully translated by linguist Genevieve Leung:

Toy Len Goon: They were asking for $500 down. He [her husband] had nothing in his pocket. So I told a lie and said, "They're asking for $300." Then I told the truth and I said, I said, "I put up $100 and I asked Aai Ngi to borrow $200. You contribute 200." He didn't even have 200. So he went to Boston to ask Bon Lam Baak" eh, Boss Bon Lam Baak to borrow 200. Then I went immediately to Aai Ngi to borrow 200. Wah, a few hundred dollars. This is how I paid for the down payment.

Janet (daughter): That's why the . . .

TLG: Otherwise I'd have no house to live in! I wouldn't have the 500 dollars! [*Janet or Doris laughs.*]

TLG: How can [he/we] not even have 500 dollars! Worked for tens of years and [he] didn't have a bank book! No bank book! Look at how useless he was! It wasn't like there wasn't money! There was a lot, the business was good! I, at that time, a lot of people used to give money to my children. I took it to the bank, under, the [shared] account under my name. At the time, you [Doris and Janet] were young, your names weren't, weren't added yet, it was under my name. The children's money, once I saved 30, I told him [husband], told him to go to the bank. I saved 30, he would take 30 to gamble. I saved 40, he would take 40 to gamble. He took even all the children's money and gambled it all away.

Unknown speaker: Do you know why . . .

TLG: And I didn't know how to read/write. Ah Thliu, little brother/cousin Thliu, you know, Ah Thliu, at that time he could read, he knew how to read/write. [He said], "Ai, Auntie, there's nothing, no money. Where's the bank book, Auntie? When did you deposit 20? When did you deposit 30? There's no money in the bank book like you said!"

So I yelled at/scolded him. I yelled at/scolded him. Nothing [there was nothing in the bank]. So then I did not save money for the children [in the account]. I didn't [save] for you guys, did not. What was the point of giving him [the money to save]? He saw 20 dollars, I would save 20 dollars, he would take 20 dollars. I would save 30 dollars, he would take 30 dollars. There was no point/He was no good/useless. Very useless. Otherwise [if I hadn't done what I did] I/we would have had nothing.[33]

Figure 2.3. Goon family, 1941. From family collection.

One reason I had wanted help with a formal and complete translation of the interview was that I had noticed that there were substantial sections of the interview that my mother and aunt did not translate. I am not clear why they didn't translate these portions. Perhaps they thought that the information was not relevant to the questions I had asked. Perhaps they had heard their mother say similar things about their father before and didn't make note of what she was saying. Or perhaps they did not want me to hear her say such negative things about my grandfather.[34]

By the time 615 Forest Avenue was purchased in 1936, all eight children had been born, seven of them in the former residence. Toy Len faced some pressure not to keep all of her children. According to Doris, her mother had told her that the doctor asked her whether she wanted to keep Doris when she was born.

> And mother said, "Of course I want this baby. She's my baby." And she said to my father that the doctor asked me if I wanted this baby. And he said, "You could have given it away." He didn't care. Because I was a girl. Five boys and three girls. There were four boys born, Carroll, Richard, Ed, Albert, and then out popped Jo and my father said, "Oh, it's a girl," . . . and then Arthur was born and then me, and then he had probably lost count by that time. The doctor probably said, "If you have a baby that nobody wants, I'll take it." Mother was so mad at him. Can you imagine that he said, "Why didn't you give her away?" She was not happy that he would be accepting of giving me away.[35]

According to Amy Guen's biography, Toy Len Goon reported that Dogan recorded each child's birth date and time based on the lunar calendar and gave them their Chinese names.[36] They were given their English names by the doctors who delivered them, as Dogan and Toy Len did not know enough English to name their children and used their Chinese names at home.

Carroll was given the Chinese name Doo Foo, meaning "son has wealth," and he was born on the fourth month, tenth day of the Chinese lunar calendar, between noon and 2:00 p.m. Dick was given the name Jien Foo, meaning "to raise wealth," having been born on the seventh month, ninth day of 1923, between midnight and 2:00 a.m. Edward was named Gwock Foo, meaning "wealth of country," and was born in 1925 on the sixth month, nineteenth day, between 4:00 and 6:00 p.m. Albert was given the Chinese name Ark Foo, meaning "wealth and virtue," and he was born on the tenth month, twenty-second day of 1927 between 2:00 and 4:00 p.m. Josephine was named Thsiew Gee by her father, meaning "beautiful pearl." She was born on the first month, sixteenth day of 1929, between 10:00 p.m. and midnight. Arthur was given the Chinese name Hem Foo, meaning "increase wealth." He was born during the fifth month, twenty-seventh day of 1931 between 8:00 and 10:00

a.m. Doris was named Nguet Gee, meaning "moon pearl," by her father. She was born on the third month, nineteenth day of 1933, between 6:00 and 8:00 p.m. Janet, the youngest, was given the name Tew Gee, meaning "autumn pearl," after having been born on the eighth month, fifteenth day of 1935, between 2:00 and 4:00 a.m.

Friends and Neighbors in Portland

I discuss the daily routine for the Goon family as it revolved around laundry work, household chores, and the children's education in chapter 5. Here, I focus on notable memories, events, and relationships that Toy Len, her children, or their spouses recall from life in Portland. Toy Len Goon's hard work and devotion to her family made a strong impression on her children as they reflected on their childhoods. My mother, the youngest, remembers her as

> a very competent person who managed many different aspects of family life all at once and did it very well. She had a wonderful sense of humor, which she maintained despite her busy schedule. . . . She was good at multitasking and being motherly. Making sure everyone got fed and got off to a good day. She would always make sure we were dressed correctly and that we had our mittens, hats, and our coats.[37]

Arthur, the sixth child, describes her as "self-sacrificing," remembering that she would buy fish for dinner and "she would make sure we would all eat our portions before she ate any of it. We had to make sure we left some for her. She really wanted to make sure we ate our portions before she got to eat any." I asked whether she took the less desirable parts and whether the children felt they had to hold back, and he responded, "That's right. She always, . . . that was something that always sticks in your mind. . . . You had to hold back. You fill yourself up with rice. And the other food just . . . we just, no one got overweight. But no one really was hungry. When we grew up no one said they were hungry."[38]

My mother similarly recalls,

> We didn't have a lot to eat because there were quite a few of us. I don't remember being terribly hungry. Maybe once in a while, a little bit, we

> would want more. But we would always eat together. It was usually a nice time. No reprimanding and fighting. We had rules about where we would be able to pick the food from the bowls right in front of us. We weren't allowed to reach in front of someone else's space, and we were very good about that. Once in a while I got a morsel because I was the youngest.[39]

She did not remember her mother holding back, wondering whether she had put food aside for herself.

Toy Len had developed good relationships with the local butcher and fishmonger, sending her daughters Josephine or Doris to shop when they were old enough to help. Doris remembers that they would shop for food daily, since they only had an icebox in the basement to store food.

> She would say, "Doris, go get string beans or cod." She would say haddock, she would call it *hatnick*. I would go there and say I want a pound of *hatnick* and they would give me the *hatnick*. I said, "Mother!" It caused me such embarrassment. I remember going next door and buying the meat. I remember the book of coupons during World War II when they were rationing the meat. I would have all the coupons ready and he would say, "You're a smart little girl." Because I would give him the coupons. I must have been ten years old or eleven. Something like that in '41, '42. I was only seven or eight years old.[40]

Amy shared with me that when she traveled with Edward up to Portland from Boston to meet Toy Len for the first time while they were first dating,

> The first thing when I met [your] Grandma, she brought me to an A&P store (in 1948 or 1949). I took the railroad from North Station and I think Uncle Ed—they had a car—they picked me up in the Portland station. . . . So the first thing, she brought me to see the meat man. "Edward's girlfriend." So she said that this man had been very good to me. . . . By that time they still make their own hot dogs in the meat department. Grandma told me about how some of the whole piece of meat, that would be very expensive, he would charge her half price. The guy would save the big fish, the mackerel. Big family. Different people. They knew her. This is how she appreciate these things and all the positive feeling keep things going.[41]

From her many conversations with Toy Len over the years, Amy also had insight regarding Toy Len's early years trying to raise her children while working in the laundry.[42] Edward had been born when Carroll, the oldest, was three years old. Richard would have been a toddler. When they needed to work and could not take care of baby Edward, they would sometimes put Carroll on a rocking chair and tie Edward to him. Sometimes, they would find Edward on the floor, and would pick him up and tie him to Carroll again. Helen (Git Hing) Wong, the woman whom Toy Len pretended to borrow money from for the down payment for 615 Forest Avenue, would sometimes go shopping with Toy Len. Dogan told Toy Len he could only manage taking care of the two oldest children, Carroll and Richard. Toy Len asked Mrs. Wong's young daughter, around eleven years old, to help her by carrying Edward while they shopped. Amy found out about this when Toy Len asked her to reserve two seats at her daughter Terry's wedding for Helen Wong because Edward owed it to her for carrying him around when he was a baby.

She was also friendly with three Portland laundrymen, whose names and addresses she shared with Amy Guen, as well as with two Chinese restaurant owners. According to Amy, one of her good friends was the aforementioned Git Hing (Helen) Wong, who had pretended to loan Dogan money for the down payment. Helen had seven children and lived in an apartment in Portland. They shared the same maiden name, so Toy Len's children referred to her as Ai Yi (aunt). Thill Wong was another friend, who came to Portland to join her husband, William, who had come to the United States as a teen. Clara Soule had served as a "surrogate mother" to William.[43] Toy Len, as an older and more experienced mother, became a mentor to Thill, who was raising three children and helping run a chop suey stand called Chung King Chinese Products. Another friend was Mrs. Ngan Ngue Yuen Ng, who came in the 1940s to run a hand laundry with her husband. As she was also a member of the Goon clan, she saw Toy Len as an older sister. Toy Len gave her advice on rearing children while running a laundry.[44] She was also close to Mrs. Kalil, a Syrian immigrant who lived next door on Forest Avenue. According to Amy, Toy Len also formed friendships with a few Chinese women who were related Goon "clan cousins" while living in Lynn,

Massachusetts, after her retirement. She also remained connected to the Chinese community in Boston through the Goon Family Association.

Taking Care of Her Family's Health

In addition to taking care of her daily responsibilities running the laundry and household, Toy Len also made sure her children received the medical care they required. Josephine, the fifth child and the oldest daughter, became very ill at the age of ten (1939). She was so weak that her mother had to feed her so she could get out of bed in the morning, and her gums bled. Toy Len took her to the dentist, who told her to bring Josephine to see a doctor. Josephine recollects that her mother, though unable to speak English, managed to take her by bus to the doctor's office on Commercial Street in downtown Portland for multiple appointments before she was hospitalized. She did not know how her mother knew which bus to take.

> They didn't know what was wrong with me. I didn't even know it. But mother. On top of all mother's work in the laundry, she had to take me to the doctor. She had to take me to the hospital. She visited me. I don't know how often, but she had to take time off to visit me. She visited me quite often. I don't know how she did it.[45]

Josephine spent a year in the hospital before they finally identified her thyroid problem and performed the necessary surgery, which was delayed multiple times because her blood pressure would rise when she realized she was going into surgery. She seemed to feel guilty about her busy mother having to take time to visit her on top of her other responsibilities, but also was in awe of her mother's ability to care for her, reflecting, "Mother, with all that she had to do, she had to spend all that time to take care of me." When I asked how her mother showed her care for her, she responded, "Through actions. She wasn't much for words. She would give me an envelope so I could buy some snacks. . . . She would always give me a hug before she left. I don't remember her being much for words. She was always working. That's why I took over the cleaning and the cooking. I wasn't much good in the laundry."[46]

Dogan's Illness and Death, and the Aftermath

Dogan's death and the illness that preceded it marked a difficult transition period for the family. Dogan was hospitalized at the Togus VA hospital from August 8, 1939, through January 24, 1940, for the amputation of his leg.[47] Before his leg was amputated, he had been in intense pain, so Toy Len had called a policeman, who summoned an ambulance to bring him to the Portland City Hospital. Dogan had to sign his own paperwork to authorize the amputation because Toy Len was reluctant to do so.[48]

In the 1992 interview I conducted with her, she described the situation:

> The doctors always, when I went to see him for a few days, his leg had turned all black. Then, they told me to go sign my name to amputate his leg, but I would not sign my name. . . . He, he could do it. I, I said I would not sign my name to amputate his leg. What if tomorrow he got his leg amputated it's also, he, he, also hadn't died yet! After his leg was amputated he still lived, lived for another two, three years! He couldn't work but he still lived two, three more years! Those eight months [he was deciding? In the hospital?], then his leg was amputated.[49]

The minister who had asked her to sign the paperwork also gave her a tranquilizer to calm her nerves.[50] Her stress level had likely been amplified by the urgency she felt to respond to the request from Hung Gee, her stepdaughter in China, to send money. Before he entered the operating room, Dogan took the three dollars left in his pocket and told Toy Len to buy a check to send to her.[51]

While Dogan was in the hospital, Toy Len continued running the laundry while taking a taxi to the hospital daily, which added to their already tight household expenses. Lo Chin Bak, a family friend from Toisan, arranged for a taxi to bring the dirty laundry to his own laundry so that he could wash it and send it back. Police officers and teachers would also check on the family, one officer one time giving each child a yo-yo.[52] The children, who had always helped in the laundry, had to increase their household responsibilities after Dogan returned from the hospital unable to work due to the amputation of his leg.

Carroll, then a junior in high school, was kept home from school to help run the laundry.[53]

Things took another turn for the worse when Dogan was rehospitalized due to his declining health. He was referred to the Veterans Administration facility in Togus, Maine, on October 17, 1940, and was declared "medically eligible" for hospital care. His Veterans Administration records show that on October 18, 1940, he applied for a waiver of fees for his care at the VA hospital. The form (P-10), "Application for Hospital Domiciliary Care," lists his NSC (non–service connected) disabilities as "Amputation left thigh, middle and Lower third permitting prosthesis Arteriosclerosis general with hypertension and tachycardia Bronchitis, chr." His date of birth is listed as May 5, 1890, color is listed as "Yellow," and birthplace as "San Francisco Cal." He is shown to have enlisted in Portland, Maine, on June 2, 1918, and was discharged in Hoboken, New Jersey, on December 21, 1918, as a private in the medical department. He was listed as receiving a pension of thirty dollars a month. The form notes that he was married, with eight children under eighteen. In response to the question "Are you financially able to pay the necessary expenses of hospital or domiciliary care?" Dogan had answered, "No."

His medical report, signed by the examining physician, N. H. Badaines, on October 16, 1940, notes that he "appears chronically ill. Pale." His chief complaints were "general weakness, fatigue, loss of appetite, headaches, extremities cold, and difficulty in urination" over the past four weeks, in addition to swelling of his right ankle and "shortness of breath and cough." His pulse was 98 and his blood pressure was 170/145. The report also notes that his "radials are sclerosed" with "a rough murmur at the apex" and "some cardiac enlargement to the left," reflected in his diagnosis of "cardiac enlargement and myocardial insufficiency with failure."[54]

During my individual interviews with them, Jo, Doris, Arthur, and Amy each talked about how Toy Len took the bus to Togus and back alone during Dogan's hospitalizations, often waiting in the cold weather for it to arrive. They marveled that she was able to figure out which bus to take, as she was not able to read the schedule or bus name in English.

Arthur recollects, "The amazing thing is that when my father was in Augusta, she would take the bus in the dead of winter. . . . She's working so hard and then traveling 100 miles in the winter. From Portland to Augusta had to be 150 miles. She was waiting for the bus in the cold." However, Arthur said, she never complained. Doris shared a similar memory, marveling at how Toy Len would travel to Togus on the bus even though

> she couldn't read. She had to remember a few letters. By herself. And must have had a photographic memory because she had to look at the bus and remember what bus she was on so she would know which bus to get back on. Yet she couldn't speak any English and didn't know how to read.[55]

Dogan passed away on May 3, 1941, at 4:00 p.m. at the VA hospital in Togus, Maine. His death certificate indicated that the immediate cause of death was "hypertension artery with myocardial damage," with acute uremia as a contributing cause. The manager, M. L. Stoddard, sent Toy Len a letter, most certainly from a standard template, expressing his sympathy, ensuring her that Dogan "received every attention" during his stay and that she "will have the further consolation of the thought that he served his country, and died honored and respected by all of us."[56]

The VA form (supply form 2237a) titled Notice of Death and Information for Disposition of Remains indicates that Dogan's body would be transported to Hay and Peabody Funeral Directors of Portland. The form also noted that the clothing would be "furnished by government." With help from the Goon Family Association and the VA, Dogan was buried in Mount Hope Cemetery in the Chinese section and was reburied in the Forest Hills Cemetery in Boston when the family moved.[57]

Veterans Administration Opinion on Marriage

Following his hospitalization at the VA in August 1939, Dogan's immigration file had been combined on September 6, 1939, with Toy Len Goon's file (number 2500/4536). In an October 27, 1939, document, the solicitor writes to Major Clark of the VA that an opinion needed to be rendered "as to whether the Veterans Administration may recognize the existence of a valid marriage between Dogan Goon and Chin Toy Len."[58] If their custom marriage in China could be deemed valid by the US Veterans Administration, Toy Len would be eligible for a pension if Dogan were to pass away and she did not remarry.

The case revolved around whether the "custom marriage" ceremony performed in Dogan's village of "Hong Tow" in China constituted a valid custom marriage per the "requirements of a Chinese custom marriage." The VA used another custom marriage, Hum Foon Wahdo, C02, 028, 511 (35 Sol. 194) from November 17, 1937, as precedent. However, Dogan and Toy Len's wedding had actually taken place sixteen years before that case.

The criteria were laid out in the memo:

> From this brief as well as from certain decisions referred to in the course of the opinion of May 31, 1935, it appears that in order to constitute a valid customary marriage under the laws of China, there must be (1) the exchange of three generation certificates relating to the bride and groom, respectively, (2) the written proposal by the groom's parents or guardians, and (3) the written acceptance by the bride's family. These three preliminaries must be gone through with no matter what adverse conditions may exist and make their performance more or less difficult. There then follow the six ceremonials, which are (1) the presentation of gifts, (2) the request for name, (3) the consultation of fortune for luck, (4) the giving of the assessment, (5) the request for the date of marriage, and (6) the receiving of the relative.[59]

The memo noted that a genealogical certificate might also be used as proof that "one of the three preliminaries has been gone through."[60]

The VA notes that no "documentary proof of the marriage" of Dogan and Toy Len Goon had been provided, so depositions were taken from both Dogan and Toy Len regarding their marriage ceremony and presented as evidence.

In a deposition dated October 10, 1939, Dogan says he was born in San Francisco on May 5, 1892. In May 1921 he left Boston by train for Montreal, and traveled via the Canadian Pacific Lines to Vancouver, taking a boat from that port to Hong Kong. A month after arriving, he married Toy Len, described in his own words below,

> by Chinese Custom; this custom of marriage is different than in the United States as matchmakers arrange the couples to be married and obtain the consent of the oldest living relative of both families. My uncle, as

> my father and mother were dead, consented to my marriage to Chin Toy Len—his name was Goon Yen Gek and he lived in the village of Hong Tow. The matchmakers obtain birth dates of both couple and take them from one home to the home of the other person to be married and after these are accepted the ceremony follows. My uncle and the parents of Chin Toy Len agreed on a lucky day for the wedding or ceremony and I believe this was on July 15, 1921 and the ceremony lasted about two or three days before the ancestors. We had a feast and then gifts were presented by relatives and invited guests. I met only my wife's sister and never went to their home although this is only permissible after the ceremony. We were married by my Uncle Goon Yen Gek, and I then lived in my eighth uncle's house who was dead but my father had half ownership in this house. We lived in this house about four months and then left China via Hong Kong to Vancouver, Canada arriving in this country around Dec. 7, 1921.[61]

Of the criteria described in the case used as precedent, Dogan's deposition mentions only three: the presentation of gifts, the consultation of fortune for luck (in the agreement on the lucky day for the ceremony), and the receiving of the relatives. The exchange of certificates, written proposal by the groom's guardians, and written acceptance by the bride's family were not discussed by Dogan and may not have occurred, since most villagers were unable to read and write.

Toy Len's account was similar to Dogan's in its reference to the matchmakers and the choosing of lucky days. She recounts details specific to her own experience of being dressed in traditional gowns, being brought to the ceremony in a carriage, and taken in on the back of a servant.

> The wife, Goon Chin Toy Len, in her deposition of October 10, 1939, testified in part:
>
> I was twenty-five years of age when my parents arranged for marriage ceremony to Dogan Goon. According to Chinese custom all marriages are arranged by matchmakers and our marriage ceremony was the same as others. After the matchmakers have arranged with my parents to my marriage to Dogan Goon the lucky days both agreeable to our parents the date is set for the ceremony. I was dressed in Chinese gowns and taken in carriage to where the ceremony was to be carried out at the

> home of my bethothed's [*sic*] uncle. When I arrived at the uncle's house Dogan Goon met me at the carriage and I was taken into the house on the back of a servant (woman) who is hired to do this. I was taken to a separate room and kept there with three maids for all day and that night. Early in the morning about eight o-clock I was taken before the names on the ancestors which is on the wall of the house and in company with my intented [*sic*] groom or husband to be we both bow before their names and we remained there about one hour. I was then returned to the room from which I came and then the maids go back to their homes. Then I came from the room to the feast and I was the host to the guests and relatives. The feast lasted about an hour and this concludes their marriage, although during the feast I poured tea and then was presented gifts by the people present. We were then permitted to go to my husband's room. We remained in China for about four months and then my husband and I came to the United States and arrived in Boston, Mass in Dec. 1921.[62]

While the procedure of assessing the validity of a custom marriage was based on the idea of precedent, there existed variation within Chinese marriage customs, based on region, class, and other factors. Marriage practices of "the imperial family and clan, the educated elite, and ordinary people" differed, and marriages both reflected and shaped inequalities.[63] Patricia Buckley Ebrey notes that "in the south, especially in areas with dominant lineages, dowries among the poor were often modest affairs, costing the woman's family significantly less than the amount they received in betrothal gifts."[64] There was no mention of a dowry in Dogan or Toy Len's depositions, just the exchange of gifts. Toy Len's family was unable to afford a dowry, and her foster family had provided the appropriate outfits for her first marriage, to Mr. Moy.[65]

The very premise of the hearing illustrates the power that the state had to regulate and verify migrants' relationships—all for a pension of fifty dollars a month. It is absurd that the Veterans Administration thought it could accurately assess the validity of their marriage with very little knowledge about what a Toisanese village marriage might look like, and eighteen years after their wedding and after the couple had produced eight children.

However, I include this discussion for another reason. Contained within the papers are depositions of Dogan and Toy Len Goon, each describing their marriage in China in their own (translated) words. Their accounts are rendered eloquently, in contrast to the hesitant English that comprises the transcripts in their immigration files. There is something very powerful about reading these comprehensive accounts of their marriage in their own words, despite having been done in the context of interrogation.

The file also notes that the deputy commissioner of the Immigration and Naturalization Service of the US Department of Labor verified in a letter on September 13, 1939, that "after a hearing held in December 1921, Chin Toy Len was recognized as the wife of the veteran and admitted to the United States as such."[66] Chi Fuey Gim testified at the hearing to the effect and that she had recently come from China; that she lived in a village in China near that of the veteran's wife; and that although she did not attend her marriage to the veteran she visited her house a few days after the marriage and that she knows them to be husband and wife."[67] In addition, Dogan's application included affidavits from white witnesses Blanchard H. Brown and James H. Pinkham saying that they had known Dogan for twenty years, that he had gone to China to get married, and that the couple had given birth to "several children."[68] Birth certificates were available for seven of the eight children. The document ends with the decision "that the evidence is sufficient to cstablish a valid marriage by Chinese custom between the veteran and Chin Toy Len." It is signed by Edward E. Odom.

Children's Perspectives on Dogan

The Goon children I interviewed, some of whom were also interviewed by community historian Gary Libby and Fenggang Yang, who conducted a series of interviews with the family and other Chinese families from Portland to establish an archive on the history of Chinese in Maine, did not have strong or numerous memories of Dogan. Not all the Goon siblings were interviewed, as Richard and Albert had already passed away when Libby and Yang conducted interviews with Edward and Amy, Josephine, Doris, and Janet. The other two surviving siblings, Carroll and Arthur, were not interviewed by Libby and Yang because they lived out of town, in New Mexico and California, respectively. Unfortunately, by the time I started doing my interviews, Carroll's health had declined, and I was advised by my mother not to interview him for fear it would tire him out too much.

Josephine talked about how Dogan's illness was challenging for her mother and the Goon siblings. She recalls, "He was sick most of the time, so he really didn't know what was going on. It was difficult for my mother when he was sick. He had sort of a bad temper. At one time he had one leg removed already. It just wasn't an easy situation for anybody."[69]

However, she recalls positive experiences with him. As the oldest girl, she was charged with helping her mother with domestic chores and spent less time doing laundry work. She remembers,

> My mother would cook the meal downstairs and bring it upstairs for him. Then I would clean up and bring the dishes back downstairs. I interacted with him a lot. . . . I actually enjoyed him. Maybe I didn't know too much. But I enjoyed interacting with him a little bit. Just together, because I had to try to look after him a little bit when mother would give him the food and I would have to clean up after him. I don't know how he got to Chinatown. But he would get these waterbugs. They were good too. He would buy them and tell me to eat them. They were good. That's kind of salty. I remember having fun with him eating those. I was probably the only one not working at that time.[70]

In my interview with my mother, Janet, she speculates that since was so young, she is uncertain whether her memories were real.

> I don't know [whether] I made that up, but I have a memory of my going upstairs with Aunt Doris, sitting by his bedside. He was on the second floor. He was bedridden. He was very warm and caring. We would bring him stuff. I think I remember sitting on his lap. I think he gave me Coke, and my mother didn't like that. I had a sensitive stomach and my mother blamed it on that. Very minimal, but whatever I have is warm. Him smiling, and sitting on his lap.[71]

Figure 2.4. Dogan, Doris, and Janet, May 1940. Courtesy of Maine Historical Society.

I reminded my mother of a photo I had seen where she and Doris are sitting on Dogan's lap, and she responded, "Maybe that's where I got the memory from. Was I three or five [when Dogan died]? I wouldn't remember a whole lot."[72] She speculated that her older brother Arthur might remember more. However, when I interviewed Arthur, he said that he did not have many memories at all about Dogan.

> I honestly don't remember a lot about my father. I remember when he came back from the Army, he had his leg amputated shortly after that and spent a lot of time in the veterans hospital. I don't recall any of that. I just saw him just a few times after he had his leg amputated. I have a lot of hazy memories. My sister keeps talking about him eating these beetles. That's one thing I recall, him sitting there eating these roasted black beetles. I never was crazy about that.[73]

The Goon siblings' varying recollections of their father show that memories are shaped by specific interactions and relationships within the family, which may stem from age, birth order, or gender.

Mother's Relationship with Dogan

The children were aware that their mother shouldered most of the responsibility for running the household and the laundry due to their father's illness. They also knew that he had gambled and at times used opium and that their mother had worked very hard in the laundry even before he became disabled. Doris observed that because they had been in an arranged marriage,

> it wasn't as though it was a big love story. My dad, I thank God for him, he gave me life. But she carried the ball for the whole family. Even when he was alive. He came from a well-to-do family and never had much responsibility. She carried the ball all the way through. It's not like she had warm feelings she wanted to share about your wonderful dad. . . . It would be something on the negative side.[74]

When I asked Josephine what she remembered about her parents' relationship, she recollected, "By the time I would have noticed, my father was sick. There were never fights. I know they didn't have a good relationship." I asked how she knew this, and she said that her mother would mention the challenges in their relationship sometimes when they were "just talking" when Josephine was in her thirties or forties.

> Because my father didn't . . . started the laundry but he really didn't work in the laundry. Someone told my mother that if you learn how to run the laundry, that job is going to be yours forever. And sure enough, she came over, and then she was working in the laundry, learned how to do all the chores, and then my father got sick. And then she had to run the laundry. She said one of her friends told her that and then she told me. She had a couple of lady friends in Boston and they would talk.[75]

However, though she was only seven, Doris remembers her mother getting emotional after Dogan died. She interpreted the emotion as reflecting her feeling for him to some extent, but also the uncertainty of what lay ahead:

> In spite of what I just said to you, he still was her husband, and some level of love there because when he passed away in 1940, he was a veteran. They buried him in Mt. Hope cemetery in Massachusetts, and we were in Portland, Maine. Anyway, he died, there is no money, for some reason these people [American Legion] stepped in, but we went in the car and drove forever. I'm only seven years old and all I know is that she was crying her eyes out and I was so scared. He was in the casket.[76]

Because all of the Goon children had described their mother as being very coolheaded, I asked Doris, "You had never seen her so emotional?" She responded,

> At that time she was hysterical because she was left with eight kids. It was, "What am I going to do now?" I'm sure she was sorry he passed away, but he was ill the last couple years of his life. So she took care of him. She had all this on her shoulders. . . .
>
> So we all moved to Massachusetts [in 1952], and after a few years, we said, "You know, we should get a family plot." We all got a plot in Forest Hills. I said, "Well, Mom, let's move Dad to the plot." Okay, that's the thing to do. So they arranged to exhume the coffin and bring him to Forest Hills. So we go to Forest Hills and I say, "Mommy, we're here," and I got out of the car and I looked back and she's standing by the car in tears. So that . . . there was feeling there. But it was just kind of covered up by the hard work and the responsibility she had.[77]

Mother's Aid

The Woodfords Corner community was understandably concerned when Dogan passed away. How would Toy Len continue to run the laundry and take care of all of the children? A City Welfare Department social worker tried to persuade her to close the business and apply for financial assistance in the form of Mother's Aid, but she did not want to apply.[78] Toy Len told Amy that Carroll had been translating, and that she had told him to tell the worker that she didn't want their money and that it was shameful to receive handouts.

Carroll was upset, but she explained to him that as the oldest child, he would have to stay out of school to help her with the laundry.[79] Later, she had also told her daughter Doris that she had been concerned not only about having to give up her assets—the laundry business she had worked so hard to maintain and the building she had purchased on 615 Forest Avenue—but also about the long-term support for her children. As she understood it, while she would receive money for each child, those benefits would end once the children reached a certain age.[80]

Amy also recalled that Toy Len told her that she had been embarrassed when the principal of Deering High School, Mr. Wiggins, came to the laundry to find out why Carroll had not been coming to school. Toy Len was not able to communicate that as the eldest son who was a substitute for the father, Carroll had to take care of the laundry. Amy explained, "If you were in China, the eldest son get double share of the legacy. You have to lead the family for the younger brothers and sister." Amy said that Toy Len was "very smart," as she was able to look at her situation from "two to three angles" in explaining her decision to Amy to not accept Mother's Aid.[81] She weighed being able to keep her children together under one roof, being self-supporting as a family in the long run, and keeping ownership of her property, 615 Forest Avenue.

Doris proudly recalls her mother's refusal of welfare and the measures she took to continue running the laundry after Dogan's death. Her mother had understood that if she were to accept Mother's Aid, she would have to relinquish both her children and her property. Therefore, she politely refused. Doris shares that though the family had little, the children's work ethic was recognized and rewarded with opportunities for higher education and upward mobility:

> After Dad's early death at the age of 47 I think it was, Mother declined welfare payments as it would mean she would have to give up her house and her business (those were the rules in those day; not now) and told her oldest son Carroll that he would have to stay home and help her so that she could keep us all together. What a gutsy lady!! It made a great impression on our neighbors and the school system. Teachers brought books to the laundry for Carroll and told him to study them and to come back to high school, which he did a year later when Richard then took over, and he graduated high school a better student than when he left. Also, the principal, who was a very stern and much feared man, asked Carroll what he wanted to do after graduation. He always knew he wanted

> to be a doctor but Mother told him it was out of the question as there was no money. But Principal Wiggins, because he admired the family (probably the way Mom handled things), got Carroll a full scholarship to Syracuse U and then Carroll earned another full scholarship to Johns Hopkins Medical School. The rest is history! We had such respect for Mom that we all strived to make her proud by getting good grades and staying out of trouble! For a treat, we would get a dime to go to the movies or have an ice cream—and, I'll never forget this, candy bars were cut and shared 8 ways![82]

Toy Len Goon was also concerned about what others would think if she received public assistance, believing that those on welfare were in a similar category to the disabled, and were not self-sufficient.[83] She prided herself on modeling responsible behavior for her children and teaching them to be self-sufficient.[84] And while she would later receive praise for her children's good behavior and academic records, she felt that she was under continual scrutiny by outsiders concerned for their health and well-being after Dogan's death.[85]

According to Judy Yung's history of Chinese women in San Francisco, accepting public assistance created stress for many women.[86] Yung shares an account by Jane Kwong Lee, who worked with Chinese women as a YWCA coordinator during the 1930s, noting that while a mother was "grateful" that the family had been provided with sufficient food and appeared to be happy, "when I talk with her further, I can sense the struggle within her. She cannot bear the thought of being on the relief roll. Her people in China think she is enjoying life here in the 'Golden Mountain.' She dares not inform them about the family's sufferings and hardships. If she does, she would 'lose face.'"

Toy Len Goon's refusal of welfare, known then as Mother's Aid or Mother's pension, has become a central part of family memory. Like her purchase of 615 Forest Avenue, this act was viewed as a testament to her self-reliance, work ethic, and the importance she placed on providing for her family and keeping them together. According to Josephine,

> When our father died, people came to the house and wanted to put us in different homes. Grandma said absolutely not. She would take care of her own children. They must have been social workers. Some people came to

> the house and wanted to take us to different homes. Not together, because there were eight of us. Mother didn't want any of that.

Josephine recalls that her mother "told that story many times, that people came and wanted to take us and give us a home so she wouldn't have to worry about us, but she didn't want anything to do with that."[87]

Doris recalls that her mother would often express negative ideas about welfare to her, even before she was offered it herself:

> Anyway she just I remember her saying to me. That lady is on welfare. The message to me is that well that's a negative. Welfare isn't something you want to be doing. When it came to be her turn, she thought about it, and figured I could keep you together if I accept the few dollars they were going to give me for each child. You get to be a certain age they would stop the payments. So if I took the payments I would not be able to keep you so she made the decision to keep the laundry, and have us all work together.[88]

Doris elaborated:

> All I know what she told me as I remember is that they would give so much money for each child but she also knew there was an ending to that scenario. She didn't want help anyway. I think she spoke to Carroll and said you are the head of the household now. You have to leave school and work with me and keep us together. So of course nobody said no to momma.[89]

Amy, in her discussions with Toy Len, had also discussed the subject of taking welfare. She reported that Toy Len was primarily concerned with what others, both Chinese and non-Chinese, would think when she refused welfare and had her children help her run the laundry. "So she was concerned?" I asked. "All the time," Amy replied. She elaborated:

> The way I've heard the story is that she refused the welfare because she would have to give up her assets, her laundry, and that kids would have to go to different homes. . . .
>
> . . . Well, she also think the Chinese way. She said a lot of Chinese in the village would say just because you can have so many children, you

> couldn't feed them. That would be somebody, people will think they are stupid. Now since you have so many children, if they were eventually hand [*sic*] out, the Chinese people would criticize her.[90]

I asked whether it would seem as though she had failed as a mother, and Amy clarified, "Not only fail, she also say that when you have so many children, it's almost say you are less, to a woman." Amy said that Toy Len was worried that people would criticize her for taking her children out of school to work. "She kept on thinking people's gonna say if the kids didn't turn out good people, they're gonna say, 'That stupid Chinese woman didn't know what she did. Make the kids work.'"[91]

Thus, Toy Len felt some pressure to make sure her children followed the rules and contributed to the household. The children remember that while she may have threatened to use force, she primarily managed her children by talking to them, and leading by example. Amy recollects what her husband, Edward, shared with her:

> But the kids had to be better. All Ed told me was this. Grandma has a stick or something to whip the kids with. But she always put it very far up, she couldn't reach it herself. She would say, "Look at that stick. If you don't behave, I'm gonna use that stick on you." So Ed said you would think she would put it very handy where she could grab it and whip. But she didn't. She used it so the kids would behave.[92]

Arthur, the youngest son, recalls that she would take the time to talk with her children if they were having problems. He shared, "I guess one of the boys said that instead of hitting us with a stick, she would talk to us and talk a lot. I guess they said that was how she controlled us, by just talking. I think if you had problems, she would talk to you."

Concerned Community

Amy Guen, who had first met Toy Len in 1948 while dating Edward, had interacted directly with a number of the people in Toy Len's life who had been concerned about how she would support her family after Dogan's death, particularly Clara Soule. Soule was a retired elementary supervisor at Portland Public Schools who worked as an Americanization teacher.[93] The Americanization movement, which arose in the 1920s, was an effort to recognize the cultural adaptability of immigrants and to facilitate the shedding of their differences through the teaching of "American" culture to help tame the threat that some of these immigrants and their differences were thought to represent. Soule had been a frequent visitor to the Goon laundry, having taken a number of Chinese families in the area under her wing.[94] She had known the Goon family prior to Dogan's death, but started to come by more frequently to check on the family after he passed away. However, her interest in Toy Len Goon and other Chinese in the area was also motivated by broader concerns. Though Soule was genuinely interested in their welfare, her role as an Americanization teacher meant that she saw it as her duty to help new immigrants assimilate to US society by teaching them US history and culture, and more importantly, the English language. But Toy Len Goon told Amy that she was not always happy when Soule stopped by. When I asked why, Amy elaborated:

> Well, it's interfering. See, Grandma liked to please Ms. Soule, but Ms. Soule happened to come more than she would have liked to because she's so busy. So there's a conflict there of feeling, ambivalence. But later on, how Ms. Soule being sensitive to everything going on and how hard she worked, Ms. Soule told me that she disapproved of her not taking the welfare offer, yeah, and kept the kids working. She would even disapprove that Carroll had to work two years. And then later on went back to school. Because that wasn't American culture at the time. Child labor, remember that.[95]

Amy said that Soule told her years later at a banquet in Boston that she had sensed that Toy Len was trying to avoid her every time she came into the laundry. Soule had wanted to teach her to read English, but Toy Len felt that she didn't have time to sit down for a lesson. Indeed, Toy Len had told Amy that she had worried she was being impolite by not being more hospitable to Soule.

Soule also told Amy that she eventually realized that she was wrong in thinking that Toy Len Goon needed aid to support her family.

> I always entertain Ms. Soule and Reverend Hough and wife. They told me things similar, how they felt saw grandma [after Dogan's death]. . . .

> But then after she was chosen [as Mother of the Year], everyone was happy. They thought that she probably had better virtue than they assume. Before they thought that was Chinese way.[96]

Still, Soule likely never fully understood Toy Len Goon's full responsibilities and priorities that blended work and domestic responsibilities, which may have resulted in her also not understanding the agency that Toy Len Goon had in managing her family's situation. Toy Len would regularly work sixteen-hour days, cooking, doing housework, and running the laundry business, and had little downtime. This context is important for understanding why it seemed that she never had time to engage with Soule when she would drop by the laundry. But it is also likely that she didn't feel that it was a priority to spend time on personal development, which would take time away from running the laundry and caring for her children. She was able to learn enough conversational English to get along quite well in her day-to-day dealings with the fish merchant, the butcher, the twine and paper peddler, neighbors, and customers. She would even speak a combination of Chinese and English to her children. Toy Len later told Amy that unbeknownst to Soule, she had actually taught herself the alphabet and how to read some basic English words on her own, using grocery flyers. She would show her children the picture of bananas in the ad, and ask them the English word. She would then learn to associate the sounds with the letters also pictured in the ad. Years later, Amy told Soule that in fact Toy Len had taught herself to read basic words on her own and using her own method, one that reflected the practical needs of grocery shopping. Though she had not become "Americanized" in the way that Soule had planned, she had become integrated into her local community and was able to run her business, patronize local merchants, and form friendships with neighbors. This example highlights some of the alternative perspectives that reflect her agency that emerge from exploring her life story, and how they may reflect different routes, methods, and goals of "Americanization," but not necessarily assimilation.

Just Knowing What to Do

The Goon children not only worked long hours in the laundry, but also excelled at school. Seeing how hard their mother worked, they knew that they needed to pitch in where possible, while also keeping up with their studies, or in the case of Carroll and Dick, taking time off of school and catching up later. They felt that they somehow knew what they needed to do without being told, following their mother's example as well as that of the older children.

Josephine recalls taking over some of the cooking when she got out of the hospital at around the age of eleven. She reflects,

> You know, we just did what we had to do. . . . She would give me instructions. "Go shopping for food." She would have me buy fish. What I needed to cook for that day. I would do the shopping. I remember when she told me not to touch the cases. She gave me a lot of instruction. I guess everything came out all right.[97]

Arthur thinks that his mother must have managed all of the laundry work on her own until her children were old enough to help out. Arthur recalls "seeing how hard she worked. Nobody said you had to do this or that. When we got old enough to do something, we just did it. I just watched what the older boys were doing, and as soon as you were old enough to do it, you did it.[98] I asked whether they ever didn't want to work because they had to study or wanted to do what other teenagers were doing. Arthur said that he did not remember, but that they were not able to do extracurricular activities at school. "But we accepted that." He added, "I don't feel we worked hard. We just did our share." I repeated a story that Toy Len had told Amy about when the football coach came to the laundry to ask her whether Richard could play football, but she had to say no, otherwise she would have nobody to help her in her laundry. Arthur remembers, "We entertained ourselves in other ways. We would build these little go-karts. Instead of playing organized sports, we would go in the back and play ball."[99]

As the oldest daughter, Josephine was charged with taking care of Janet, who is eight years younger than she, and therefore missed out on playing with her siblings. She recalls,

> I used to resent it because I couldn't play. Everybody was out there playing and I had to take care of my sister. I used to babysit her. Take her outside in the carriage to get fresh air. I think I probably changed diapers.

Figure 2.5. Goon children playing, Portland, ca. 1934. Courtesy of Maine Historical Society.

> As she got older, she wanted to play school with Doris. . . . They were playing ball outside. I wanted to play ball too. But I couldn't because I had to watch her.[100]

I asked whether her mother would ever ask anyone else to help take care of Janet. She replied, "It was always me. The boys were working at the laundry. We all kind of had jobs. That was my job. One of my jobs." She continued, "You know, all these things, you just do it. Whatever needs to be done, you just do it."[101]

Studying

The Goon children remember studying in between doing their laundry chores. Josephine recalls, "While you're doing your chores in the few spare moments you had, we looked at the books. Somehow we got it done on time." I asked whether her mother had to remind them to study, and she replied, "She didn't have to really enforce it. We knew that she wanted us to get our homework done. So we were obedient children, at least most of the time. And we tried to do what we were supposed to do." Josephine elaborated,

> I think maybe we knew we didn't want to do these kinds of jobs the rest of our lives. Maybe we knew that. Mother wasn't very forceful. Very seldom would she have to raise her voice with us. From my own limited memory, we just knew what we had to do and we just did it. Whether we liked it or not, we just did it.[102]

When I asked whether some of the older siblings led by example, something I had heard my aunts and uncles say of Uncle Carroll, the eldest, Josephine responded, "Could it be innate? We just knew what we had to do. Could that be possible?"

In an interview with Arthur in 2019, he reflected, "Actually I think it's because for me, I see my older brothers going to college and studying, so it seemed like the thing to do." I asked whether she told them to study, and Arthur replied, "I don't think she did that with any of the kids."[103]

Despite her concerns about what others in the community thought about how she was managing her family after Dogan's death, Toy Len Goon also felt that she had been supported by many people. Principal Wiggins brought books to Carroll and encouraged him to return to school when he was able. He helped Carroll get a scholarship to Syracuse University, and later helped Richard get a scholarship to Rensselaer Polytechnic Institute (RPI). All of the children developed a reputation among their teachers and their principal for being hardworking and achieving good grades. Each ended up going on for further education after graduating high school, whether a four-year college, secretarial, or court reporting school. Carroll, the oldest, became a doctor. Richard studied physics at RPI and opened his own television and electronics store. Albert became a lawyer. Edward received his PhD in chemistry and went into industry. Josephine went to school to become a secretary and eventually became the office manager for Doris, who went to stenotype school and started what would become one of the largest court reporting firms in Boston. Arthur studied engineering at Tufts University on the GI Bill. And Janet, the youngest, eventually received her MSW from Simmons College and became a clinical social worker.

The Good Old Days

Contrasting the current climate to the era in which she and her siblings grew up, Doris believes that the climate in the United States has changed since the "good old days," when hard work was rewarded and people got along. In a 2018 interview, she reflected,

> That's how things worked in those days. It was a lot easier and they . . . America is a great country. It's interesting. It's not that you felt accepted in a total way, a societal way, but nobody bothered you. As long as you did your share, worked hard and were good kids, they left you alone. A lot of people helped, but a lot of people just left you alone. They were not your friends and not your enemies. Which is fine.

I asked how things were different now. She replied,

> I think it is a lot more volatile now. I don't know why, but there seems to be an awful political divide. Everything is driven by politics. It's all political. People are a lot less civil. It's so bad. As the elections come and go one [every] four years you might win the next four years, you might lose, and you just get along. But something happened the last election when Trump, who wasn't supposed to win but had the right message obviously to the people. It has been unbelievably uncivil. I'm not saying that anything would happen necessarily between the Chinese race . . . It's more Black and Hispanic, a lot of strong feelings. I don't think, the Asians are not so much as a part of it. It's basically because of the culture. They are quiet people, they obey the laws, they study hard, all the things that make life workable.[104]

The family story of upward mobility attained through hard work and good behavior, which fueled the development of the model minority myth in the 1950s, also had long-lasting effects on how later generations thought of their own successes and the circumstances that shaped their opportunities. While the ideas expressed by Doris do not reflect those of all family members, the changing social and political climate and evolving ideas of the model minority myth have shaped their ideas about the opportunities and challenges faced by themselves and their children.

3

Kinship Ties Across Borders

A Transnational Family Separated by the Cold War

ANDREA: Can you ask if she, if she wishes that she could have gone back to China?

JANET: Mmm, that's a big question.

DORIS: Andrea mun o haai ni um, ni zung ji faan hui Hong Saan ni. [Andrea asked, wants to see, if you want(ed) to go back to China.]

TOY LEN GOON: If I were to go back now, who would I know [in China]?

D: In the past, when [your husband] was alive, did you want to go back?

TLG: When he was alive, we had plans to go back to China. When he was alive. We thought we'd take you all back, to see what China was like. And then come back here [to the United States].

J: We were all supposed to go back and visit when my father was alive.

TLG: Wanted you all to go back and visit.

J: We were all supposed to go. And come back [to the United States] to live, though. Aa sun faan loi koi zi, right? [We planned to come back (to the United States) to live, right?]

TLG: Yeah, yeah, faan e haai a Hong Saan ja. [Yeah, yeah, go back to take a look at China.]

J: The plan was to visit.

TLG: Jiu hui jiu faan loi koi zi aa. [And then come back here to live.]

D: She just wanted us to see it but uh it, never came to be.

TLG: Jit loi kui jiu, kui oi je u thlai ne ngaan, ngi loi, kui daau goi heu, jiu mot aa. [First, when he (husband) came, he gambled all our money. Second, he's gone, so what was left?]

A: But does she wish that she could have?

J: Yeah, she does, that's what the plan was.

D: Her plan was to go back and visit. Not to live.

J: Not to live.

D: But to visit.[1]

In this chapter, I explore how Toy Len Goon carried out her filial duties to both Dogan's family and her natal family, despite the state-imposed challenges of connecting to kin in China. I trace the significance of filial ties, which not only reflected affective bonds between family members, but also dictated the place of Chinese migrants and determined their social connections and obligations within a transnational social universe that extended not only back to China but also to other Chinese in the United States.

I also consider how the specific point in time when Toy Len Goon received her US Mother of the Year award, an honor that might be seen to represent a pinnacle of acceptance as an American, marked the interruption of generations-long patterns of transnational relations. The Cold War politics that produced the model minority stereotype, which the Goons were seen to exemplify and from which they had benefited, also cut them off from their ancestral homeland for decades to come and shaped the relationships of future generations to China. The migration of women and the formation of families in the United States enhanced the development of US-based community organizations and kinship networks. However, despite their filial obligations and affective connections to China, Cold War tensions between the United States and China weakened homeland ties for Toy Len Goon and other Chinese Americans who were separated from kin in China. Rather than existing solely within the bounds of a nation-state, these obligations were transnational in scope, linking parts of a community separated by distance and time.

Growing up in a predominantly white suburb of Boston, I did not think much about my family's relationship to China. If anything, I sometimes wished that I wasn't Chinese American, particularly when a second-grade classmate, an intimidating boy much larger than I, told me that his father was a policeman and could send me back to China. In that desperate moment, I remember returning home and asking my mother why we had to be Chinese. Though I did not believe that the boy's father could send me to China, I wondered what China would be like, and imagined how out of place I would feel there, as I had never been before. What I did know was based on the little I'd learned in school or seen in the media. I was a child in the 1970s during the Cold War, when relations between China and the United States were tense, and information was limited to dramatic news reports about diplomacy efforts or the evils of communist China.

Though she lived to be almost 102 years old, Toy Len Goon never returned to China to visit. She would have been in her eighties in the early 1980s when, under the leadership of Deng Xiaoping, mainland China reopened to the outside world after the death of Chairman Mao. My mother recalls her mother having talked about her unfulfilled plans from time to time—that while their father was still alive, he and Toy Len had hoped to take the family back to visit someday. She does not remember her mother planning to take the family back after Dogan passed away.

In truth, it would have been unlikely that the family could have made the trip prior to Dogan becoming sick. Dogan passed away in 1941 and had been in poor health for two years prior. Before he became ill, they would not have had the time or money to travel to China. In addition to running the laundry, Toy Len Goon gave birth to eight children between 1922 and 1936. She saved any extra money for the down payment for 615 Forest Avenue and to send back to relatives in China. Had the Chinese Communist Party not taken power in 1949, effectively closing mainland China off from the rest of the world and deeming the Chinese abroad "capitalist roaders," it is possible that they eventually would have been able to return for a visit if Dogan had not died, or once the family got back on its feet after Dogan's death. However, the Goon family, along with the entire Chinese diaspora, was cut off from their ancestral homeland when Chairman Mao shut mainland China off from the outside world between 1949 and 1978 This unfortunate timing meant that Toy Len was never able to return to China to see her parents, siblings, and other friends and relatives. Though she had built a full life for herself in the United States enriched by her many children, friends, neighbors, and customers, I have often wondered what she, like many migrants, had left behind, and the impact those losses must have had on her, despite what she may have felt she had gained in the United States.

Toy Len Goon and other Chinese immigrants of her generation may not have expected to return once arriving in the United States due to the expense, time, and navigation of legal hurdles required to travel back. Furthermore, funds spent on a trip home would reduce remittances that could be sent back to support families. Their work did not allow for vacations or time off, and returning to the United States under the regime of Chinese Exclusion would not have been a simple proposition either. The responsibility that Chinese migrants felt to stay in the United States and earn money to support their kin in China has been well documented.[2] In this sense, staying abroad, earning money, and sending remittances and sometimes goods back to the homeland were also expressions of affective bonds, sometimes in the absence of physical return.

The US media, in its efforts to craft a new image for Chinese Americans, obscured a long history of transnational migration and continued emotional connections to the homeland.[3] The Cold War politics within which Toy Len Goon's story became entangled, in combination with Mao's revolution, which largely cut China off from the outside world from 1949 to 1978, temporarily suppressed these filial ties that spanned time, space, and political borders. It is these nuances, silences, or omissions in the official media and other narratives that I hope to fill in by bringing together other versions of her life story throughout this book as told by those who knew her and as contextualized by the historical literature. These omissions smooth over the complex and varied relationships that Dogan Goon, Toy Len Goon, and their children had to China as a homeland, to other Chinese Americans from their area of origin, and to the United States, and how these sentiments overlapped and shifted over time. The relationships significantly affected what it meant to them to be American and what they thought they needed to do to achieve the status of "good minorities" in this context. It also shaped the ways that they thought of themselves as Chinese or Chinese American, and how they viewed the relationships between these identities. Exploring these tensions between official narratives and family stories allows for insights into how the Goon children navigated their identities as successful, patriotic, assimilated Chinese Americans in the context of an upbringing that was decidedly still influenced by Chinese values, and by experiences of sacrifice and hard work.

From Exclusion to Inclusion

Even though Toy Len Goon never returned to China, her experiences in the United States were shaped by relations between the United States and China. The inclusion or exclusion of Chinese migrants in the United States cannot be separated from US interests in Asia and China-US relations. Asian exclusion emerged as a means to exclude immigrants deemed undesirable in the context of labor competition in the United States. The Exclusion Laws were then repealed in 1943 as part of the politics of US empire building, and of China-US politics during the Cold War, in an attempt to redefine some Asian immigrants as "good" and the United States as a welcoming place for these "good" immigrants.[4] As Jane H. Hong observes,

> In the same way that the timing and shape of Asian exclusion's rise in the United States during the late nineteenth and early twentieth centuries tracked American expansionism in the Pacific, the movement for repeal charted the development of the United States' new informal empire in Asia after World War II. Framed most broadly, repeal was part of the larger transformation and expansion of US empire during the era of Asian decolonization.[5]

Similarly, Madeline Hsu notes the connection between immigration policy and the United States' political motivations in discussing how the Exclusion Laws' exceptions for students "laid the ideological and legal foundations for the role of Chinese students and refugees in enabling this dramatic turn in American immigration strategies, racial ideologies, and foreign relations, as immigration controls turned from emphasizing restriction to selection, with the aim of enhancing America's political and economic agendas."[6]

A Transnational Social Field

The Goon family was not part of the student population or political refugees discussed by Hsu. However, their portrayal in the US English-language media in coverage of the Mother of the Year award echoed the theme of selectivity that was applied to these groups. The media attributed their success to their Americanization, made possible by a welcoming and inclusive US democracy. Those who remained in China were seen as being victims of the Communist government. However, English-language coverage did not consider the importance of the broader network of kin and hometown mates (*tong heung* [C], *tong xiang* [M]) that the Goon family relied upon for support, whether while back in China or in the United States.[7] These relationships were socially and culturally important as a means of establishing their social identities within the Chinese community, and both affective work and financial resources had to be put into maintaining those ties. The Cold War drastically altered that transnational social field, cutting the US migrant community off from their kin in China, with financial and other repercussions.

Before 1949, there had been long-standing transnational relations between the emigrant regions of southern China—particularly the Pearl River Delta region, where the Goon family originated—and its diaspora. Migrants from the Pearl River Delta and their friends and family back in their home villages constituted a transnational social field.[8] They occupied a social space that extended across national borders and connected parts of a community that was separated by distance, but whose members still imagined themselves as part of the same social and cultural universe.[9] This transnational community emerged due to migration following the forced opening of China to trade with the West during the Opium Wars and the unevenness of global capital development that compelled men to move abroad as laborers. The sustained social relations between Toisanese villagers at home and abroad were built on filial ties that were part of a larger system of kinship and ancestor worship that organized rural Chinese society, particularly in the south, which was known for its strong, single-surname villages.[10] These filial ties were also manifested in migrants' deep sense of rootedness to their ancestral village and lineage, defined by affective sentiments to their native place. The "searching for roots" (*xun gen* [M], *cam gan* [C]) metaphor often used to describe migrants returning to their native villages refers to affective ties to native soil and water.[11] Males born abroad were included in genealogy books, tying them to kin at home with the expectation that they should return to worship ancestral graves. Prior to 1949, bones of migrants who died abroad would often be shipped back to China to be buried in the ancestral soil to be worshiped by their descendants. As anthropologists have observed, ancestor worship was a means of defining and strengthening lineage identities.[12] Though women were traditionally excluded from the genealogy books of both their natal families and their husbands' families and were not allowed to set foot in ancestral halls, they were still expected to be filial, and to encourage their children, particularly their sons, to fulfill their obligations. For example, though women, particularly menstruating women, were not allowed in ancestral halls, they were expected to bring their young sons to participate in ancestor worship.[13] This sense of filiality is so powerful that it could extend to nationalism to China as a whole.[14]

In a practical sense, the transnational community was connected by the remittances migrants sent back to support family members, the appointing of overseas members to political positions back home, the inclusion of news of village members abroad in local publications, return visits to the village, and ideally a return home to retire in a new home built in the village.[15] While the formation of families in the United States would have reduced the back-and-forth travel and also the overall strength of social ties back to China, advances in communications and travel such as telephones and air travel would have eventually made it possible for migrants to maintain contact with friends and relatives in their home villages in new ways.[16]

The Goon Family's Kinship and Native Place Ties

Dogan Goon purchased war bonds through the Chinese Consolidated Benevolent Association to support China in the defeat of Taiwan and purchased US war bonds during World War II. These investments illustrate that he felt allegiances to both the United States and China at the time he made those donations. As Mae Ngai, citing historian Him Mark Lai, notes,

> Racial exclusion and segregation nearly guaranteed that Chinese in America would remain interested in China politics and not in American political affairs. In both Chinese American and Japanese American communities, the ethnic presses featured homeland news and politics, and ethnic elites held power over their co-ethnics in part by maintaining both official and informal ties with their respective countries' consuls. The leaders of the Chinese Consolidated Benevolent Associations in the United States were usually members of the Kuomintang (Nationalist) party.[17]

Dogan's sense of patriotism toward China might likely have shifted when the Chinese Communist Party took power, with the political climate in the United States making it difficult for him to openly identify with a communist power even if he had wanted to do so.[18] But his filial sentiments toward his kin at home would have continued.

As Amy Guen notes in her biography of Toy Len Goon, Toy Len began taking responsibility for seeing that her relatives in China were supported to the extent possible, both in her natal family and in Dogan's family, even before Dogan passed away.[19] She ensured that money was set aside to send to them, even if their own finances were tight. While living in the Goon village for three years before Dogan returned to marry her, she had memorized the Goon family tree. The generational naming system assigned males ceremonial names, different from the names they used daily, when they got married. Each lineage followed a cycle in naming generations, oftentimes based on a poem. Thus, males of the same generation could be identified by the shared characters of their married names.[20] According to Amy Guen's biography, since she could not read or write, Toy Len memorized the names by sound, from the fifteenth generation through the twenty-fourth, following the cycle "Edd, O, Sing, Chiao, Jung, Fung, Ngien, Yiao, Born, Doang)."[21] Amy provides the corresponding Chinese characters in her biography:

> Beginning with the 15th generation, (Edd 迪, O 道, Sing 聖, Chiao 朝, Jung 重, Fung 宏, Ngien 仁, Yiao 耀, Born 本, Doang 宗) through the 24th. She explained that Dogan's father, being the 21st generation, carried the name Ngien 仁 and his name is Goon Ngien Wei 阮仁渭. Dogan, being in the 22nd generation, his married name is Goon Yiao Hung 阮耀騰.[22]

When her sons were married, Toy Len made sure to give them ceremonial married names. Following the naming cycle, she gave them names including the character "Bon."[23]

The significance of these traditions and the relationships they reflected were more than symbolic. They defined a Chinese person's social position in relation to their kin in China and to the broader Chinese community in the United States. Thus, Toy Len's maintenance of these practices did not serve only as a means of carrying on family traditions. It also placed her children—specifically her sons, who carried on the family lineage—within a broader social and cultural system that defined their places in relation to the Chinese American community in the United States and back in their homeland. While having a place within this system may not have been important to all her sons, Toy Len Goon's actions demonstrate that it was important to her.

Traditionally in Guangdong lineages, ancestor worship was a means of reinforcing the cohesion of the lineage based on devotion to a shared common ancestor, and clan members who migrated abroad were expected to carry on these practices.[24] Kinship and native place ties to fellow lineage members played key roles in organizing Chinese immigrants. *Huiguan* (M) and district associations, also known as *tong xiang hui* (M), were based on region of origin, and provided migrants with basic needs such as shelter and food.[25] The Chinese Consolidated Benevolent Association was led by merchants and developed out of the six major *huiguan*, "prompted by a growing sense of community that crossed clan or regional lines and the need to respond to anti-Chinese agitation."[26] Clan associations were based on shared surnames, and thus could encompass people from different lineages who based on a shared surname saw themselves as descended from the same ancestor, despite not necessarily having demonstrable kinship relationships.

Though he lived in Portland, Maine, where there was a small Chinese community, Dogan remained connected to other Chinese immigrants.[27] When he made trips to Boston for groceries, he would go to the CCBA to read the Chinese newspaper.[28] He and Toy Len were also part of the Goon Family Association, and Toy Len was connected to the Chinese Women's Association even when she was living in Portland.[29] She likely was introduced to the association via relationships with other Chinese women, some likely from the Goon clan. According to Amy Guen, Toy Len said that Dogan, who was part of the twenty-second generation of the Goon lineage, "was a proud member of the Goon Family Association in Boston, and every year never failed to offer annual incense and oil money to the Association."[30] Following Dogan's death, Toy Len made offerings in her oldest son Carroll's name. And in 1952, Toy Len herself went to the Goon Association to "make offerings in her five sons' names." After Leo Guen, Toy Len's first grandson, was born to Edward and Amy in 1954, Toy Len charged Edward with making the annual offerings for Toy Len and her family. "Now," she told Amy, "you have my first grandson and you and Ed (generation 23) should carry on Dogan's legacy."[31] As Amy and Edward Guen were Catholic, Leo was baptized at St. Mary's Church in Winchester, Massachusetts, at the age of three weeks. However, as soon as he was born, Toy Len requested that as her first male grandchild, he be given a traditional Chinese one-month head shaving ceremony and celebratory dinner. She asked Amy to make sure to invite important representatives from the Goon clan, and charged Bon Man Bak (George Mook), head of the Goon Family Association, with making plans for the dinner in Boston Chinatown. Bon Man Bak suggested that "bees building a new nest need not be extravagant," meaning that since Edward and Amy were in the beginning stages of building their family, they did not need to spend too much on the occasion.[32] However, he advised that they should invite two members from each branch of the Goon clan, and including family and friends, more than seventy people were in attendance. In addition to traditional banquet dishes, "red dyed hard-boiled eggs, red pickled ginger slices, vinegary pigs feet, and sweet and sour sweet potatoes," customary for one-month ceremonies, were served.[33]

This celebration not only marked the momentous occasion of a child's birth, in this case the first grandson of Dogan and Toy Len, who would ensure that the lineage would be carried on, but it was also a way of cementing the family's social relationships to the rest of the clan. Therefore, Toy Len was aware that she should invite the appropriate Goon Family Association members in Boston for this event but needed Bon Man Bak's advice to ensure she did everything according to custom and her new social standing.

Amy recollects that her wedding, which had been planned before Toy Len Goon's selection as Mother of the Year in May 1952, was scheduled to happen in August, after she had been awarded the title and received national attention for it. Amy writes, "As Bon Man Bak said, everything she did had to conform to her newly elevated status in the Overseas Chinese circle, from whom she received accolades and high regards."[34] Several meetings were held at Bon Man Bak's house to determine how to proceed, with another Goon "clan cousin" appointed to take notes on the developing plans. Originally, Amy and Edward were going to be wed in a double ceremony along with Richard (Edward's older brother) and Helen (Amy's older sister). However, it was decided that Richard should be wed first, so that the brothers would be married according to birth order.[35] The Chin clan "uncles" also took pride in the formal weddings of Amy and Helen. Both their father, surnamed Chin, and their mother had passed away. They "were expecting some traditional ritual, significant for the brides to be" and decided that the grooms' family should send pastries to be distributed by the brides' family. Pastries were ordered from Chinatown in New York City, and a large, organized effort was made to distribute them appropriately.[36] As many wedding gifts came in, the Chin family also arranged for a space for them to be publicly displayed.[37]

Toy Len's Mother of the Year award had raised her status and visibility within the clan, and with the Chinese community more broadly, making it even more important that her family act in accordance with her social position. Her award occurred the same year as her sons' weddings, and only two years prior to Leo's birth. Toy Len did not have experience planning such affairs, and therefore sought advice from a senior male member of the Goon clan, indicating that she had both the social connections and the social knowledge about how to navigate these events. These social occasions were not only important rites of passage for the family, as they would be for any family, but became important for Toy Len Goon's family, the Goon clan, and those associated with them. These examples reflect not only the importance of kinship ties in the US context, but also the additional pressures that Toy Len Goon faced in having to live up to the prestige associated with her title. Fortunately, she had retired by this time, and her older children were self-sufficient and could help finance these events.

Despite the media's focus on the Goon family's assimilation to and success within mainstream US society as measured by their careers and educations, the Goon family remained connected to Chinese American institutions and practices and continued to invest in social capital within that community. They did this in tandem with developing their careers and raising their children, which for the most part involved cultivating social ties outside the Chinese American ethnic community. Over time, some siblings participated more than others in Chinese American networks such as the Goon Family Association and doing charitable work in Chinatown. In contrast to how unfamiliar she had been with the pageantry and festivities in Washington, DC. which constituted public formalities in the form of meetings with Bess Truman and other officials in which she had been made into a symbol of Chinese American assimilation and success, Toy Len knew how to navigate the Chinese American social world of which she and Dogan were a part, even if this meant knowing who to ask for help.[38]

The Significance of Names

All of the children had Chinese names in addition to the English names that they used with one another, with friends, and at school. The multiple names that the Goon children were given reflected different aspects of their identities and social positionings. As previously noted, the Chinese names were given to them by their father, who also recorded the times of their births according to the lunar calendar.[39] As it was common for the sons to share a character in their names, and for daughters to share another, each of the sons had the character "Fu," meaning wealth, in their names, and each of the daughters had the character "Gee," meaning pearl. It was not uncommon for Chinese names to reflect desirable characteristics or goals, including prosperity or peace, and for this naming to be gendered, with males given names reflecting strength or leadership, and females given more beautiful and gentle names. Toy Len and Dogan would refer to their children by their Chinese names, though their Chinese names were not part of their legal names. The English names did not carry as much Chinese cultural significance, as they were given to them by the doctor who helped deliver them. Another important aspect of naming was the Goon surname itself. Dogan's surname, 阮, would be romanized as Yuan in Cantonese and Ruan in Mandarin in accordance with current naming systems. However, at the time he arrived in the United States, there was no standardized procedure, and immigration officials would have likely written down the name as they heard it. Some of the Goon siblings felt that the officials may have been hostile in romanizing their name as a homonym for a common English-language word meaning "a stupid person" or "a man hired to terrorize or eliminate opponents." Toy Len Goon's daughters took their husbands' names when they married. However, of the sons, only Carroll, who moved to Utah to open his medical practice, kept the name Goon. The other sons changed their last name to Guen, an alternative spelling that sounded more like the original name in Toisanese, or Len, in honor of Toy Len. The power of the immigration system to name—or rather, rename—immigrants, particularly with names that are unflattering in the lingua franca of that nation, is just one of the many ways that the state can enact a form of symbolic violence on them. Though they were able to find alternatives, the names they would use on an everyday basis seemed to be in stark contrast to the layers of meaning behind their Chinese names.

The Goon children had to navigate both mainstream US and Chinese American social universes, reflecting the multiple, and perhaps sometimes competing, pressures in their lives to act as "assimilated" Americans and to participate in family traditions that were important to their mother and the broader Chinese community. This was done in different ways by different children. Carroll moved to Utah and forgot much of his Chinese, but kept the name Goon, while Edward engaged in community service and leadership positions in Chinatown but changed his name to Guen.

Supporting Relatives in China

The Cold War and the communist takeover of China had made it more difficult for Toy Len Goon to connect back to her parents, siblings, and other relatives and friends in China. Though she would cultivate ties to other members of the Goon clan in Boston, these ties would not replace those to her family back home. Fortunately, daughters-in-law Helen, Amy, and Rose had lived in the same area of Toisan that Toy Len had come from and had friends who were in touch with people in the Goon village. With their help, she was able to reconnect with her relatives in China, write them letters, and send them a "token amount" of money.[40] My mother, who was still in high school when they moved from Portland, Maine, to Lynn, Massachusetts, remembers her mother corresponding with people in China via letters written by Helen, who lived downstairs, as do some of Helen's daughters.

One of the people that Toy Len would have Helen write to was her sister Toy Kuen, who had married a man named Yin Ming Jong in Fook On village.[41] Most villagers were not able to read and write and would hire others to help them correspond with relatives abroad. Amy remembers Helen commenting that the penmanship of whoever was writing letters for Toy Kuen was poor. Years later, Amy would find out from her hairdresser's father, who had since emigrated to Boston, that he had written letters on behalf of everybody in the village—except for Toy Kuen. He said that Toy Kuen's husband had encouraged her to learn to write so that she could communicate with her sister in America. Amy told me that if they had known that the letters were written by Toy Len's sister, they would have saved them.[42] Toy Kuen passed away in 1983, and the two sisters never were able to see one another after Toy Len emigrated to the United States. However, in fulfillment of her sister's wishes, Toy Len asked her son Edward as executor of her will to set up a $5,000 account at First National Bank of Boston to help Toy Kuen's children, Tew Kam (a daughter born in 1964) and Gow Lan (a son born in 1969), emigrate to the United States.[43]

It would have been rare for a Chinese woman of Toy Kuen's generation living in the village to know how to read and write.[44] In addition to the instrumental benefits of being able to write to Toy Len to ask for money or other forms of aid, the effort that Toy Kuen had put into learning how to read and write is indicative of her strong desire to keep in touch with her sister. Thus, this is a poignant example of the losses that Toy Len Goon and other immigrants of her generation, and their kin at home, must have felt because of never being able to reconnect in person. During the Cultural Revolution (1966–1976), it would likely have been even more difficult for them to correspond, as those with overseas relatives were in danger of being persecuted for their ties to capitalists abroad. During this period, ancestral halls, ancestral tablets, and genealogy books were destroyed, though in many cases they were hidden, memorized, or preserved by relatives living overseas.

According to Amy Guen, after the communist takeover, it was still possible to write to their relatives in Toisan.[45] Their letters would be opened by government officials, so if you tried to send money, it would be confiscated, though Amy observed that the Cultural Revolution did not affect the village as much as it did the city. Helen helped Toy Len Goon write to relatives on Dogan's side of the family that she was helping financially support, including the three great-grandchildren descended from Dogan's deceased brother's line. In a 2018 interview, Amy explained that Dogan's brother, Doo Wong, had died while still a child, leaving that branch of the Goon lineage with no descendants.

As is customary, Dogan's mother adopted a son to continue that line.[46] That son had a son named Jeong Nguen, who in turn had three sons, as mentioned earlier. This family was not entitled to government benefits due to its overseas connections, so they relied on remittances from Toy Len Goon for school tuition.[47] The youngest of the three sons inherited the home that had been passed down his father's line. Amy had reconnected with them when she and her sisters, and the three Goon brothers to whom they were married, visited the village in 1984. Later, with the help of Yuen Shiao Ow, a clan cousin living in Hong Kong, Jeong Nguen wrote to Toy Len appealing for her help in building a home for him and the two older sons, who were about to get married, to inhabit.[48] The youngest son would inherit half of the ancestral home in which Dogan had been born. The letter said, "Nobody will marry my sons unless they have a house in the village. A house means you have status." Toy Len asked each of her sons to contribute money toward building the new home, as according to traditional Chinese kinship practices, they remained in the Goon lineage, while the daughters now belonged to their husbands' lineages.

The above examples illustrate the continued importance of patrilineal, male-focused customs to Toy Len Goon. As Amy Guen notes, she was "a typical woman of her generation" and was therefore concerned with carrying on the Goon name through the birth of a grandson.[49] Citing the Goon tradition of only celebrating the births of sons, she did not hold one-month parties for the two granddaughters who were born prior to her first grandson.[50] She expected her sons to carry on responsibilities associated with being part of the Goon lineage, such as contributing to the home she helped build for Dogan's brother's descendants, and for helping with specific tasks such as bringing over other Goon relatives from China.

As will be discussed in the following chapter, she also expected her daughters to do the more traditional women's roles of housekeeping, cooking, and childcare. It was not surprising that she would try to reproduce the patriarchal structures she was raised with. However, she did not duplicate them precisely. She was fine with her daughters pursuing further education and careers after high school and was proud of what her sons and daughters, grandsons and granddaughters, and great-grandchildren accomplished. According to Judy Yung, Chinese women in the United States were to some extent freed from traditional gender constraints as they worked as wage earners alongside their husbands and were not under the direct control of their mothers-in-law, who were still back in China. As scholars of Chinese kinship note, one result of the traditional patriarchal Chinese kinship system was that women were considered "goods on which one loses" because they are raised by their parents, only to marry out into their husbands' families.[51] Under this system, a woman was to first serve her parents, primarily her father, then her husband. The only time a woman would have authority over another person would be when her son would bring home a daughter-in-law. However, based on the accounts of Toy Len's daughters-in-law (Amy, Helen, Dottie), they had strong relationships with her. Of course, memories are selective, but it is also important to consider how Toy Len Goon would have appreciated having other women to talk with, especially daughters-in-law who could speak fluent Toisanese and help her connect back to family and friends in China.

While Toy Len Goon broke new ground in terms of the role she took on in managing the family and household affairs, she did not necessarily see herself challenging traditional gender or social roles. Rather, her goals were to provide for her family and to use the family's eventual upward mobility and financial stability to carry out the family's responsibilities to other members of the Goon clan, whether in the United States or in China.

The acceptance of the Goon family and other Chinese Americans as model minorities and good Americans facilitated their upward mobility, enabling them to contribute money to relatives in China and to host the marriage and birth ceremonies appropriate to their social standing and their social responsibility. However, the politics surrounding their acceptance were a product of the same Cold War tensions that made it challenging for them to connect with their kin in mainland China, and for those kin to continue carrying on the traditions surrounding family and ancestor worship.[52]

Like many other Chinese immigrants, Toy Len would also show herself to be flexible, not strictly following "American" or "Chinese" traditions. Rather than understanding these traditions and cultures as discrete and mutually exclusive wholes, we should think of cultural practices, and people, as being malleable. While I do not want to resort to a wholly functional explanation, it is more productive to think of traditional behaviors as being connected to social relationships and social capital. Thus, while Toy Len Goon insisted that her sons have traditional Chinese married names and that only the birth of grandsons be recognized with red egg ceremonies, she also followed US politics, became an avid Boston Bruins fan, and learned how to cook perfect apple pies.[53] This did not necessarily mean she was an assimilated American.

Even as she reached an advanced age, Toy Len Goon remained concerned with maintaining contact with and fulfilling her filial obligations to family members in China and Hong Kong. Amy relates a memory of her son Timothy being home from college one weekend in the late 1970s and receiving a late-night phone call from Toy Len, who had fallen quite ill with pneumonia. In great discomfort due to chest pain and a severe cough, Toy Len shared her wish that if she were to die from her infection, she would like to make sure that Edward and Amy continued to help Jeong Nguen and his family. She told Amy, "I am praying to Jesus for a few more years of life so I can help this family a bit longer."[54] Amy recalls being "upset at the thought that Toy Len might die without someone helping fulfill her dutiful desire."[55] Toy Len would have only been in her eighties then and would live for another fifteen years. The house was completed in 1992, the year before Toy Len Goon passed away at the age of 101.[56]

Toy Len Goon was in touch with several other relatives in China and Hong Kong, many of whom she helped, or asked some of her children to help.[57] These included her sister's son (previously mentioned), the Zhen family of Toy Len Goon's side of the family, and the grandchildren of Dogan's older daughter, Hung Gee. She was also in touch with Kong Poo Yuen, who fled from mainland China to Hong Kong in 1949 after the communist takeover. The fifth son of Dogan's cousin Yue Ng, he had graduated from Peking University and had been an official in the Guomindang (the Chinese Nationalist Party) the previous ruling party of China. Toy Len sent him money in the early 1960s to help with his research on the Goon genealogy.[58]

Despite the media's portrayal of Toy Len Goon as a loyal new American, her desire to financially support relatives in China in the Goon village, many of whom she had never met in person, indicates a transnational orientation that goes against the rhetoric of Americanization and resultant separation from communist China during the Cold War. Her selection as US Mother of the Year was meant to signify the height of symbolic acceptance as an American. However, the Cold War politics that informed her selection ironically made it much more difficult for her to connect back to China. Toy Len Goon remained devoted to those she felt responsible for in China, and once she was able to reconnect with them, spent time and energy ensuring that they were supported. However, this part of her story gets erased in the US media's one-dimensional portrayal of her as an assimilated American, as do the losses she experienced when the long-standing transnational networks between residents in Guangdong, China, and their kin in the United States were cut off during this time period.

Toy Len Goon's social worlds were shaped by her social positioning as a Chinese American woman, both in the context of the United States and in relation to her family and friends back in China. These relationships were constrained by geopolitics involving the US and Chinese states. As noted previously, Toy Len Goon remained insistent that Dogan was born in the United States when I interviewed her in 1992. Her experiences of immigration and exclusion not only regulated the nature of her connections to the United States, shaping her life course, but also framed how she was able to narrate her life.

4

Counter Cultures

The Place and Space of the Chinese Laundry

In this chapter, I discuss the Chinese shop entryway as an interstitial space separating the public and private parts of the laundry, and the Chinese laundry overall as a nexus for cultural contact. While Chinese laundries may have shared some characteristics with other small ethnic businesses, the work demands of the laundry also defined the physical layout of the laundry and living spaces, and the rhythm of family life, in specific ways. Family dynamics were also shaped by the delegation of both business and household duties, which were allocated according to age and gender. I focus on the Goon laundry in relation to both its internal workings and its external relationships in the community, while also placing the Chinese laundry and Chinese families within the broader context of Chinese American immigration history.

The summer after I graduated from college, I was living with my parents in the Boston suburbs, and decided to visit my college friend Kim, who was living and working in Portland, Maine. This was prior to cell phones and GPS, so I called her to confirm her address and get directions to her house. When she told me that the apartment she was renting was at 615 Forest Avenue, I thought that the address sounded familiar. As soon as I hung up the phone, I asked my mother about the address, and she confirmed that she had grown up above the family laundry at 615 Forest Avenue in Portland. I drove up to Portland to visit Kim, arriving at a nondescript three-story wooden building in the Woodfords Corner neighborhood, the first floor occupied by a retail shop, and the second and third floors being rented as housing. Kim and her roommate lived on the third floor in a cozy two-bedroom apartment. As I walked through the apartment, I tried to imagine the family of ten living there. My mother, the youngest, remembers sleeping in the same bed as her mother. The other sisters, Josephine and Doris, slept in the living room. And the boys slept in the other bedroom, though this configuration changed over time as the older boys left for college. Though I was not able to access or photograph the first and second floors where they had lived and worked, I took numerous photos of the third floor. I got the photos developed and brought them to show my grandmother. She looked them over carefully, and it didn't take her long to point out all the things that had been added or removed since she moved out in 1952. I still marvel at the coincidence that of all the places in Portland, my friend lived in the building that my grandmother used to own, above where the laundry had been. However, despite having visited the building, it was still difficult for me to imagine what it was like to live and work there, particularly the daily rhythm involved not only in completing household responsibilities, but also in working in the laundry business and going to school.

The Chinese laundry holds an iconic status in Chinese emigration history as a small business that operated outside Chinese ethnic enclaves, evolving out of the marginalization of Chinese workers in the mainstream economy. As such, it has historically played a role in the imagining of Chinese American difference. Chinese laundries and their proprietors were viewed in stereotypical and Orientalist ways by non-Chinese patrons. As John Kuo-Wei Tchen notes, "the image of a pig-tailed, 'no tickee, no shirtee' 'Charlie' jabbering away in nonsensical monosyllables was long set in the public's mind by melodramas, songs, pulp paperbacks, cartoons, and films."[1]

In the late nineteenth and early twentieth centuries, Chinese laundrymen were subject to overtly discriminatory legislation designed to disadvantage them. In the 1930s, Chinese hand laundries faced systematic attacks by non-Chinese-owned mechanized laundries that tried to outcompete them, but also were able to organize their own alliance to advocate for themselves.[2] Though they may have appeared to be isolated, Chinese laundry workers were part of numerous networks, both formal and informal, that tied them to other laundry workers, but also to kin and clan (surname) members in both China and the United States.

Paul Siu's book *The Chinese Laundryman: A Study of Social Isolation* focuses on Chinese laundrymen who left families behind in China while they tried to earn money to remit back home. Siu came to the United States as a student and eventually studied under William Burgess of the famed Chicago School of Sociology in 1932. His study is significant not only for the ethnographically rich fieldwork he carried out in the Chicago laundries of his "cousins" that he frequented, but also for his theoretical reframing of the assimilationist assumptions of the Chicago School. Rather than viewing Chinese laundrymen as "deviant" and socially disorganized because of their difference from mainstream European Americans, he understood their experiences as stemming from being part of an "immigrant economy," their only option in a US society that excluded them from other opportunities. In describing Chinese laundrymen as "sojourners," he recognized their racial marginalization.[3] Siu's work is invaluable for understanding not only the lives of Chinese laundrymen, but also how they were perceived by non-Chinese scholars and citizens. While additional details from Siu's research will be discussed later in this chapter, for the purposes of introducing the Chinese laundry, I begin with an account of an interaction with a Chinese laundryman from the perspective of a non-Chinese observer from Siu's now classic ethnography:

> I took a batch of laundry to a Chinese laundryman once in Philadelphia. The Chinese laundryman, short, tubby, somewhat greasy, perhaps it was sweat from his steamy work room . . . steam pipes along the low ceiling . . . works late . . . careful, honest . . . always precise though slow, methodical, calm, doesn't worry if something should go wrong. Probably has a lot of money stored up somewhere, though he leads a humble life, desires little, face expressionless except slight smile infrequently, restrained in conversation . . . still says, "No ticky, no washy; com again Fliday," holds hands together in front of stomach and bows slightly as he says this, smiling slightly . . . usually a tubby wife hovering in the back work room behind the partition, . . . with some kids running around . . . whole family lives in the tiny shop, . . . she cooks in it too, in the back, inside room. Usually has a son who is well dressed, a white collar worker in the city, . . . comes home frequently . . . all in one family . . . keep in close touch . . . see each other whenever possible . . . lots of other Chinese (probably family) constantly dropping into the shop to talk a little or just sit and smoke.[4]

Interestingly, though Siu himself was quite familiar with Chinese laundries and could have begun with an "insider" perspective on

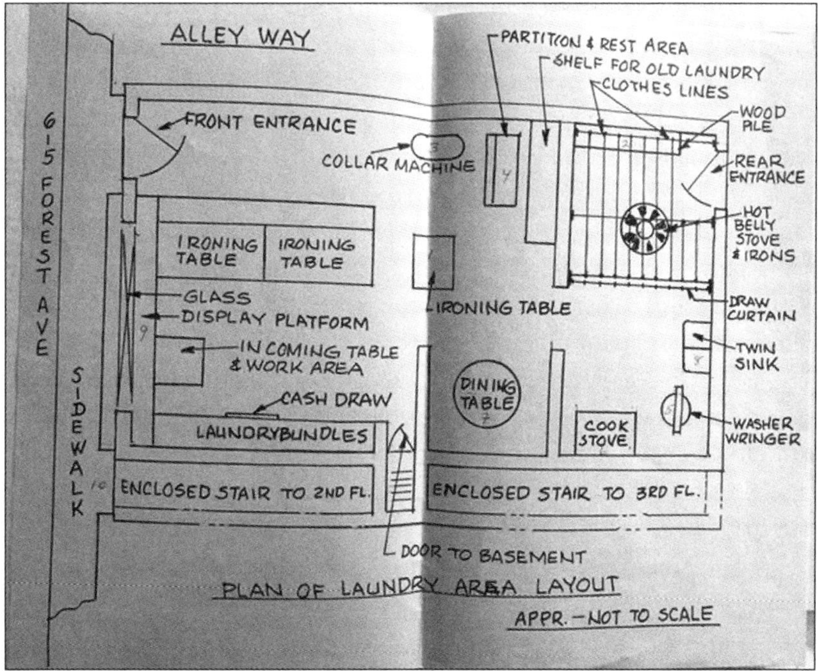

Figure 4.1. Tony Moy's hand-drawn diagram of the Goon laundry.

laundrymen's lives, he chooses to start his ethnography from the perspective of an outsider, with descriptions of how Chinese men and their laundries were viewed by non-Chinese. He likely believed that "entering" the laundry from the customer's point of view would be the more effective way to draw the reader into a world that was both familiar and "exotic" to most non-Chinese, as most Americans would have interacted with Chinese laundry owners as customers. However, the uncredited passage is notable for its mention that the laundryman's family lived with him in his shop, including his wife, who remained in the back in the private part of the laundry, where she helped with both laundry and domestic work, and their children. The account also includes the well-dressed son who is a "white-collar" worker. Unlike other descriptions that Siu included that take a more negative tone, the laundryman is described here as "honest" and hardworking, while still defined and perhaps constrained by his limited English and seemingly quaint Chinese customs. This passage highlights themes that will be discussed in this chapter, including the transition of Chinese laundries from being run solely by men to being family businesses, the upward mobility of the next generation, and the division of public and private space within the laundry, the latter which includes both workspace and family living space. I do this through the lens of spatial metaphors as they reflect cultural, gender, and power differences. While the Chicago School of Sociology played a role in creating popular spatialized understandings of cultural differences and assimilation, these conceptualizations can be further problematized in relation to theories of space, place, and identity from cultural anthropology and cultural geography that do not permanently tie peoples and cultures to places.[5] They view place as being dynamic, rather than static, and social relations as existing both within and across space.[6] Doing so enables us to think about the Goon laundry as a fluid social space that allows for the varied experiences of the Goon family members within it.

"Counter Cultures"

According to Siu, most Chinese laundries were designed in specific ways around the workflow of laundry life, but also for the safety and security of the laundry workers, who both lived and worked in the back area of the shop that was hidden from customers' views. He describes the very deliberate design of the laundry counter, which served both practical storage and protective functions:

> Immediately after one enters the laundry shop, one faces a counter of unusual height. Shelves are built underneath the counter; usually some supplies and all sorts of miscellaneous items are stored on these shelves. Generally, one cannot get into the laundryman's office-workshop because the counter is built around it. The entrance to the inner chamber is through a low swinging door attached to the counter. It is locked from within. In order to get in, the loose section of the counter has to be lifted and the hook underneath unlocked.
>
> Why is the counter built this way? It seems the counter in the Chinese laundry serves two purposes: it is a customary facility for business trading, and it is also some sort of protective measure.[7]

A similar description was given by Richard Chin, Superior Court judge, in an oral history interview with Shauna Lo in 2009. Chin's family owned a laundry in Brockton, Massachusetts, called Jimmy's Laundry from the 1950s until the early 2000s.

> Yes, it was very simple. There was a counter in front, and on the side were shelves to put the wrapped packages of shirts and behind it were racks and behind that was the machinery. And to the front of that was where all the pressing took place and in the rear of the laundry was where the laundry was actually washed. And in the middle there was a little area where you could eat and watch television.[8]

While not all laundries were constructed in this exact way, the laundry counter has served as both a metaphorical and physical division between the entrance space occupied by customers and where the work and family life took place. As noted in the first quote from Siu, the work and personal lives of Chinese laundrymen "behind the counter" were left largely to the public's imagination. And as indicated by the second quote, this separation was purposeful, as a means of regulating contact with an outside world that was often hostile to the Chinese. Chinese shop counters have been theorized as a "cultural contact zone throughout the Chinese diaspora."[9] A 2011 conference held at Ryerson University expanded on this theme as a means of understanding how "life behind the counter—in laundries, groceries, restaurants, shopping malls and general stores—has shaped the ways in which Chinese migrants have survived their migrations and interacted with the larger communities into which they have migrated."[10]

Chinese laundries have been viewed by scholars as a livelihood developed in response to restrictive opportunities for Chinese created by racism, exclusion, and economic marginalization in the United States.[11] Siu points out that Chinese did not run laundries in China, but rather took on laundry work when other types of work were not available to them. The lives of Chinese laundrymen were characterized by isolation, which Siu saw as an alternative end product of the famed Chicago School assimilation cycle, which predicted a process of competition, conflict, accommodation, and assimilation through which immigrants could become Americans.[12] Siu argues that due to racism, assimilation was not an option for the Chinese; they instead took on a sojourner mentality in which they remained oriented to their families and Chinese homeland. He surmised,

> Perhaps the Chinese laundryman behaves like a sojourner because this conduct represents a solution to a race problem, and his isolation may be considered as a form of accommodation. It seems clear in our study that the laundry as an occupation is related to the laundryman being isolated; the laundry is an instrumentality for isolation.[13]

The historical pattern of sojourning has been well documented in the literature on emigration from South China from the mid-nineteenth century until the mid-twentieth century, though it is not always labeled as such.[14] Siu's book describes a typical life course of a Chinese laundryman as migrating to the United States as a young man, going back to China to get married and have children, and then returning to the United States, where they can earn money to send back remittances to support their families. Because his research was conducted in the 1930s, and was focused on the isolation of laundrymen, he rarely mentions the presence of women and children. However, he does observe that some laundrymen had wives and children and that while the wives worked along with their husbands, "if there are any children it becomes necessary to have the home and the shop conveniently located. The wife has childcare problems while helping her husband."[15]

Chinese Laundries in Boston and Portland

According to Shauna Lo, who has conducted research on Chinese laundries in Boston, there were over a hundred laundries in Boston in 1880, with around three thousand Chinese living in Massachusetts in 1900. Of that population, 90 percent were laundry workers.[16] Lo says that Chinese, who had been forced into self-employment due to discrimination, were able to open laundries in the Boston area because of increasing urbanization as well as industrialization that followed railway lines. Their clientele consisted of non-Chinese who lived in these neighborhoods, including apartment dwellers and people who needed their dress shirts cleaned, starched, and pressed. She emphasizes that they were not located in Chinatown, as they were located near where the customers they served lived or worked.[17]

Chinese laundries in Portland, Maine, date back to around 1877, when the first Chinese hand laundry was opened by Sam Lee, who was just fourteen years old.[18] A year later, the number of Chinese laundries had grown to five, with fifteen workers total. Gary Libby notes that the newspaper coverage of Chinese laundrymen showed that they were the subject of both curiosity and hostility. For example, the wife of a white barber lost her laundering work when a nearby Chinese laundry opened; she asked her husband why he didn't "cut the 'Chinese heathen's' throat."[19]

Libby reports that by 1890 there were ten Maine towns that had Chinese laundries, and that number would eventually grow to thirty.[20] In 1886 conflict arose in Augusta when the Augusta Knights of Labor requested to a property owner that a Chinese laundry no longer be able to operate there, out of concern for the labor competition the laundry posed. However, records showed that the laundry was still present at that location the following year.[21] An account in the East Argus newspaper by reporter Alfred York, published in 1881, describes the Wah Lee laundry in depth, after York had been invited by the proprietor to eat dinner. The proprietor and worker lived and worked together in the laundry, which consisted of two rooms. Customers were received in the front room, which also housed office supplies, including an abacus, ink and paint brush, and account book. The front room was also used for ironing and storing finished bundles of laundry. The second room in the back was used for washing and drying clothing, but was also where they ate and slept, and observed religious rituals.[22] This arrangement was remarkably similar to the spatial division of the Chinese laundries from later eras described above, with the distinct demarcation between public and private spaces, but also the mixing of work and living spaces in the back of the laundry. As described below, the Goon laundry also fit this pattern, with some modifications once they moved into their own building and were able to divide their working and living space across two floors, which was necessary to accommodate their large family and heavy workload.

Amy Guen writes in her biography of Toy Len Goon that she and her husband, Edward, had conducted research in Portland trying to figure

Table 4.1. Laundries Owned by People Surnamed Goon in Portland, Maine

Year	# of Goons	Goon laundries	Other Goon details
1913	1		Lived at 87 Center St.
1914	8		
1915	10		
1916	9	Shoon Goon at 640 Forest Ave., corner of Revere St.	Including Shoon Goon
1917	12	Same as previous year	Same as previous year
1918	11	Gun Goon took over laundry at 640 Forest Ave.	Including Gun Goon (Dogan)
1919	9		Same as previous year
1920	6		
1922	3		Plus Dogan and Chin Shee (Toy Len)
1923	2		Same as previous year
1924	0		Same as previous year
1925	0		Same as previous year
1926	1		Another Goon male plus Dogan appeared at 640 Forest Ave.
1927		Frank Goon Laundry; Gun Goon Toysan Laundry	
1928		Frank Goon Laundry; Sing Goon Laundry; Gun Goon Laundry	
1929		Goon Laundry; Gun Goon Laundry	
1930		Shing Goon Laundry; Dogan Goon Laundry	
1931		Goon Laundry; Dogan Goon Laundry	
1932		Goon Laundry; Dogan Goon Laundry	
1933		Dogan Goon Laundry	
1935		Dogan Goon Laundry	Dogan Goon Laundry moved to 550 Deering Ave. House moved to 544 Deering Ave.
1936			Rented 615 Forest Ave.
1937			Purchased building at 615 Forest Ave.
1941			Last time Dogan was listed.
1942			Laundry listed under Chin Toy (Toy Len)

Data compiled by Edward and Amy Guen from Portland city directory (duplicated from Guen, *The Toy Len Goon Story*, 28).

out why Dogan may have chosen to settle there. Accessing the city directory at the Maine Historical Society, they searched for the name Goon and recorded the residents and laundries and their locations. Table 4.1 is based on the chart created by Amy and Edward. Amy notes that she and Edward "generalized the findings to assume that the city of Portland must have been a place where the early Goon Clan members congregated; that is why Dogan settled there."[23]

From "Bachelor Society" to Families

While the Chinese immigrant population in the United States has historically been viewed as a "bachelor" society organized around single men, in the period following World War II, representations of Chinese Americans shifted to a focus on nuclear families, coinciding with the rise of the model minority myth.[24] The Goon family had great potential to serve as a model of an assimilated, model minority Chinese American family, with Dogan having been in the Army, Toy Len singlehandedly running the laundry and raising her children (without government assistance) after Dogan's death, and the children moving into white-collar jobs after going on to secondary education. As discussed earlier, the Goons were not alone in being featured as an assimilated Chinese American family by the US media, and the positive portrayal of Chinese Americans as "Americans" during this period was quite deliberate. The transition of Asian Americans from being an "Oriental Problem" to a model minority occurred within a broader set of changes in the United States as the nation was trying to understand the possibilities for the integration of large and varied groups of immigrants into US society, at the same time that it endeavored to prove itself the rightful leader of the free world during the Cold War.[25] Asian Americans were painted as exemplary, exceptional citizens who had benefited from opportunities offered by the United States. As Henry Yu elucidates in detail in his book *Thinking Orientals*, the Chicago School of Sociology, under which Paul Siu trained, was at the center of producing the spatial and conceptual frameworks for these debates about the assimilation of immigrants into US society. In the process, it defined the terms through which Americans thought about cultural difference and assimilation, and, particularly relevant here, the place of Asians in the United States. "The

Oriental Problem," Yu notes, emerged as part of the Chicago School's theoretical framing that encompassed a broader vision of US race relations including both European immigrants and what Chicago School sociologists termed the "Negro Problem." As Yu notes, "The Oriental represented a way for them to bridge these two separate issues, a subject that could amalgamate their studies of immigration and of race."[26]

Under Robert Park, the Chicago School of Sociology developed theories that, similar to the idea of cultural relativism discussed by anthropologist Franz Boas, argued that the perceived difference of immigrants and Blacks from mainstream US society stemmed from their unfamiliar cultural practices. Rather than being biologically fixed racial characteristics, these practices changed as immigrants adapted to US society.[27] But in studying immigrant communities, Chicago School sociologists also spatially bound these communities to their ethnic enclaves, both through mapmaking projects and assumptions that the existence of ethnic enclaves reflected actual cultural differences rather than segregation, racism, and discrimination.[28] As Yu argues, cultural differences became spatialized such that "cultures became self-contained objects with clear physical boundaries. Culture was bounded, with a borderline demarcating the difference between one culture and another."[29] In addition, reflecting Orientalist thinking that was prevalent in the West, the East was viewed as a static, backward place, while the West was seen as modern.[30] Theoretically, Asians could become American by migrating to the United States, crossing into "American" spaces, and assimilating to US culture.[31]

The spatialized understanding of places and cultural difference has been well documented in cultural anthropology and cultural geography, whose retheorizing of place, space, and the problematic territorializing of people's identities in specific locations is contextualized within assumptions that power and capital flows shape social relations.[32] In the remainder of this chapter, I consider the Goon laundry as a porous social space through which the Goon family interacted with their community, and as a locale that was defined by a spatial dynamic reflective of class, racial, cultural, and gender differences both within and extending outside the laundry building interactions. Thus, the spatial politics of the laundry as a home and business evolved in response to both internal family dynamics and family members' interactions with the broader Portland community.

I focus on four key areas:

1. The mixed-use space of the laundry, which was shaped by the rigors of laundry work in a small space that combined living and work tasks, and reflected the social and economic marginality of laundry workers.
2. Laundry work, space, and gender: The gendered nature of both housework and laundry labor that defined roles for the Goon children, but that also were challenged by Toy Len Goon as a homemaker and businesswoman.
3. The laundry as an immigrant space: The laundry as a business whose social relations and business interactions positioned it to interact in specific ways in relation to the non-Chinese community. While some ethnic businesses attempt to relegate any signs of "non-American" identity to behind the scenes, there was some fluidity between the "front stage" and "back stage" of the Goon laundry.[33]
4. Out from behind the counter: This previously hidden labor was brought out from behind the counter as a result of the attention garnered from Toy Len Goon's award and the framing of this labor and her role in particular ways within the public imaginary.

Mixed-Use Space of the Laundry—Layout of 615 Forest Avenue

Below I share portions of three accounts of the laundry's layout. The first is from Josephine Moy, the fourth child and oldest daughter:

> Our hand laundry was situated right on Forest Avenue, a very busy thoroughfare, lots of activity and also a family atmosphere with many households in the area. Our laundry was a three storied building, two upper floors used as apartments and the street floor was our laundry. Entrance to the laundry [was] through the front door. As you come in, you will meet a counter where customers would come in to pick up their laundry or drop off laundry to be cleaned. On the right of the counter were two areas for ironing shirts. In back of that area was a place to note the customer's laundry and tags attached to the clothing. . . . Directly in back of the counter as one entered there was another ironing board and a big

> machine for pressing the collars. To the right of the area was our dining room. And then further back there was the kitchen with a potbelly stove for drying the laundry. Hand irons were placed on the stove to heat up as needed. Also in the area was a kitchen to cook all of our meals. The bathroom was downstairs in the cellar where also was the furnace to heat the laundry and our living quarters upstairs.[34]

As Josephine notes, the laundry was located at the edge of the busy Woodfords Corner, in Portland, where Forest Avenue, Woodford Street, and Deering Avenue meet. The neighborhood had evolved over time to include not only residential buildings, but also social clubs, schools, a fire station, and small businesses.

In considering Josephine's description and the very precise drawing produced by her husband, Tony, who was a professional draftsman and had visited the laundry on numerous occasions, we see a spatial division that differs slightly from that described by Siu. The L-shaped counter where customers were received and clothing was sorted was located at the very front of the store, along the wall where customers entered. There were also ironing tables and storage for clean clothes bundles in that area. Further toward the back, located near the partition that divided the front entrance from the rear work area, was a machine for starching collars and a round dining table where the family ate their meals. Behind the partition was a potbellied stove used to heat the irons and provide heat for drying the clothing, a washer and a wringer, and a small cooking area. Clothes lines were hung along the ceiling above the back.

The mixed use of living and workspace was notable, with the family's dining table located in front of the partition, along with the laundry equipment for starching and ironing clean clothing. In contrast to the laundry described by Siu, a customer entering the Goon laundry would have likely seen some of the Goon children or perhaps at times Dogan or Toy Len ironing, sorting clothes, or eating at the table in front of the partition. They might have seen some of the Goon children doing their homework in between carrying out household and laundry duties. Doris, the seventh child and second daughter, describes the laundry in the passage below, providing detail regarding the daily rhythms of life there, including the washing, drying, ironing, and pressing of shirts, and shopping for groceries. In her description, she inserts herself into that space, as both an observer and a participant, relating memories of hand ironing shirts, washing dishes, shopping for groceries with food stamps, and playing games outside. She remembers how physically taxing the laundry work was, having seen her mother and brothers work the heavy machine that was used to press shirt collars and cuffs. She recalls the hand-crank washing machine that would later be replaced by a Maytag washer (see Edward's comment below), as well as the arduous process of hanging up laundry in the stifling hot back room to be dried by the heat of a potbellied stove. Her memories span different time periods, from the early 1940s during World War II, until right before the family sold the laundry, when Doris and her mother ran the laundry (sending out the clothes to be washed and then pressing and packaging them at the laundry) so that she could earn her tuition for court reporting school. I quote Doris in full here:

> The layout of the laundry was thus: Customers came through the front door (as we all did) and the tables we ironed on were right there. Behind the tables was the cash register and shelves for the clean packages of laundry to be picked up. When the laundry was brought in, the customer was given a slip with a number and we kept the other half and attached it to the package for pickup.
>
> Also a little back in the area was a heavy hot press for collars and cuffs of shrits [*sic*]. I remember seeing Mom and the boys using it. The rest of the shirt was hand ironed. I did that the last year we had the laundry which I ran with Grandma. (That's how I earned my $200 tuition for Stenotype school!!)
>
> Also in back was a table where we ate all our meals—breakfast, lunch, dinner. Of course there was a gas stove and an ice box so ice was delivered and paid for daily, I think. And food had to be bought daily. We lived on a main street, Forest Avenue, thank goodness, and I remember doing much of the food buying for Grandma. I remember having to use food stamps for the rationing that took place during World War II so that had to be in the early '40s. Of course there was also a sink where I washed many a dish standing on a box!!
>
> Also in back was a washing machine that was used to wash the clothes brought into the laundry. I think it was the hand crank style. Don't know

> how Mom and Dad did it. Then they had to starch the collars and cuffs of shirts, some hard, some light. (Don't know how they remembered which was which). Then they hung the clothes/shirts up in the very back room to dry on lines strung across the ceiling, using a wood-fired stove. That stove also served to heat up the irons to iron the shirts. I remember it being stifling hot in there when the process was going on. I can't remember what part of the day this was going on but it must have been late in the day.
>
> There was a back door from this area which led to a yard where Mom tried to do a little gardening, as I recall, and there was also a swing. We didn't have much in the way of toys. We amused ourselves playing with marbles, hopscotch, hide-go-seek, etc.[35]

Edward Guen, the third-oldest, provided more detail on the daily work of washing, drying, and ironing laundry in a 2001 interview with Gary Libby and Fenggang Yang. The older sons were responsible for the labor-intensive process of washing, drying, and pressing the clothes.

Figure 4.2. Toy Len Goon's iron, Portland, Maine, 1950. Courtesy of Maine Historical Society.

Over time, the Goon family purchased a few new and updated pieces of equipment for the laundry. Arthur remembers Dick buying electric irons for the laundry with one of his first paychecks, which replaced the old irons that were heated in the potbellied stove, and were very hot and dangerous to work with. Here, Edward mentions the Maytag washer, which replaced the hand-crank machine:

> It was just a regular Maytag washer with an electric mechanically run roller for drying the washed laundry. We would do perhaps seven or eight loads a day in the washer, then we would take those, the shirts from there and next to the washer there would be a sink and we would make starch in the sink and we would actually starch the collars, the cuffs and the front of the shirt where the button hole side and after starching the shirts we would then hang them up in the drying room where we had these wires running length-wise in the room. . . . There were two stoves in the drying room. One was a coal stove for heating irons. . . . And next to that stove would be a pot belly stove that both burned coal and we would light up the pot belly stove and heat the room until it got real hot and . . . it was like a sauna room. . . . After the shirts were dried we would cool down the room, take off the shirts, bring them into the front of the laundry there would be a table next to the gas fired mangle. The mangle consisted of a steel roll, very fine finish, gas fired, . . . we would bring the shirts out, we would dampen the shirts on the table . . . and then we would fold them, and then we would individually press the collar, the cuffs, and the front of the shirt and then we would re-stack it next to the other pile and from this re-stacked pile, the people that were ironing would take the shirt to the ironing table, one at a time, and do their ironing. We did this six days a week.[36]

Laundry work was monotonous and required long hours and intense labor to be carried out by all members of the family, in addition to usual household work and school. The rhythm of daily life revolved around their work, which occupied more than a standard 9:00–5:00 shift. The blending on the ground floor of the laundry business with daily activities of cooking, eating, homework, and other household chores likely arose out of practicality and the need to multitask or move quickly between tasks. Toy Len Goon would cook meals, or supervise

Josephine's cooking, in between the numerous responsibilities in the laundry. She would rise at 6:00 a.m. and not finish her work and get to bed until 11:30. In the winter, she would need to go down two flights of stairs to the basement to stoke the furnace.[37] She would then cook a hot breakfast for her children before school. She would do laundry work until lunch, when the children would come home from school and she would once again cook for them. Doris recalls that breakfast and lunch would be "American style" and dinner would consist of Chinese food. However, Josephine remembers her mother making things that the neighbors had taught her to cook, including apple pies. She also fondly recalls that her mother would also learn to cook whatever recipe she brought back from home economics class at school from memory, and it would somehow taste much better. She learned many years later from her oldest brother, Carroll, that their mother would wait until they all ate so that she could eat what was left over, despite his pleas for her not to do so.[38] The children would do their homework on the first floor after school along with fulfilling their duties in the laundry, whether that be going through batches of clothing to make sure the pockets were empty, ironing shirts, or doing the heavier work of washing and drying the clothing. After the amputation of his leg, Dogan would spend his days upstairs in bed, but the rest of the family would spend most of the day downstairs in the laundry.

The spatial arrangement of their shop and living area as defined by mixed use of business and personal (public and private) spaces and crowded conditions also reflected the economically precarious position of the Goon family within their Portland community and within US society. Carrying out the physically demanding labor of washing other people's clothes for a living necessitated that they live in cramped quarters both within and above their shop, though the fact that Toy Len had the foresight to purchase the property put them in a much stronger financial position than they would have otherwise been in.

Laundry Work, Space, and Gender

The relationship between capital flows and space has been discussed by geographers, who argue that the unevenness of capital flows and people's access to them creates the social relations that shape places in particular ways. Rather than viewing space as a neutral container, geographer Doreen Massey sees places "as particular moments in such intersecting social relations, nets of which have over time been constructed, laid down, interacted with one another, decayed and renewed."[39] She continues, "Thinking of places in this way implies that they are not so much bounded areas as open and porous networks of social relations. It implies that their 'identities' are constructed through the specificity of their interaction with other places rather than by counterposition to them."[40] This conception of place and space shapes my analysis of the Goon laundry as a place and space that was both defined by and played a role in shaping the relationship of the Goon family members to the community and US society more broadly. This model enables us to think about these relationships as fluid and as connected to varying experiences and memories of individuals. We can consider that while the laundry as a space to some extent reproduced a traditional gendered division of work, the laundry was also a dynamic space, with work responsibilities and job assignments shifting over time. We can also consider how the process of carrying out this labor shaped not only the spatial layout of the laundry and living space, but also relationships within the family, and family members' relationships with friends, neighbors, and classmates.

Massey understands places to be defined by an unequal "power geometry," reflecting the unevenness of capital flows and investments. She describes the "power geometry of time-space compression" as being shaped by the ways that people and "social groups" are positioned in different ways in relation to flows of capital.[41] She notes that "it is also about power in relation to the flows and the movement. Different social groups have distinct relationships to this anyway differentiated mobility: some people are more in charge of it than others; some initiate flows and movement, others don't; some are more on the receiving end of it than others; some are effectively imprisoned by it."[42]

Massey theorizes that just as spaces and places are constructed, so are meanings about gender. She argues that the mobility of women "in terms of both identity and space, has been in some cultural contexts a crucial means of subordination."[43] She adds that "home" is often seen as "a woman's place" and therefore "a source of stability, reliability, and authenticity."[44] While these associations may seem inconsequential, they can result in women's roles, identities, and mobility being controlled in ways that limit their opportunities outside the home due to their symbolic association with domestic spaces. However, over time, these gender constructions can have unintended effects, such as when in the 1960s and 1970s, regional policy shifted the economy of northern and western Britain from mining to decentralized industry work. The women of the region, who had been shunted into traditional gender roles as wives and mothers within their mining households, made ideal workers in the eyes of employers. They were a "cheap, flexible, untrained and trapped pool of labour," which made them willing to work for low wages on a part-time basis. In addition, they were not unionized.[45]

Massey would have been interested in the ways that family members of different genders and ages operated within and outside the space of the laundry across traditional household spatial divisions. She would also likely have found the integration of domestic and work space to be significant to understanding how Toy Len Goon's labor was categorized under her domestic role.[46] Toy Len Goon's labor was central to running the laundry, even before Dogan fell ill and passed away.

In this sense, the Goon laundry was quite different from the more common male-run laundry described by Siu and imagined by the public, in that Toy Len Goon took on the bulk of responsibilities for both laundry and domestic duties, which were deeply intertwined. However, the ready association of women and laundry work in mainstream US society, and the location of the laundry within the space of the household, may have made her remarkable achievements appear to be a natural extension of her role as a woman, a mother, and a housewife. As in the example from Massey above, preexisting associations of mothering and housekeeping with laundry work likely obscured her skills as a businesswoman and head of household. During the 1950s, manufacturers promoted—and the middle class became obsessed with—labor-saving devices such as the automatic washing machine, whose modern technology promised to make the work of (always female) homemakers much easier. The existence of this technology likely made Toy Len Goon, a poor working-class woman who labored long hours daily washing other people's clothes, seem even more noble, or perhaps further differentiated her from the middle class. In contrast to the wife of the laundryman who stayed behind the partition, described in the excerpt from Siu at the beginning of the chapter, Toy Len Goon became the public face of the laundry and oversaw not just domestic work but the whole business, a departure from the type of work more commonly done by Chinese women in the United States.

Doris recollects that her mother had already become quite proficient at running the laundry and the household at the time of Dogan's death, and even prior to it:

> She and Dad worked the laundry together but she was the real moving force as he would take off to visit his opium-smoking friends on a regular basis, from what I understand. She knew how to "run" the laundry business, the various steps that needed to be taken from the laundry coming in until it was ready to be packaged and returned to the customer. She even made the purchases of paper and twine and starch from a Jewish peddler who came around every so often. I kind of remember that he also sold some groceries like rice and potatoes which Mom would buy in bulk, since there were 8 of us![47]

Though Toy Len's duties departed from traditional gender roles, the work done by the children fell along more traditional gender and age lines, with the older boys helping with the heavy work alongside their mother, the girls doing domestic work as well as doing lighter laundry work and childcare. In response to my question, Doris recalls, "Mom most certainly took age and gender into consideration when giving out our duties; i.e., Aunt Jo was to clean the living quarters; I washed the dishes; the boys ran the hot press; did the bulk of the ironing; the older taller boys hung the clothes to dry; the girls helped Mom preparing meals as we got older." According to Doris, each child was given a task to carry out, with the older siblings (boys) ironing, washing, and hanging clothes to dry. Doris and Janet remember sorting the incoming laundry and checking shirt and pant pockets.

Josephine's recollections were like those of Doris, though hers focus more on helping her mother with the cooking, as well as being charged with cleaning the living quarters upstairs, which included dusting, vacuuming, and changing bed sheets. She also took care of the younger siblings, particularly Janet, the youngest. She added that Doris had to do the dishes because Jo had eczema on her hands. While the Goon children shared many experiences in common, they also had their own specific experiences and memories, in part due to age and gender, but also extraordinary circumstances such as the illness that put Josephine in the hospital for almost a year.

As an outside observer who married into the family, Amy Guen, wife of Edward, remembers that the girls, particularly Josephine as the eldest, were expected to help with domestic chores. In response to my sharing that Josephine had to take care of my mother and help with the cooking and cleaning rather than working in the laundry, Amy commented, "Oh yeah, being the oldest girl. I think something [*sic*] that girls are expected to do. I remember when I visited, all the boys were listening to the radio or reading comic book when the girls were cleaning up the dishes."[48] Amy viewed this gendered division of labor as something that traditional Chinese families practiced, though she also did not believe it was unique to them.

The division of labor by gender and age in the laundry may seem to be a natural outgrowth of the practicalities of carrying out rigorous laundry work. Though Toy Len was able to do the heavy work of washing and hanging the clothes done in the back room, it was understandable that the sons, who were also older, stronger, and taller than her daughters, would be asked to work alongside her. That is why when Dogan fell ill, Carroll, as the oldest son, took time from high school to help his mother with the heavy laundry work. Household and laundry duties shifted over time, as the older siblings left home for college, military service, or secretarial school, and younger siblings grew older and were able to help with more tasks. My mother, Janet, recalls being patiently taught to iron by her brother Arthur, but being quickly taken off ironing duty after burning too many shirts, causing them to lose customers. In a 2019 interview, she said that she eventually caught on and "graduated" to ironing. As the youngest child, she did not bear the same responsibilities of childcare or household and laundry work as her older siblings while growing up.

The Goon children say they never questioned having to carry out these duties. However, the time they spent together working shaped their complex sibling relationships. In addition, those responsibilities mediated their relationships with those in the community, some of whom didn't fully understand their circumstances. Work also created burdens and stressors for some of the children, particularly the older ones, who shouldered more responsibility and had to sacrifice other activities as a result.

The Laundry as an Immigrant Space

Small immigrant businesses have been a well-studied subject, both because they represent a form of immigrant adaptation to a new society, and because they connect immigrants through networks to both co-ethnics and others in the community.[49] Today, the success of these small businesses is often seen as evidence of American exceptionalism, and as proof that immigrants can pull themselves up by their bootstraps to become self-supporting in a neoliberal society where self-reliance and entrepreneurship are valued.[50] Immigrant entrepreneur success has also been viewed within the public imagination and the media as an indication that immigrants have achieved full cultural citizenship and belonging in the United States, without their racial and ethnic differences providing barriers to their success.[51] In his study of Gujrati Indian motel owners in the midwestern United States, Pawan Dhingra notes that this misconception "obscures the reality of their tenuous position within the hierarchies of capitalism, race, gender, economic and political opportunity, and culture."[52]

Though hoteliers and laundry workers appear to have little in common, I refer to Dhingra's study both for the broader debates regarding immigrant entrepreneurship within which he frames his discussion of immigrant small business owners, and for the specific ways he discusses the use of space within these ethnic businesses. Toy Len Goon's celebrated journey from struggling widow to business owner and Mother of the Year was touted in the media as evidence of the potential that the United States as a liberal democracy held for immigrants of all backgrounds, regardless of race. Though framed within Cold War politics, this rhetoric was a precursor to the neoliberal logic applied to Dhingra's Indian motel owners.

In the case of Indian motel owners, a central goal was to ensure that their businesses did not appear to be "ethnic." In analyzing the spatial dimensions of the midwestern Gujrati Indian-owned motels he studied, Dhingra observed that owners would try to present a "front stage" that obscured the fact that the hotel was owned by an Indian family.[53] This was true both before and after September 11, 2001, when racial profiling of both Muslim and non-Muslim Indians became even more prevalent. Drawing on Goffman's concept of "front stage" and "back stage," Dhingra describes how motel owners would hire a local worker of non-Indian descent, most often white, to work the front desk. Unlike some "ethnic" restaurants that might highlight Asian décor to establish a sense of atmosphere or authenticity, Dhingra discusses a motel owner who decorated the lobby with a set of hands in prayer, implying that the establishment's owners were Christian when they were not. Perhaps most noteworthy is how they made efforts to render the presence of their family, who also lived in the hotel, invisible, by making sure no odors from Indian cooking permeated the areas of the hotel that visitors occupied, keeping their children out of the lobby as much as possible, and not renting rooms close to where the family resided to prevent guests from hearing noises made by the children.[54] Dhingra also discusses how wives remained "backstage," cleaning, doing laundry, and sometimes bookkeeping, while men remained "frontstage" at the front desk, did repairs, and dealt with vendors.

In contrast, the Goon laundry, like all Chinese hand laundries, was clearly a Chinese space. The Goons did not make special efforts to adorn the space with Chinese décor, and in fact did not own many Chinese decorations. However, the presence of eight Chinese children and their parents working and living in the laundry was quite obvious and at times piqued customer's curiosity. Doris recalls,

> I remember Mom telling me that when they first arrived in Portland and had children, customers would come in to see the Chinese babies. She knew that because they would come in with just one shirt and look!! She didn't mind at all. She loved her babies and was proud to show them off![55]

While Siu mentions some Chicago laundries hiring local women, often Black, to help in the laundry, this was not a common practice in Maine.[56] And even if the Goons had wanted to hire a non-Chinese worker to run the front counter, they would not have been able to afford it. Far from remaining "backstage," Toy Len Goon was front and center as both the proprietor of the laundry and the mother of her children.

After the older boys left home, they were able to arrange to send some of the laundry out to be washed and dried, while Toy Len, and later Arthur and Doris, took care of the ironing and pressing.[57] Arthur recollects,

> Actually I took over the laundry after I graduated from high school. I was waiting to go to college. That would have been when I was seventeen? Around 1948? I went to the Navy at nineteen. . . . Essentially I did it by myself. The business at that point was getting lower so I could handle it. At that point I sent out the laundry to be washed. They would come once a week to pick it up and then they delivered it.[58]

Because their home was also a place of business frequented by customers and other visitors, the Goon family had multiple opportunities to interact with neighbors and others in their community. As such, they were quite visible. Though there was not a strict dividing line between them, with the dining table and ironing tables in front of the partition, the laundry still had a front stage and a back stage.[59] For example, as mentioned previously, when the teacher Clara Soule would visit, Toy Len would feel inconvenienced by the latter's desire to spend time teaching her English, as Toy Len did not have the luxury to chat extensively with visitors or customers during the workday, which would have required her to neglect her duties in the back of the laundry, and for the household. The children remember not being able to have friends over often, because there was no leisure space inside the building. However, my mother shared both during my interview with her and during her comments as part of the unveiling of the historic marker at 615 Forest Avenue that she fondly remembers how her mother let her have two non-Chinese friends over one day, even taking the time to make them snacks.

Toy Len and her children established good relationships with their non-Chinese neighbors, some of whom shared local customs and knowledge—such as how to make a pie. Doris recollects,

> There were some very regular customers but I don't remember any that could be called friends. But there were neighbors that befriended us. I remember Mom telling me how someone came to the laundry

> when she first arrived and told her about how to celebrate Christmas with a tree; someone who told her to buy iodine for a cut or scratch; how to make a pie or a cake. Don't know whether they were customers or neighbors.[60]

My mother also recollected that her mother would often talk with the next-door neighbor by shouting across the alley way (driveway). According to Amy Guen, this neighbor was named Mrs. Kalil, an immigrant from Syria.[61] Her husband, Joe Kalil, was "a traveling salesman with a dry goods inventory storage in his garage."[62] Amy describes their friendship with Toy Len Goon as "affectionate" and was touched when Mrs. Kalil wanted to give her and Edward a wedding gift. Mrs. Kalil and Toy Len Goon kept in touch, even after Mrs. Kalil was paralyzed after a stroke in the 1980s and moved to Oklahoma to live with her nephew. The two friends reunited in July 1987, when Mrs. Kalil visited Toy Len in her condominium in Swampscott, Massachusetts, where they "embraced and talked with intermittent emotional expressions of laughter and lamentation while holding hands."[63]

Sometimes, the private and public aspects of the laundry overlapped. My mother remembers one awkward situation when a customer inquired about the set of curtains they had left to be laundered. In fact, after many weeks had passed, the Goons had assumed that the customers were not coming back for their curtains and had decided to hang them in the second-floor kitchen window. The family hoped that the customers would not notice them.

Dhingra's study took place in the early 2000s, and with immigrants who were often the only Indian family in their small communities. He notes that one of the priorities of the Indian families was to pass on their culture to their children. Devoting time and energy to thinking about culture and how to pass it on would have been a luxury and privilege Toy Len Goon didn't have. Though Toy Len Goon raised her children based on her Chinese cultural background, there was also strong external pressure for them to assimilate to US culture. The children would have received these messages at school, from missionaries who came to the laundry to try to get the Goon children to attend church, and from friends and classmates. What it means to assimilate—what one is supposed to gain and what one is expected to give up or change—can be a complicated prospect, particularly for a Chinese immigrant family that is being held up as an exemplary "American" family.

Out from Behind the Counter

Toy Len's success in raising her family and running the laundry after Dogan's death was recognized as extraordinary by those who knew her story, even if seen as an extension of her role as a mother and a woman. In their recollections of their childhoods, the Goon children viewed the hard work and cramped living conditions they left behind as a testament to their work ethic and grit, something they did not believe was demonstrated by all immigrants. They emphasized that they did not know anything different, only that they should follow their mother's lead and do their part to help her out. These family narratives from Doris and others reinforce the idea of the hard work ethic and sacrifice of mother and children, in the laundry and at school. They don't remember ever complaining or misbehaving badly, as they wanted to please their mother.

Toy Len Goon's selection as Mother of the Year, and the resultant focus on her dual roles as mother and business owner, seemingly marked a transformation of the Chinese laundry from an immigrant space to an ambiguously American one. In celebrating her achievements, the media brought the family's labor out from behind the counter to exemplify the American Dream. However, what was portrayed was a selective account of their work. As Chiou-Ling Yeh observes, the full extent of their labor was not recognized by the media:

> Indeed, the coverage failed to mention Goon's self-employment and her financial struggles. Rather, it painted Goon as a proper middle-class gender model—a good wife and mother. Even though accentuating Goon's humble economic background could demonstrate upward mobility, the author instead chose to stress Goon's domestic role and the myth of the attainable American dream for female immigrants to maintain heteronormativity.[64]

Regardless of what the media may have underplayed in terms of the family's struggles, the Goon children saw themselves as having benefited from the opportunities afforded by US education, freedom, and democracy, as they were eventually able to leave laundry work behind, thus moving from manual labor to skilled work. Their labor in the laundry and their mother's sacrifice enabled them to transition from their immigrant parents' working-class lifestyle to a solidly middle class "American" one. They accepted this narrative, not only as a testimony to their mother's sacrifice and their own hard work, but also because it was how the American Dream was supposed to operate. In this origin story, the laundry could be seen as a transitional space within which the Goon children's efforts and their parents' hard labor successfully transformed the children into high-achieving Americans.

The celebration of the success of Toy Len Goon and her children was thus a testament to capitalism, entrepreneurship, and the United States as a meritocracy. The Goon children demonstrated strong work ethics in their duties in the laundry, around the home, and at school. But between the predominant narratives of Americanization circulating in popular discourse at the time and the media coverage of Toy Len Goon's award, the Goon children were not given the opportunity to think about their family story in any other way than in terms of assimilation and being exemplary minorities who have achieved the American Dream. The Goon children could be seen as having kept their end of the bargain, and were rewarded by becoming solidly middle-class and experiencing a level of material comfort that their parents could not have imagined. They were able to buy homes, have successful white-collar careers, and provide their own children with opportunities they themselves could not have dreamed of. But one wonders whether the praise lavished upon Toy Len and her high-achieving children minimized or reframed the challenges they may have endured.

Toy Len Goon's story was retold in public discourses as one of Americanization, maternal sacrifice, and the resultant success of her second-generation Chinese American children. However, as discussed by Dhingra above, it is important to consider that the existence of narratives of immigrant success do not necessarily mean that immigrants did not face challenges or structural barriers. While the Goon children did not necessarily remember experiencing discrimination, they also appear hesitant to recognize the possibility that structural racism and discrimination might have negatively affected them, even though these social issues have been well documented, from the arrival of the first Chinese immigrants to the United States until the present. They recollect that they were treated well and did not feel that there were any barriers to their success.

While they do not recall having been treated significantly differently by their friends, neighbors, and teachers, given the focus on assimilation and Chinese Americans as "good minorities" during that period, they also would likely not have had the vocabulary to think about their experiences in terms of continued structures of marginalization. Nor were they likely aware of how the media's portrayal of them as a model minority family fit within the broader context of the Cold War. The Goon story not only seamlessly figured into the public's imagination of Chinese American belonging, assimilation, and exceptionalism of Chinese immigrants in the United States, but also appeared to parallel the Goon children's own narratives.

Toy Len Goon's selection as Mother of the Year made the Goon laundry into a focal point that enabled Americans to go behind the counter via the filtered lens of the media to discover an assimilated "American" Chinese family. While the laundry remained "Chinese," in the form of the Chinese language, cooking, and customs practiced by the Goons and their children, this part of the story took a back seat to the idea that they were being accepted as Americans. As I discuss in my previous work, I do not view "Chinese" and "American" as being discrete cultures, as one does not leave one to enter another.[65] Rather, I focus on how Chinese American and other diasporic cultures are dynamic and evolving, involving elements of both continuity and change, rather than straight-line assimilation and the loss of cultures of origin.[66]

The integration of the Goon family into their Portland community and into US society more broadly may appear to be the culmination of the Chicago School's assimilation cycle, thus proving Paul Siu's sojourner thesis wrong. While Robert Park and Paul Siu believed the Chinese to be stuck at an earlier stage of the cycle and therefore unable to see it to its assimilation endpoint, the Goon family and other assimilated Chinese American families appear to have cracked the code. But as discussed earlier, the concept of assimilation in Park's theory did not adequately address the existence of constructed racial differences and viewed the assimilation process as being entirely positive and unidirectional.[67] The Chicago School also problematically based its ideas about assimilation on ideas about the inferiority of "Oriental" culture and the celebration of the marginal man who had transitioned from his old culture.[68] However, the cultural geography–based ideas of culture and space discussed earlier in this chapter facilitate movement beyond the idea of cultures acting as undifferentiated wholes, and of these whole cultures moving toward assimilation.[69] It also allows thinking beyond Siu's idea of the sojourner as a solo figure who remained socially, economically, and culturally bound to China and Chinese culture because of his marginalization from mainstream US society. By understanding space as fluid, and the laundry as an interstitial space, we find it possible to think of the relationship between the Goons, their laundry, and their community in a more dynamic and nuanced way. Siu's conceptualization of the sojourner views the Chineseness of Chinese laundrymen as being contained within the laundry and the social networks of laundrymen, which extend to other Chinese immigrants, as well as back to China. In this sense, he inadvertently reproduces Orientalist ideas of Chineseness as being contained and preserved in these "Chinese spaces" that are distinct and separate from American ones, though he recognizes that these differences are not essential but rather the result of structural racism. The media portrayed the Goon family's story as one of unidirectional Americanization, as a movement away from both traditional Chinese culture and the threat of Chinese communism faced by those in their homeland. Massey's conceptualization of space enables places to contain multiple and sometimes competing identities. It thus allows for thinking beyond the idea of culture being a self-contained entity, and instead for the existence of new hybrid forms of Chinese American identity that are not wholly "Chinese" or "American." Rather, these forms of Chinese American identity shift over time, along with the changing experiences and identities of individuals. They are a product of the relationships within the Goon family and laundry, their relationships to people in the community, and even their sentiments toward their homeland and to the Chinese immigrant community. They are intertwined with changing ideas of gender, family, and home in the context of the Goon family's changing relationships to broader US society as structured by the social, political, and cultural capital they endeavored to build.

There is no doubt that this hardworking family achieved its successes through its members' ability to cooperate and to endure challenging labor conditions as a family. However, when examples of Asian American families like the Goons are held up as models of success against other immigrants, particularly other minorities, this success narrative becomes problematic. While the myth has its origins in post–World War II, Cold War America, the model minority myth continues to shape Asian American experiences today, particularly in the way they are used as a foil to other minority groups. As Cindy I-Fen Cheng argues, in the late 1950s, as part of the Cold War project of promoting the superiority and inclusivity of US democracy in contrast to communism, the focus on Chinese American cultural citizenship would eventually move from an emphasis on assimilation to a refocusing on "'Chinese' as a marker of racial difference."[70] The inclusion of Chinese American families into integrated suburban neighborhoods, a process for which Chinese women were seen as key, helped reinforce Chinese Americans' proximity to whiteness, while also sending the message that these suburban spaces weren't exclusive. Rather than erasing their differences through assimilation, which could only be accomplished on a limited basis, the Chineseness of these Chinese Americans became strategically important within the Black and white racial politics of the United States.[71]

5

Mother of the Year Award

Being "Good" Chinese Americans During the Cold War

Clara Soule's Nomination Letter

Mrs. Toy Goon, the mother named in this application, being presented by Business and Professional Women's Club of Portland, Maine, is a woman of the highest type of character, strictest integrity, amiable disposition, deep understanding and gentle pleasing appearance.

She has proved herself to be an outstanding mother, always sacrificing herself for the good of her children. Her husband was in ill health after his return from service in World War I and finally had one leg amputated. He died around twelve years earlier. During his illness, Mrs. Goon carried on the laundry and cared for her family, the children assisting outside of school hours, but she was the controlling force.

We, who have known her through the years have learned to admire and love her. While she has never been privileged to attend school, she has a keen mind and carried on her business. I taught Americanization in Portland for twenty-one years and I proved to my entire satisfaction that lack of education in no way affects intelligence. Some of the most intellectual could not read in any language, never having had time even in early childhood to learn to read. She has always sent her children to school regularly, had them attend church and Sunday school and always her family was the first contacted to participate in inter-racial and inter-cultural programs. She was always ready, overworked and burdened though she might be, to encourage the children to take part in any civic or community project, assuming the extra responsibility of doing the children's work in addition to her own. We have marveled at her uncomplaining,

THE AMERICAN MOTHERS Committee
OF THE
GOLDEN RULE FOUNDATION

Devoted worker, who established on the solid foundation of motherly love a home and a life that are model in their every spiritual and material appointment; - - - -

Who reared her children in reverence for God and in an atmosphere of love, sympathy and understanding; - - - - -

Whose successful service to her own State and community have made her widely recognized for her self-sacrificing efforts;

Benefactor of her neighborhood and of that greater area which comprises humanity, a living exponent and exemplar of the truth that motherhoods finest function is helpfulness:

Mrs. Toy Len Goon Ideal American Mother, the glorification of American womanhood, whose love and loyalty have been woven into the red, white and blue of the Stars and Stripes, an inspiring example to others, she has added glory to the American Flag.

Beloved by all who know her, by the authority of The American Mothers Committee of The Golden Rule Foundation, she is hereby honored as

The American Mother
For 1952

PRESIDENT, THE GOLDEN RULE FOUNDATION

NATIONAL CHAIRMAN THE AMERICAN MOTHERS COMMITTEE

CO-CHAIRMEN, THE AMERICAN MOTHERS' COMMITTEE

SECRETARY OF AMERICAN MOTHERS COMMITTEE

PRESIDENT, ASSOCIATION OF STATE MOTHERS

TREASURER OF AMERICAN MOTHERS COMMITTEE

Figure 5.1. Toy Len Goon's American Mothers Committee Mother of the Year 1952 certificate. Photo courtesy of Linda and Doug Fifield.

untiring, cheerful attitude. The loyalty and acts of genuine thoughtfulness of their mother now bespeak of her children's deep love and appreciation.

One of her sons was president of his class in Deering High School and another son was vice-president of his class.

I can recommend Mrs. Goon highly as a mother who lives by the Golden Rule and has taught her children to do so.[1]

Mary McLeod Bethune's Editorial

My first thought on reading of the selection of Mrs. Toy Len Goon, widow of a World War One veteran and mother of eight splendid American citizens, was to wonder how far America would back up this choice in terms of the opportunity to tell all of its Chinese citizens. This is the third

180 High St.
Portland, Maine
Feb. 5, 1952

To Whom it May Concern:

Mrs. Toy Len Goon, the mother named in this application, being presented by Business & Professional Women's Club of Portland, Maine, is a woman of highest type of character, strictest integrity, amiable disposition, deep understanding and gentle pleasing appearance.

She has proved herself to be an outstanding mother, always sacrificing herself for the good of her children. Her husband was in ill health after his return from service in World War I and finally had one leg amputated. He died about twelve years ago. During his illness, Mrs. Goon carried on the laundry and cared for her family, the children assisting, outside of school hours, but she was the controlling force.

We, who have known her through the years have learned to admire and love her. While she has never been privileged to attend school, she has a keen mind and carried on her business. I taught Americanization in Portland for twenty-one years and I proved to my entire satisfaction that lack of education in no way effects intelligence. Some of the most intellectual could not read in any language, never having had time even in early childhood to learn to read. She has always sent her children to school regularly, had them attend church and Sunday School and always her family was the first contacted to participate in inter-racial and inter-national programs. She was always ready, overworked and burdened though she might be, to encourage the children to take part in any civic or community project, assuming the extra responsibility of doing the children's work in addition to her own. We have marvelled at her uncomplaining, untiring, cheerful attitude. The loyalty and acts of genuine thoughtfulness of their mother now bespeak of her children's deep love and appreciation.

One of her sons was president of his class in Deering High School and another son was vice-president of his class.

I can recommend Mrs. Goon highly as a mother who lives by the Golden Rule and has taught her children to do so.

Signed ________________________
Clara L. Soule,
Formerly Elementary Supervisor
& Director of Reading in
Portland Public Schools

Figure 5.2. Clara Soule, nomination letter, February 5, 1952.

time that the Golden Rule Foundation's American Mothers Committee has selected for its annual honor a mother not of the Caucasian race. The other two were Negro and Indian respectively. And it grieves me to recall the instances of rejection of others of those races that became matters of national concern subsequent to the awarding of those honors.[2]

Toy Len Guen's Description of Award

ANDREA: Tell me about Mother of the Year.

TOY LEN GOON: Hah?

A: Mother of the Year.

TLG: Mother Year. Ne ngin zung ji ngoi, zung ji ngoi ne children. [People liked, liked my children.] . . .

TLG: Like my children. I no husband. My children every one good. School enjoy ngoi ne children. I good mother to good children. Like that. . . .

TLG: I, I tell them, every day everyone listen to me. Yeah. That kind of mother of the year. I wish more Goon come my school. Uh, ko, nek gong. [Uh, like that, you all tell it (tell her).]

JANET: The teachers would say they wish more Goon children would come to their school. We were goody two-shoes, that's what were!

DORIS: We were all good kids [*laughs*].

TLG: Wish more children come.

J: We were easy.[3]

This chapter focuses on the political and historical contexts that enabled the Goon family to be seen as "good" Americans. The Goon children's desire to be seen as "good" and their ability to be seen as such were intertwined with perceptions of Chinese American integration that were being reshaped by changing ideas of ethnic liberalism. The shifting racial positioning of Chinese Americans was facilitated by Chinese Americans' own perceptions of racial discrimination, or lack thereof. I discuss Toy Len Goon's nomination by Clara Soule and contextualize the latter's relationship with the Goon family and motivation to put Toy Len forward for the award. I then detail the festivities following the award and discuss her children's recollections. I then analyze the ways that news coverage in both the US-based English-language and Chinese-language publications framed her award in the context of the Cold War, newly positive portrayals of Chinese Americans, and changing gender roles. I end with a discussion of the marginal inclusion of Chinese Americans that these changes produced.

The three excerpts above represent different perspectives on Toy Len Goon's selection as US Mother of the Year. The first is from the nomination letter penned by Clara Soule, an Americanization teacher and friend of the family who was interested in helping Chinese immigrants but was also aware of the political implications of a Chinese American woman being selected as Mother of the Year. Soule seemed to genuinely respect Toy Len Goon and her ability to raise her children while running the laundry after Dogan's death. However, her letter focuses on what would appeal to the selection committee, highlighting not only Dogan's military service, but also Toy Len being the "controlling force" in the family after Dogan's death, her "keen mind" despite her lack of formal education, and her raising of good citizens. The letter concludes by emphasizing that Toy Len lives by the Golden Rule and has taught her children to do so. Soule also describes Toy Len as "uncomplaining, untiring, cheerful" and as "a woman of the highest type of character, strictest integrity, amiable disposition, deep understanding and gentle pleasing appearance." Thus, while she is depicted as a "force," the portrayal is balanced by a characterization of her as nonthreatening in personality ("amiable," "cheerful") and even in appearance ("gentle pleasing"). Though the nomination letter was meant to extoll Toy Len Goon's positive qualities, Soule's depiction has all the makings of a model minority stereotype, focusing on her hard work, extraordinary accomplishments, strong family values, and good citizenship, while also emphasizing that she was well-behaved and gentle.

The second depiction is by Mary McLeod Bethune, a well-known Black educator, writing for the *New York Age*, an independent Black newspaper. Her editorial also emphasizes Dogan Goon's veteran status and the good citizens that Toy Len Goon had raised. She also realizes the significance of a Chinese American immigrant being selected for the national honor, following "Negro" and "Indian" recipients of recent years. From her perspective, the selection of non-white women for this honor was overdue, and Bethune saw this as an opportunity for the United States to live up to its promise and potential as a democracy. However, she did not appear to view Chinese Americans as occupying a racial category distinct from the other non-white recipients she mentioned.

The third excerpt is from Toy Len Goon herself in response to my question during my 1992 interview with her about her selection as Mother of the Year. At the age of one hundred, she recounted the familiar narrative in a combination of Chinese and English (the latter for my benefit). She saw the award as being based on how well-liked and well-behaved her children were, commenting that the teachers liked having Goon children in their classes. She also refers to Dogan's passing, recognizing that she was given credit for continuing to raise her obedient, studious children in the absence of a husband. During the interview, her daughters Doris and Janet served as more than translators, freely adding in their own comments regarding revelations they hadn't been aware of previously, or in response to a comment their mother made. When I asked my grandmother about her selection as Mother of the Year, my mother joked that we were in for an hour-long response, knowing how proud her mother was of that honor. When my grandmother talked about people liking her children, my mother commented, "We were goody two-shoes," and Doris agreed.

While the opening excerpts do not wholly represent the diversity of ways Toy Len Goon's story was depicted, they appear to share the same basic form and emphasis. This template for her story served as a starting point for various parties who saw different implications for her success story. Clara Soule not only admired Toy Len Goon's parenting and work ethic but saw broader potential for the public dissemination of her story for discussions of the inclusion of minority immigrants in US society through the route of education. Mary McLeod Bethune thought it important to bring the accomplishments of various US minorities into the spotlight. And unlike the previous two excerpts, Toy Len Goon's own account focuses less on her own accomplishments and more on those of her children, consistent with the prevalent narrative in media stories.

All discussions of Toy Len Goon focused on how she had produced "good" and likable children who were upstanding American citizens. While I am certainly not questioning whether the Goon children were well-behaved, upstanding citizens, what exactly did it mean to be a "good citizen" or to be "a goody two-shoes" in the context of the early 1950s? Particularly, what did it mean for Chinese Americans to be "good" during this time, and what might have compelled them to try to be so? And while it may be possible to argue that there are ways to objectively measure good behavior and success based on grades, educational attainment, awards, reputation, and adherence to the law, what standards or expectations were the Goon children living up to in trying to be "good"?

The context that enabled Chinese Americans to be considered "good immigrants" was international in scope, and situated within specific historical currents, including public discourses about the integration of Chinese American families into US society.[4] A *Reader's Digest* story from 1944 discusses Gordon Mah, who went from being a houseboy in San Francisco to a restaurant owner in Hartford, Connecticut.[5] Mah credited the fact that they were not raised in a majority-Chinese environment for the success of his children, who were educated at elite institutions such as MIT and the University of Chicago and held positions in the US military. The article emphasized that while they remained proud of being of Chinese heritage, they were also proud and loyal US citizens.[6] A 1944 photo in *Look* magazine shows a Chinese American man, Mr. Chan, from San Francisco Chinatown reading an English-language newspaper with his grandchildren.[7] The caption also notes that both Mr. Chan and his wife had purchased war bonds.

A similar picture of Dogan Goon appeared in the *Portland Press Herald*, with the caption noting that the family had purchased US war bonds. Interestingly, another article in the *Portland Evening Express*, dated October 10, 1944, features a photo of six of the Goon family siblings reading a War Chest publication with a visiting War Chest worker, the caption noting that their native land of China was in its thirty-third year as a republic. The article, titled "Chinese Family Joins Appeal for Success of Chest Drive," notes that "members of Portland's oldest Chinese family" were visited by a worker from the War Chest campaign, which included aid for the Chinese homeland.[8]

The article informs the reader that the family has bought both Chinese and American war bonds, and that Toy Len Goon has "sisters, nieces and nephews in China" who have not been severely affected by the war. The article quotes her son Edward Goon as saying that he hopes the funds will help "lessen the suffering in China," and points out that Edward was nominated by Representative Hale as an alternate to West Point.[9] It describes sentiments from the other children about their desire to help China by providing them with clothing, footballs, dolls, and comics. At the conclusion of the article, it is revealed that the largest portion of the funds for Allied relief in the next War Chest campaign will go toward relief in China, a US World War II ally.

There was much at stake in the United States' efforts to call attention to the successful integration of immigrants. As Ellen Wu observes,

> The failure of the nation to live in accordance with its professed democratic ideals endangered the country's aspirations to world leadership. The United States' battles against fascism and then communism meant that Asiatic Exclusion, like Jim Crow, was no longer tenable. Seeking global legitimacy, Americans moved to undo the legal framework and social practices that relegated Asians outside the bounds of the nation.[10]

Much of the media coverage of Toy Len Goon's award, like the newsreel quoted in the introduction, emphasized her accomplishments as a good mother who raised "fine American citizens." An article in the *Dallas Morning News* quoted the Portland Women's Club as highlighting how well she had been integrated into her community, saying, "She has proven herself a wonderful mother, a good citizen, and is highly regarded in the community in which she has lived for thirty-eight years," and quoted Soule as commenting, "I can recommend Mrs. Goon as a mother who lives by the Golden Rule and has taught her children to do so."[11] A *Portland Press Herald* article titled "Mrs. Goon Overwhelmed, Happy as She Prepares for American Mother Ceremonies in New York City" illustrates the connection that Soule saw between Toy Len Goon's immigrant success story and its implications for the image of the United States abroad, particularly in the communist nations.[12] The article quotes Soule as saying, "It could never happen in China. . . . And really, it's a great boost for democracy too, coming at this time. I guess it will mean something when it gets behind the Iron Curtain."[13] The story points out that Toy Len Goon came from China thirty-eight years ago, and that her homeland was "in the grips of Communism."[14] The symbolism of Toy Len Goon, a Chinese immigrant widow of a US veteran, being selected as US Mother of the Year was deployed on many fronts via the media to spread the image of the United States as a democracy.

Cold War Context

While the picture of a patriotic Chinese American family contributing to the war effort out of concern for their ancestral homeland certainly is consistent with the other media efforts at the time to portray Chinese Americans as assimilated US citizens, the situation would change in 1949 when Mao Zedong and his Communist Party took power. The *Portland Evening Express* article emphasized the family's ties to both the United States and China, without these connections seeming at odds with the fact that the family's children were also assimilated, loyal Americans.[15] In contrast, the coverage of Toy Len Goon's selection as Mother of the Year only eight years later, in 1952, shows how their portrayal as loyal US citizens occurred at the expense of any transnational ties to China.

As Madeline Hsu discusses, "Cold War politics laid the groundwork for transformations associated with the Civil Rights era in repositioning Chinese Americans, as capable of, and even ideally suited to, participating in American democracy and capitalism."[16] She notes that during and following World War II, the United States aimed to present itself as diverse and inclusive, reminding us that the integration of Asian and African Americans became ideologically connected to decolonization abroad and the promise of capitalism.[17] Finding itself on the same side of World War II as China, the United States saw the repeal of the Chinese Exclusion Acts as "a symbolic gesture of international friendship towards its Pacific ally," giving Chinese Americans a "newfound acceptance and stature in American society."[18] Key to this reframing of Chinese and Japanese Americans as part of the nation was the idea of racial liberalism, "the growing belief in political and intellectual circles that the country's racial diversity could be most ably managed through the assimilation and integration of nonwhites."[19] Under racial liberalism, the internal issues of race-based discrimination such as Exclusion and Jim Crow segregation became challenges to the United States' "global legitimacy," and thus needed to be dismantled to enable the inclusion of Asians.[20]

Quoting Christina Klein, Hsu notes,

> "Questions of racism thus served to link the domestic American sphere with the sphere of foreign relations, proving their inseparability: how

> Americans dealt with the problem of race relations at home had a direct impact on their success in dealing with the decolonizing world abroad." And so the Chinese Exclusion Act had to be repealed in 1943 so that Chinese and later other Asian allies of the United States gained naturalization rights.[21]

Cold War containment, understandings of difference as cultural rather than racial, and the need for the United States to demonstrate its openness to diversity created the conditions for immigration reform and the integration of certain ethnic immigrant groups. These changes paved the way for the promotion of Chinese Americans as model minorities.[22] In his book *Orientals: Asian Americans in Popular Culture*, Robert Lee traces the development of the model minority myth, illustrating how the portrayal of Asian Americans as an assimilable racial minority "whose apparently successful ethnic assimilation was a result of stoic patience, political obedience, and self-improvement was a critically important narrative of ethnic liberalism."[23] Lee observes that in the context of the Cold War, "the narrative of ethnic assimilation sent the message to the Third World, especially to Asia where the United States was engaged in increasingly fierce struggles with nationalist and communist insurgencies, that the United States was a liberal democratic state where people of color could enjoy equal rights and upward mobility."[24]

Thus, the coverage of Toy Len Goon's selection as US Mother of the Year in the US media reflected more than just respect for her accomplishments. Rather, it resonated with ongoing efforts to portray the United States as a democracy and thus as the rightful leader of the free world in the context of Cold War containment. These concerns were entangled with efforts to promote the domestic sphere as a safe haven, one in which women were imagined as playing a key role. In *Homeward Bound*, Elaine Tyler May connects "the containment of communism in Cold War politics with the containment of women in the postwar domestic ideal. In the midst of Cold War anxiety, 'the family seemed to offer a psychological fortress,' a buffer against both internal and external threats."[25] While women had made some gains during the World War II era, Joanne Meyerowitz notes that the focus of historians on the push for the return of traditional gender roles as part of the conservative turn in the postwar period "tends to downplay women's agency and to portray women primarily as victims."[26] She asks us to consider that "in the years following WWII, many women were not white, middle class, married, and suburban; and many white, middle class, married women were neither wholly domestic or quiescent."[27] Meyerowitz compiled a series of essays that examine women's intersectional identities and that "suggest that the postwar public discourse on women was more complex than often portrayed. . . . They investigate the competing voices within the public discourse on women and the internal contradictions that undermined and destabilized the domestic stereotype even as it was constructed."[28]

The success of women, and minority women in particular, was viewed by those conscious of the United States' international image in the context of the Cold War as a barometer of the United States' ability to craft a strong reputation as a land of opportunity, countering accusations by the Soviet Union and other communist powers that its poor treatment of women and minorities belied its claims of liberty and justice for all.

Complicating Gender Roles

The story of Toy Len Goon as a working-class, non-white, immigrant woman complicates the association of the postwar era with the return to traditional gender roles, as well as the idea of domesticity itself. As an immigrant to the United States from China who was being portrayed as a new American, she held an in-between status. Neither Black nor white, she was less easily slotted into the entrenched racial categories of the United States, making her racial positioning open for reinterpretation and debate as part of a broader repositioning of Asian Americans in the United States at the time. She was a single mother, but as a widow rather than an unwed mother, she was viewed as a victim turned hero, rather than being scorned. She became a convenient vehicle for the media to create—and to some extent debate—rhetoric about pressing questions surrounding women, mothering, and immigrant assimilation. However, her life challenges and accomplishments were certainly more multifaceted and multilayered than the one-dimensional portrayal of her as a traditional mother onto which the various politicized versions of her story were projected. Despite being constrained by the traditional rural Chinese gender roles and familial responsibilities into which she was placed, and by the relative isolation she experienced as the wife of a laundryman in a small city in the United States, she ran her home and business by going outside traditional gender roles. Mixing domestic and business space and her nontraditional gender roles in the context of her laundry work allowed her to break these boundaries.

Meyerowitz observes that though there existed in the postwar era strong public messages about how women should retreat to their traditional roles in the domestic sphere, there were also many women who did not fit this mold. The postwar ideologies surrounding women were more complex than retrospectively presented in Betty Friedan's influential book *The Feminine Mystique*, which "investigate[d] the competing voices within the public discourse on women and the internal contradictions that undermined and destabilized the domestic stereotype even as it was constructed."[29]

As Toy Len Goon entered the national spotlight as a celebrated, exemplary mother, much of the coverage of her life story and selection as US Mother of the Year reflected (and was likely intended to shape) debates over the appropriate role of women at the time. The newspaper coverage portrayed Toy Len Goon sometimes as "a modern woman" and sometimes as traditional, and occasionally as a modern woman with traditional values. An article titled "Immigrant Named Mother of the Year; Born in China" proclaims, "Some people say women should stay home and take care of the house, of children, and of husbands. Toy Len Goon didn't have that choice."[30] After describing her struggles and the success of her children, it goes on to conclude, "Now that's a modern woman." However, other portrayals paint her as traditional, rather than modern. Commenting on the dramatic changes in motherhood over the past thirty-nine years since Mother's Day had been celebrated in the United States, a 1952 editorial in the *Portland Press Herald* by May Craig comments, "Mrs. Goon is old-fashioned, thank God, old-fashioned enough to believe in a large family, old-fashioned enough to believe her major duty to her children is to teach them to know right from wrong, to follow the Golden Rule, to place 'spiritual' values above material values." The editorial praises her traditional family values as being like those on which the US nation has been built, criticizing those who have given up these values to be modern:

> Ideas about bringing up children, training them religiously, ideas about hard work and personal sacrifice have changed tremendously, and not entirely for the best. Mrs. Goon, who came from China to make her way in the famous land of opportunity and free enterprise; has not abandoned her old ideas for the sake of being modern. We honor her because she embodies that fundamental character, that combination of energy and humility and wholesomeness, which helped to transform this land from barren fields and forests to bustling communities.[31]

The fact that a Chinese female immigrant is being lauded for living "traditional" family values in the United States involved interesting logic. Her hard work and grit were seen as evidence of her adoption of traditional US values, and thus as a marker of her successful assimilation. However, an alternative framing focused on her as a Chinese immigrant woman who embodied virtues through her traditional Chinese family values that American women were seen as abandoning in their efforts to become modern. Both reinforce the idea of Chinese Americans as model minorities.

An editorial in the *Boston Herald* stated that Mrs. Goon was "typical of the best meaning of the word mother and of the wonderful family tradition in Chinese Culture."[32] It is not clear what exactly these writers were imagining as traditional Chinese family values, or how it was that these values were thought to flourish in America, seemingly in ways that they could not in China. Many Chinese family traditions were rooted in patriarchal kinship systems in traditional Chinese society, ones that afforded women little power and influence within the family. And despite the many harmful policies enacted by the Chinese communist regime that the United States so feared and hated, it was also endeavoring to reform this system that disadvantaged women by providing them with opportunities for education, putting women in leadership positions, and giving them credit for their work outside the home. Chairman Mao famously proclaimed that "women hold up half the sky."

One way of addressing this apparent lack of clarity regarding traditional Chinese and American values was to present Toy Len Goon as somehow melding the best of both. An article by Jeannette Pomeroy in the *Portland Press Herald* described Toy Len Goon's recipe for Chinese lobster. Titled "How to Prepare Lobster Dish Using Recipe of

No. 1 Mother," the article discusses the cooking of Maine's well-known seafood delicacy with Chinese cooking techniques, producing an apt symbolic metaphor for the blending of cultures that Toy Len Goon was supposed to represent. The author describes the Chinese ingredients required, including black beans, soy sauce, and scallions, as well as the process of cooking them in a large fry pan. She delights in sharing that Toy Len Goon insists on eating the dish with chopsticks but leaves out the part where the live lobster is chopped with a large cleaver before it is stir-fried. It is also suggested that baked beans or mushrooms could be substituted if Chinese ingredients were not available.[33]

The controversy surrounding Amy Chua's "Tiger Mother" style of parenting presents an interesting contemporary twist on the immigrant and model minority narratives that have historically surrounded Asian Americans. In presenting her tiger parenting style, Chua, the daughter of Chinese parents from the Philippines, essentializes the supposedly Chinese values of hard work and discipline. According to the model minority myth, the hard work and discipline of Asian immigrant parents produce a population that is overwhelmingly successful, thus differentiating them from other immigrant groups in general, and other minority groups in particular. The media's presentation of the story of Toy Len Goon—of mothering and of immigrant grit and success—represents an early version of the model minority myth that presents some interesting parallels yet also striking contrasts to today's "Tiger Mom." Toy Len Goon did not have the time or resources to tiger parent her children, nor did she have the literacy to write a book about it. Her voice, as well as a full understanding of her life story that is contextualized within the realities of her life experience, is largely absent from the picture painted by the media.

Other Mothers

Toy Len Goon was not the first Chinese American maternal figure to capture the public's imagination or to challenge traditional gender roles. Though earlier portrayals of assimilated Chinese American families focused on the male heads of Chinese American households, prominent Chinese women such as Madame Chiang Kai-shek helped reshape the American public's view of Chinese women on a national political scale, fostering a sense of nationalism to China as a homeland. In discussing the support of Chinese Americans for China during this period, Ngai observes,

> Gender did the work of Chinese nationalism to particular effect, especially with the American public. The beautiful, Wellesley educated Soong Mei Ling (madame Chiang Kai Shek) won the hearts of Americans in her tour of the United States. Over twelve thousand Chinese American men and women served in the US armed forces, and many construed their contribution to the war in terms of patriotism and national loyalty to both the US *and* China.[34]

Mom Chung was a trailblazer who bent gender norms and became a doctor and surrogate mother to US soldiers.[35] Toy Len Goon and Mom Chung were of different generations, with Chung attracting national attention in the 1930s and 1940s, and had different relationships to white society and education. However, both of their stories had a "propagandist function" that was based on their public maternal image. Judy Wu describes Mom Chung's ability to "transcend social boundaries."[36] Toy Len Goon did not break social boundaries in the same way. However, though she did not have much control over how it was told to the US public, her story was used to shape national conversations about the place of Chinese Americans in the United States. Wu asserts that Chung's story, though seemingly atypical, elucidates "the shifting margins and changing mainstreams of American society" in contrast to many histories of Asian American women that focused on "class exploitation, racial segregation, and gender oppression."[37] In a similar sense, the story of Toy Len Goon as a woman who went beyond traditional work and gender boundaries marked an important shift in the portrayal of Asian American women in US society.[38] However, while Chung to some extent intentionally crafted an image for herself, Toy Len Goon was not well positioned to do so. As will be discussed later in the chapter, the media crafted its coverage of her Mother of the Year award to highlight issues of motherhood and domesticity in the context of Cold War containment, which only partially reflected her reality. Chung was highly educated—a medical doctor—and took many white GIs under her wing. Wu documents how even though Chung remained single and had a "male gender persona," she became a mother figure "to all-American sons and daughters."[39] She notes that "Chung's maternal identity and her surrogate kinship network mediated gender and racial tensions that resulted from the international conflicts of the 1930s and 1940s" during the Sino-Japanese War and World War II.[40] In contrast, Toy Len Goon was praised by many for being a traditional maternal figure, despite being forced to take on duties beyond traditional gender roles. Though she was not an activist in any traditional sense, like Mom Chung, she became a maternal symbol—a national mother—who served a larger political purpose in US foreign relations.

Being "Good"

Thus, while the Goon children were undoubtedly "good," the historical tenor of the time allowed them to be seen and celebrated as such. It also made them desire to be "good," while at the same time defining just what it meant to be a good Chinese American, or more specifically a good mother or a good daughter or son, at that time. While Toy Len Goon's parenting certainly played a role in helping them learn right from wrong, the social pressures of the time would have also pushed Chinese Americans to behave in ways that would lead them toward the promise of full inclusion and participation in US democracy. The end of Exclusion created new opportunities for employment, while also revising previous restrictive immigration laws and barriers to citizenship.[41] Similarly, additional occupational opportunities became available to Chinese Americans during World War II, bringing them outside the previously restrictive realm of the Chinatown ethnic enclave and of hand laundry and restaurant work for white customers.[42]

But Ellen Wu also emphasizes that they experienced pressure to behave in an exemplary fashion, as

> various authorities—both within and outside their ethnic communities—checked their autonomy to choose their own futures by pressuring them to behave as praiseworthy citizens Some gladly complied, others inadvertently went along, and not a few refused to succumb to these demands. All found their lives conscripted into the manufacture of a certain

narrative of national racial progress premised on the distinction between "good" and "bad" minorities.[43]

Discrimination?

The Goon children undoubtedly saw that they had opportunities available to them that their parents did not. They saw their good behavior paying off in the positive recognition they received at school and in the opportunities the older brothers had to go off to college. However, they deny feeling any pressure to behave as "praiseworthy citizens," and do not recall having faced discrimination. Like many other Chinese American families of that era, the Goon children found themselves coming of age at a particularly fortuitous moment. While the upward mobility of the second generation is a common immigrant trope, this would not have been possible for Chinese Americans during an earlier time period. Ellen Wu notes that prior to the 1940s and 1950s, Chinese and Japanese were seen as "unassimilable aliens unfit for membership in the nation" and were therefore marked as "definitively non-white" and denied opportunities for "civic participation through such measures as bars to naturalization, occupational discrimination, and residential segregation."[44] The Goon children were born in the 1920s and 1930s and were thus moving into their teenage and young adult years during the post–World War II era, when national narratives were shifting to emphasize the inclusion of Chinese Americans and some structural barriers to civic participation were being removed. Together, these factors would have facilitated their seeing themselves as citizens whose good behavior and hard work were paying off.

Yet discrimination against Chinese was still very much present during this time. According to Chiou-Ling Yeh, "In 1950, 21 percent of San Francisco employers specified their reluctance to hire 'Orientals,'" and many were barred from moving out of Chinatown into white areas despite changes in legislation in 1948 that outlawed housing covenants.[45] A case involving Sing Sheng generated international outrage when he was not allowed to move into a South San Francisco white neighborhood. This occurred in January 1952, shortly before Toy Len Goon's award.[46]

During a panel presentation titled "Laundry Rock: Histories of Laundries of Boston Chinatown," three sons of Boston area laundrymen,

Richard Chin, Dr. Ray Chin, and Walter Wong, shared their experiences growing up.[47] As laundries were located outside Chinese ethnic enclaves to provide convenient service to local communities, often between different non-Chinese racial and ethnic enclaves, the three men reported suffering racial taunts from some of the local children. Though they sometimes did stand up for themselves, they were also aware of the external pressure from their fathers to stand down from or avoid conflict for fear of violent retaliation. One incident was related by Richard Chin, whose family owned a laundry in Mission Hill District, sandwiched between an Irish American neighborhood and another consisting of a mix of people from different racial and ethnic backgrounds. He vividly describes an incident from one hot day in 1959 when he was around nine years old, when he asked his father whether he could go outside to escape the heat inside the laundry, something his father usually did not allow him to do. Though he was supposed to stay right outside the door, he ventured ten feet away and was met by a group of four boys around his age from the Irish neighborhood, who approached him while "giggling" and then began to taunt him by imitating the sounds of Chinese and reciting racist nursery rhymes. He asked them to stop, but they did so only momentarily. Incensed, he picked up a "boulder" from the ground, planning to chase them and smash one of them over the head with it. Three of the boys ran away, but one stood "defiantly" and asked, "Chinaboy, what are you going to do?" Richard then distracted him and slammed the rock onto the boy's right foot. Richard's father asked what had happened, to which he replied in Toisanese, "I threw a pebble at his leg." Soon, the boy's father appeared at the back door demanding to know what would be done to "make this right" or he would call the police. Richard describes feeling a "hard slap" on the side of his face from his father, followed by instructions to apologize to the man and his son. After they retreated inside the laundry, his father told Richard that he had to "publicly shame and embarrass" him, otherwise the man might come back and burn down the laundry at night. Richard said that he "lost his innocence" that day. Reflecting upon the incident, he realizes that it made him understand that his father "wasn't the protector" he had believed him to be because he "had succumbed to the white man's power politics." His father had emphasized that the laundry was the only place he and the other four Chinese laundry workers could make a living together and they would have no recourse if it was burned down. Richard reflected that this had been a "poignant lesson on race politics of that neighborhood" and that he regretted that "they were second or third class citizens" and that his father's fear of repercussions rendered him powerless to stand up for himself and his family. Richard also made a point of sharing that he befriended other Irish kids from that neighborhood and would visit them in their homes. Nevertheless, this incident remains a "painful reminder" that is "deep rooted" in his soul.[48]

Though I did not have a chance to interview all of the Goon siblings, as some had passed away before I started this project, none I spoke with recall experiencing the kind of racism and discrimination related by the Boston men, who were also second-generation children of immigrants, though younger than the Goon children. Perhaps living in an area where there were fewer Chinese (and non-white) families made it more likely that they seemed less of a threat and more of a curiosity to the local white majority, and less likely that they would find themselves caught in the middle of tensions between ethnic enclaves. While those interviewed (by me or Gary Libby) did not recall any incidents of physical violence or intimidation, it is possible that they viewed any negative encounters they may have had with non-Chinese as individual acts not related to structural racism and discrimination.

I interviewed Helen Chin Schlichte in June 2022 via Zoom. The eldest of nine siblings, she grew up in the family laundry in Charlestown, Massachusetts. Her father died when she was a teenager and the youngest was an infant. Her mother continued to run the laundry with the help of her children. Like the Goon children, Helen does not remember experiencing racial discrimination, and she and her family still reside in downtown Charlestown and consider themselves "townies," a term used for locals.[49]

Though the Goon siblings may not have recalled facing racism or discrimination, there was a historical precedent for anti-Chinese sentiment and violence in Maine. Gary Libby documented many of these cases, occurring from 1879 until around 1907. There were numerous reports of laundry break-ins, assaults, and rocks being thrown through laundry windows. Libby writes,

> In January 1890, three hoodlums assaulted laundryman Sam Lung without provocation, kicking and beating him. A few days later two Irishmen

were convicted in the Portland Municipal Court for a brutal assault on Chin Foo. They were sentenced to six months in jail. The *Portland Daily Press* described their punishment as "deserved." In November 1890, two young bullies entered a Chinese laundry. One of them presented a claim check to the laundryman and, when he turned to find the package, the other man hit him on the head, knocking him to the floor. The laundryman then grabbed a hammer that he kept behind the counter, and rose, stunned. He hurled the hammer at his assailants, who immediately fled the shop.[50]

Oftentimes, cash was taken from the laundry, but some incidents also involved assault or verbal abuse, such as an incident in 1902 when an inebriated man accused Augusta laundryman Charlie Tong of eating rats.[51] In this case, as in many others, the laundrymen defended themselves by chasing the intruders out of their shops, and in many cases, the police were able to find the suspects.[52]

Assimilation and Integration

Like the Asian Americans discussed by Wu, the Goon children may have engaged in a process of self-stereotyping, emphasizing the value placed on "family and education, and unflagging industriousness."[53] They credited their mother's strong leadership and their own hard work and discipline for their success and did not appear to believe that they were affected by historical and systemic forms of racism.

It was thus perhaps fitting that the Goon family was held up as a symbol of assimilation and integration of Chinese Americans, as their relative isolation from larger urban Chinese communities may have meant that they were able to feel more integrated into their local community. As previously discussed, they in fact were not totally isolated, as they were connected to the Goon Family Association and the Boston Chinese Women's Association.

However, Toy Len Goon was not as connected to the politics of the Chinese American community, including those surrounding her award. According to Yeh, Dail-Ming Lee, who wrote for a bilingual San Francisco–based newspaper called *Chinese World*, saw Toy Len Goon's award as a sign of ethnic integration, suggesting in his editorial that she embark on a nationwide tour of the United States to help spread positive images of Chinese Americans through her exemplary motherhood.[54] Toy Len Goon was likely not aware of this request, and was certainly not interested, as the stress of the Mother of the Year festivities had taken a lot out of her. Amy suspects that the travel, combined with her worrying about getting dressed up to be presented publicly, made her develop anxiety that made it hard for her to sleep well upon her return to Portland.

According to Yeh, the New York–based *Chinese-American Weekly* saw her selection as an important recognition of Chinese laundries and the families who ran them, but also recognized the continuing discrimination toward Chinese.

> Chinese had immigrated to the United States for more than one hundred years. Many of them encountered discrimination politically, economically, and socially. Most Americans dubbed Chinese immigrants "Chinamen" or "laundrymen." The prejudice toward the Chinese hardly subsided even in recent years. This could be seen in the example of Sing Sheng who was excluded from a white neighborhood in San Francisco. Nevertheless, Goon's title informed those ignorant Americans that we "Chinamen" had made significant contributions to the society and we "laundrymen" had exemplary character.[55]

An editorial in that same publication praised US democracy for selecting a poor Chinese mother to represent the nation, viewing her honor as an example of how the United States was a meritocracy that did not discriminate based on race, noting, "In the whole world, the United States was the only country that would choose someone like Goon who was from a humble background to be a model mother. In China, the same award could only go to wives of elites."[56]

Some leaders saw these apparent moves toward the acceptance of Chinese Americans as a reason to aim for assimilation, writing in an editorial, "If we, overseas Chinese, made tremendous contributions to the United States, Americans would end discrimination toward us."[57] According to Yeh, the editor placed the responsibility of "eliminating racial prejudice" on Chinese Americans, asserting that it was up to the Chinese Americans to "prove their worthiness" to be treated equally.[58]

Another column in the *China Daily News*, based in New York, titled "Overseas Chinese Activities" summarized a discussion overheard in a restaurant in which two Chinese American men debated the significance of Toy Len Goon's award. One reportedly said, "Even though we should be excited about Goon's award, we should not get carried away by the news, because this was due to the one-time 'openness' of a few people. Racial discrimination was still deeply ingrained in the society. It was not an easy task to make a fundamental change." The other pointed out that the United States was "hypocritical for championing freedom and democracy daily, while immigration officers continued to harass Chinese immigrants."[59]

Yeh's discussion of Chinese American press coverage of Toy Len Goon's award illuminates debates within the Chinese American community about the severity of continued racism and discrimination, and whether Goon's recognition can be seen as a shift toward acceptance. It also signals disagreement about whether Chinese Americans need to show that they deserve to receive equal treatment, which implies that it is the responsibility of the individual to rise above adversity to become exemplary within the United States' meritocracy. The focus on individual achievement is problematic, however, as it ignores structural racism and other barriers to success for minorities. Thus, as Yeh observes, Toy Len Goon's story was essentially an argument for assimilation—playing by the rules of the majority society and excelling at them—as a route toward upward mobility. As Ellen Wu notes, this focus was consistent with the "nation's cultural conservatism at midcentury," which included an emphasis on traditional gender roles.[60] Wu concludes that "self-representations of Japanese and Chinese American masculinity, femininity, and sexuality, purposefully conforming to the norms of the white middle class, were crucial to the reconstruction of aliens ineligible to citizenship into admirable—albeit colored—Americans."[61]

Clara Soule and Americanization

Clara Soule was an advocate of assimilation and was frequently mentioned and photographed in the news coverage as a companion to Toy Len Goon and as having spearheaded her nomination for the Mother of the Year honor. Doris remembers that Soule came in one day and said, "Mrs. Goon, I would like to nominate you for Maine Mother of the Year." Doris, after translating Soule's message, told her mother to just say yes.[62] As an Americanization teacher, Soule frequently visited the laundry, hoping to find an opportunity to teach Toy Len Goon how to read and write in English. For Soule, a retired school teacher, literacy was not just a practical skill, but an indicator of assimilation, and thus of the inclusiveness of US democracy. As part of a national movement, Portland public schools held "Americanization" classes for immigrants from 1922 to 1945, led locally by Clara Soule.[63]

The Americanization movement was a response to the American public's concerns about belonging and loyalty that the entry of new immigrant populations raised.[64] The 1924 National Origins Act, also known as the Johnson-Reed Act, created entry quotas based on national origins for certain European immigrants, increasing quotas for some groups, particularly those from Western Europe and the British Isles, while reducing quotas from other areas of Europe. The act also cemented the exclusion of all Asian immigrants, with language barring those ineligible for citizenship from entering the United States. The underlying goal of the act was to maintain the ideal of a homogeneous (Western European) US society in the context of increasing fears stemming from the entry of diverse immigrants. It was Clara Soule's goal to employ "public education to demonstrate that American democracy was indeed, inclusive."[65] Her "target population" was the 1,453 illiterate foreign-born whites in the 1920 census.[66] Her goal of teaching them literacy in English was in part a response to other, much more hostile reactions to the new immigrants by the Ku Klux Klan and other anti-immigrant and anti-minority groups. The *Portland Sunday Telegram* published photos of immigrant children dressed in patriotic garb, with the aim of sending the message that immigrants from Southern and Eastern Europe and from Asia could become assimilated American citizens. The paper reported that "there were students of 'twenty nationalities, but all Americans'" at one of the schools.[67]

In 1917 Soule, then director of Americanization in Portland, wrote and produced an ambitious production, titled "Pageant of the History of the United States: E Pluribus Unum—Out of Many, One."[68] Taking the form of "patomime [*sic*] of the high lights of the history of the United States acted by the pupils of the Portland Public Schools and given under the direction of its authoress assisted by the teachers of the Portland Public Schools," the show was set to music and even included a horse, on loan from a local resident for the Spanish-American War scene. The first three "episodes," covering the "Period of Discovery (1000)," the "Period of Exploration (1513–1678)," and the "Period of Settlement (1565)," documented the process of settler colonialism in the United States, presenting it as a sequence of discoveries by European explorers, gift exchange with "Indians," and the "acquisition" of and settlement of territories. The next few periods include the Revolutionary War and Independence, Washington's inauguration, the War of 1812 and the Mexican-American War, westward expansion, the Civil War, and the Spanish-American War, focusing on the United States defending its territorial boundaries. The penultimate episode (11 of 12) is the "World War" (not numbered because it was the first). In this section, the pageant program reads,

> The entry of the United States into the World War in 1917 caused the whole country to organize into groups for the purpose of giving their best aid to the government in its huge task of not only feeding and clothing its own army but also feeding most of the rest of the world.[69]

The final episode is titled "What American Stands For," in which various children represent Humanity, Democracy, Justice, Uncle Sam, Goddess of Liberty, Religion, Education, Literature, Music, Science and Invention, Drama, Agriculture, Industry, Child Welfare, Community Spirit, Play, Forest Preservation, Boy Scout, Camp Fire Girl, and finally, Immigrants.

The inclusion of immigrants at the end of this grand march of US history was intentional and significant. The finale included an Ensemble March to "America the Beautiful" and an Exit March to "Stars and Stripes Forever." The final words of the program assert that America, as a Christian nation, should welcome hardworking immigrants from other nations who come for a better life and freedom:

> Humanity is the same the world over, having like hopes, fears and aspirations and clinging most closely to religion in all crises of life. America is called a Christian nation. As a nation we must look well to our spiritual life for therein the hope of the United States lies. Therefore, religion,

> representing the eternal things, must stand first in our private and national life and guide us in all our progress. The United States with all she stands for attracts people of other countries. Immigrants, seeking better living conditions, freedom of religion, and better remuneration for their services, come to the United States and, while they love the land of their birth, they give their brain, brawn, loyalty and their children to the land of their choice in return for the opportunities and privileges given to them. The United States explains that there is room only for those who are willing to accept responsibility in proportion to the opportunities and privileges given to them. The immigrants, accepting these terms, pledge themselves before God to give their all to the united [*sic*] States of America.[70]

Clara Soule focused her efforts on immigrant mothers, enrolling ninety-nine women in eight "Mother's classes" in 1922. The Maine Historical Society's online exhibit speculates that she may have been motivated by the Cable Act of 1922, which legislated that women could only be naturalized separately from their husbands. Soule also believed that education could help immigrants beyond the classroom, holding Mother's classes in various neighborhoods and employing teachers to visit the homes of immigrants starting in 1923. She helped create a social service bureau that provided resources on immigration and naturalization, among other issues, to the immigrant population.[71] "The term Americanization, as applied to our work," Soule wrote in the 1926 Annual School Report, "means the educating of the illiterate and the foreign born in the use of the English language, in the manners, customs, government, history and ideals of America, as well as the industrial and social privileges of American citizenship and fellowship."[72] Clara Soule began teaching a class specifically for Chinese restaurant workers in cooperation with their managers, to accommodate their nontraditional working hours.[73] The Americanization program ended in 1945. However, Soule remained involved with immigrant families.

Regardless of Soule's broader motivations, the Goon children thought of her as a supportive and kind woman. My mother, a high school student at the time, says that she did not read the newspaper coverage of the award or think about the broader political implications of her mother being chosen as Mother of the Year. It was only when I explained during my 2019 interview with her what scholars had written about how Toy Len Goon's award could be contextualized within the Cold War politics of culture and containment that she understood this larger framing of her family's story.[74]

However, Amy Guen, who had talked with Clara Soule on numerous occasions, and had also talked with Toy Len about Clara Soule, had a different sense of what the latter's goals were. In a 2018 interview, Amy remarked that Soule told her "about how they like to see all Chinese people become Christian. . . . She and couple churches have Sunday school for all Chinese immigrants." Soule had told Amy that "she almost had a monopoly, even before Dogan arrived. . . . When she knew there was a new immigrant, she took the initiative to go to them, ask if they want to join the Sunday school." Amy showed me a photo of a group of Chinese people gathering after Sunday school, observing that "Ms. Soule was involved in that, though her picture was never there. She told me that when she knew [Toy Len] came that very month, she approach [Toy Len], . . . teach you English. Toy Len was scared of her, such intrusion, aggression." According to Amy, Soule wanted Toy Len to attend church and convert to Christianity, speculating, "English may be a medium . . . how they get people to become Christian. It's nothing new on that." I asked why Amy believed that Toy Len thought that Clara Soule was being pushy. Amy recollected,

> Well, earlier days she came and asked if the children were seeing doctors—very genuine concern. But then Grandma would say, "Busy busy busy," and she's watching her working hard. So Ms. Soule said she felt awkward doing that. So she said she prayed that Grandma might become Christian. So after Grandma was baptized, she felt her prayers were answered.[75]

Mother of the Year

Toy Len Goon found out about her selection as Maine Mother of the Year in May 1952, with a visit from Clara Soule to the laundry. Jo and Tony Moy happened to be visiting Maine at the time and took photos of the press photographers taking pictures of Toy Len at her laundry.

The official press photos, which were then circulated as part of media coverage, showed her in her usual attire—a housedress and work apron, hair up in a bun—smiling while operating various laundry machines or in front of paper-wrapped bundles of laundry. She was honored locally by organizations such as Woodford Merchants Association, presented by Norton Lamb, the real estate broker who helped her buy 615 Forest Avenue. An article titled "Gov. Payne Joins Portland Groups to Honor American Mother of Year" notes that the governor "characterize[d] her as the symbol of what Americans believe. In giving Mrs. Goon a US Savings Bond, he likened it to a symbol of the faith you have had in America."[76] In another article, Governor Payne is quoted as saying,

> It's a tribute to Maine and to the Nation . . . that a homemaker such as Mrs. Goon can be so honored. It vividly illustrates that the principles of our founding fathers have meaning and evergrowing strength today. A person today does have the right to life, liberty, and the pursuit of happiness regardless of race, creed or color. I extend the congratulations of the State of Maine to Mrs. Goon and say to her that we are honored and proud to have her as a neighbor. Her contribution to this State and to the whole country through her inspired motherhood will serve as a shining guide to all the mothers of the land.[77]

His characterization of Toy Len Goon as a "homemaker" and mother, rather than a businesswoman, and his emphasis on "life, liberty, and the pursuit of happiness" for all races are noteworthy. Referring to her as a neighbor, he made it clear that his message was that the integration of Chinese Americans into the nation was made possible by the United States' founding principles that espoused freedom for all. She would later meet Thomas P. O'Neill Jr., Speaker of the House, in Boston on May 27, 1952.

She received additional bonds from the Kiwanis Club on behalf of all of the men's service clubs in town. The women's organizations gave her a mink scarf. Her son Albert spoke to the gathered group, noting that despite his mother's lack of education, she can "still teach us a thing or two." The article makes a point of emphasizing that Albert was a recent graduate of Boston College. The event was sponsored by a committee of citizens who emphasized the significance of her award by noting that "the City's presentation of a scroll at a recent Council meeting wasn't enough." Other sponsoring organizations included Altrusa Zonia Rotary, Women of Rotary, Kiwanis, the American Legion Auxiliary, Women's Literary Union, Soroptimist, Lions, Lioness, Business and Professional Women, Elks, and Emble Club.[78] Local merchants such as the Maine Dairy, Casco Bottling Company, Hannaford Brothers, A&P Stores, National Biscuit Company, Cushman Baking Company, and others supported the event.[79]

James J. Metcalfe, who ran a regular poem-panel in the *Portland Press Herald*, penned a poem in her honor, emphasizing her humble nature, hard work, friendliness, and sacrifice:

> God Bless You, Mother Goon
> God bless you, Mrs. Toy Len Goon . . . Our mother of the year . . . America salutes your name . . . With pride and joy . . . You well deserve the honor and . . . Our words of glowing praise . . . For your accomplishments in life . . . And for your friendly ways . . . For all the years of constant toll [toil?] . . . To raise your family . . . And give your daughters and your sons . . . Their opportunity . . . No sacrifice has ever been . . . Too much for you to make . . . But you have humbly lived your life . . . For your good children's sake . . . This Mother's Day is truly yours . . . As much as it can be . . . God bless you, Mrs. Toy Len Goon . . . And all your family.[80]

The Portland Kiwanis Club arranged for her daughters Doris and Janet to accompany their mother to Philadelphia, where she attended church services and a Mother's Day ceremony at the Chapel of the Four Faiths, and then travel on to Washington, DC, the following Monday and Tuesday. Over fifty teachers from the Portland Teachers Association honored the Goon family with a defense bond signed by teachers who had taught her children, with the president commenting, "If all the children in the schools were as fine and willing students as the Goons, . . . teachers wouldn't have any problems."[81]

Doris and Janet both recall that Valle's restaurant put on a party in their mother's honor, and a luncheon was given by the Maine Mother's Association. According to Janet, the Valle's event was the first time the family had eaten out, and she recalls not knowing which utensils to use for which course:

> And when all the festivities started, it was like a different world. We ate out for the first time at Valle's, a steakhouse. Certainly nothing we would have been able to afford on our own. I remember we sat next to this young, nice-looking priest, and I remember he asked if we knew how to use a fork. But we were both shy. I remember going to that right away, and all the trips to DC and New York and Boston and a sweet little ceremony in the little movie theater up the street at Woodfords Corner. Which was very meaningful because it was the local merchants and teachers. There were some speeches. They gave my mother a new stove. . . . That was the most meaningful thing you could give her, a modern stove.[82]

Though she was living in Washington, DC, and was not able to attend most of the festivities, Josephine remembered, "She's really a ham. She really loved the title. She really didn't say, but you can tell that she really enjoyed it that she won Mother of the Year of America. She knew it was a big honor. You know, my mother's kind of like that anyway."[83]

Reflecting on the festivities, Doris remembers, "She had the parades in Boston, New York, Philadelphia, DC. Margaret Chase Smith gave her a luncheon at the Senate, Ms. Truman gave her a tea party, [we met] Wellington Koo."[84]

I asked my mother, Janet, what she recalled about the meeting with Bess Truman. She recalled,

> I do remember her bounding into the room. We were all herded into I don't know which room. She came rushing in, big smile, and looked rushed. She was shy, you know. She disliked her role of first lady very much, and it showed. She came in and shook our hands, cordial, and then had a photo op, and that was it. You didn't get the feeling that she was very involved.[85]

Arthur remembers,

> I shook hands with her. It was a very short handshake. I heard she was not too crazy about minorities. I don't know who I heard it from. It makes sense because it was a twenty-second meeting. We had dinner in the congressional dining room. I think I remember the Kennedys were the hosts.

> Massachusetts. Mother of the year from Massachusetts. I think—some reason I don't know if Joe Kennedy was there or not. I might have a faulty memory there.[86]

When I asked Doris whether she spoke to those dignitaries, she replied, "I'm nineteen and as dumb as a doorknob. Never left the house, so I had no idea." I observed that their mother hadn't had any similar experiences either, and Doris said,

> But she smiled. She was very gracious. Beautiful posture. She just wore the right thing and the right hat. They didn't expect any speeches from her or anything. It was given for her and it was nice. Went to Chinatown and felt more at home there. Her own people and the language was different. They had banquets for her.[87]

In contrast to the photos taken at the laundry with Toy Len Goon in her housedress and work apron, later photos of her trip to Washington and of the Chinatown parades showed her in a new formal outfit, purchased by Clara Soule, one she would not have considered buying due to its impracticality for her everyday life, and could likely not have afforded. Together, the photos create a narrative of the transformation of a modest laundry worker into a nationally symbolic figure. Unfortunately, I am not able to include most of the official press photos of her Mother of the Year festivities in this book because the family does not own the copyrights and the fees to publish them are too expensive, which serves as an illustration of how she did not have ownership of her own story.

The speech given in her honor by Governor Payne described earlier extolls her virtues as a homemaker and mother, but credits US democracy and the freedoms it allows to all despite "race, creed, or color" for her success. But though she had learned quite a bit of English during her time in the United States, Toy Len Goon would likely have been able to understand only part of his speech without translation. While the family's transition from hardworking, struggling immigrants to middle-class professionals over the course of a generation was certainly a product of hard work and discipline in the face of extraordinary challenges, the media coverage of her award illustrates that her award was also a reflection of a particular historical moment.

Media Coverage

Toy Len Goon's selection as US Mother of the Year made headlines across the United States and abroad. It was not only covered in depth by her local paper, the *Portland Press Herald*, it was also distributed nationally by the Associated Press. The media touted Toy Len Goon's accomplishment of raising eight upstanding US citizens while running her own business, but the subtext of their rhetoric included messages, both implicit and explicit, about her role as a woman and a mother, and the ability for minorities to thrive under US democracy. The extensive press coverage of Toy Len Goon's selection as Mother of the Year told her story in a manner that both essentialized her Chineseness and presented a sanitized view of her family story and of the US treatment of Chinese Americans.

Toy Len Goon's story was also covered in Chinese-language newspapers such as the *Chinese-American Weekly*, which provided a detailed account of her visit to New York Chinatown. I quote it here at length:

> It was a Saturday, and because of the event, every shop in Chinatown was hanging [ROC] flags and red flowers in celebration. Especially at New York Chinese School [華僑學校] and Chinese Consolidated Benevolent Association [中華公所]'s front doors, whose decorations were extra vibrant. At the beginning of Mott Street [勿] hung a white banner that said the words: "紐約全僑歡迎全美模範母親阮陳彩連女士" [All the Chinese in New York Welcome American Mother of the Year Mrs. Toy Len Chin Goon]. It was written in red words with a white background, and the text was very eye-catching.
>
> With the Wu [伍] Association, there was a large flag with the Wu last name flying in the air, the banner and the ROC flag were flying in the air together.
>
> The students from New York Chinese School [華僑學校] gathered together on Canal Street [堅尼爾街] to welcome Mrs. Toy Len Chin Goon at the intersection of the street. They were holding Chinese [ROC] and US flags. The welcome procedure commanders 陳以立 and 何耀 planned the ceremony. Law enforcement sent some policemen and police cars to the event to keep the event organized and civil. People started to cheer, and firecrackers began to go off when Mrs. Toy Len Chin Goon's car arrived.

> During that time, many people surrounded the car. Chinese and American reporters all surrounded the car and took photos as well. Chinese American leaders all rode in black automobiles in a car caravan. Viewing the caravan from behind, it looked large and majestic.
>
> The caravan rode around Chinatown three times. Then, Mrs. Toy Len Chin Goon got off of the car at 南園酒家 Restaurant. The Council General Mr. 張 and Captain of the Chinese Veterans Edward Hong [湯鴻業] came to welcome Mrs. Toy Len Chin Goon. Then, Chairperson Leung 梁 [of the restaurant] brought everyone to the third floor. The wives of [embassy members] Chang Ping-chun [張平羣] and K. L. Yuen [阮崐利] came over to receive the guests. A lot of Chinese female leaders came to enjoy the event as well.
>
> After tea time at 南園酒家, everyone went to the Chinese American School. A student delegate from the school gifted Mrs. Toy Len Chin Goon two bouquets of flowers in front of the school gate. After that, there was a welcome ceremony at the Chinese American Hall [僑校禮堂] in the school. There were a lot of people inside and it was difficult to move around. The emcee was 劉錦柏. The representative of the school was Chairperson 梁聲泰. Apart from Council General Mr. 張 giving a speech, there were also five souvenirs given by the following organizations: Chinese Consolidated Benevolent Association [中華公所], 中美聯誼社, Gee How Oak Tin Association [至孝篤親公所], Goon Shee Association [阮氏公所], and [politician and reporter] Y. Y. Phen/Pan Kung-chan [潘公展]. Also, Council General Mr. 張 introduced Mrs. Toy Len Chin Goon's three daughters ["princesses"] and Maine Working Women's Association chairperson and Mrs. Toy Len Chin Goon's Western friend from New York. Lastly, Mrs. Toy Len Chin Goon was asked to give a speech. She simply said thank you to all the Chinese Americans in New York. In the meantime, the audience members gave her a large round of applause.[88]

However, the Goon children do not recall being very aware of the media coverage. My mother recalls, "I don't think I was that into it at that age. I don't remember doing a lot of that. I mean, there was so much live action. All of the presentations in DC, New York, and Boston. All of the parades. And all the nice clothes my mother got."[89]

May Craig

A key figure in the media's coverage of Toy Len Goon's award was *Portland Press Herald* reporter May Craig. Craig (1889–1975) was the Washington correspondent for Gannett newspapers, a Maine-based corporation, known for her "Inside in Washington" column, which ran for almost fifty years.[90] A trailblazing female member of the Washington press corps, she was described as having "a mind as sharp as cider vinegar, as retentive as a lobster trap." Described as "feisty" in her *New York Times* obituary, she was known for wearing floral hats and asking presidents "dodge proof" questions.[91]

Craig's May 19 editorial in the *Portland Press Herald*, titled "Mrs. Goon in Washington," complimented Congressman Hale of Maine, who "struck a blow in the cold war for Asia" in bringing Toy Len Goon to Washington for a luncheon at the Capitol, a meeting with First Lady Bess Truman, and a visit with the Chinese ambassador (from Taiwan), noting that Japanese and other foreign correspondents would be given the story. She observes,

> All over the world, the Communists are telling the hordes of non-white people that Americans are hypocrites, that they do not mean what they say about democracy. They picture all non-whites as downtrodden, scorned, mistreated, in these United States. I know, because I have been around, in Middle and Far East, and I see the slimy trail of these lies and the effect they are having against us, where we want friends and allies.

As a senior member of the press, and as a Washington insider, she was a journalist whose words were influential and were shaped by the pressing political issues of the time. As Craig saw it, Congressman Hale's arrangement of Toy Len Goon's visit to Washington to meet Bess Truman and Wellington Koo, the Taiwanese ambassador, was not only a fitting way to honor Toy Len Goon, but also was an opportunity for the media to disseminate her story for public consumption.

According to Craig, the honors bestowed on her at the White House were irrefutable evidence that minorities were not "downtrodden, scorned, mistreated" and this news would be spread via the State

Department's foreign service and foreign correspondents to the communists in the "Far East." Craig proclaims,

> Wherever the State Department foreign service can reach, the story of Mrs. Goon will reach mothers in the Far East. The story of her children and their accomplishments here, will be told; the doctor son in Salt Lake City will be told about, the son in the navy, the daughter in government service here, the son who owns his own shop in Lynn, the son who is a MIT graduate, now a teacher, the daughter who is going to school in Boston in September, the daughter in high school in Portland—how can the Reds say this is not the land of opportunity?[92]

Her observations about Senator Hale's motivations for bringing Toy Len Goon to Washington, and the intended effect of the press coverage of her visit, were part of what Christina Klein has called the "cultural cold war." Ideas about race began to change in the early twentieth century, with anthropologist Franz Boas's research on immigrants proving that physiological differences between so-called races did not reflect various stages of evolution, but rather were primarily the effect of environment.[93] In the context of a Nazi agenda focusing on racial purity, Boas's reframing of diversity in terms of cultural rather than "racial" or biological differences helped back a US policy that was open to these immigrants whose differences could be absorbed or "accommodated."[94]

Craig notes that Hale "was quick to appreciate the international value of the honor to Mrs. Goon," saying that "she herself said that America is the land of opportunity and her own life, and family, are proof of it." Her selection as Mother of the Year, Craig believed, "is living proof that we are not what the Communists preach to the world" and that the international dissemination of the recognition bestowed on her in Washington via foreign service channels "cannot be laughed off by the Communists." She notes that an official White House reporter and State Department photographer were present to document the story, and that "machinery is already in motion at the State Department to get this out." She goes on to detail the ways that the information will be spread in Japan, Korea, Formosa (Taiwan), and the Pacific Islands, hoping that when the story of the Goon children's success reaches "mothers in the Far East," it will be difficult for the "Reds [to] say this is not the land of opportunity."[95]

While the Goon children were undoubtedly successful, Craig's immediate assumption that "mothers of the Far East" would compare the opportunities of their own children to those of the Goons illustrates how integral the rhetoric of the cultural Cold War had become in US media and politics, as well as the confidence that the media had in its role in shaping public opinion.

From 1949 to 1952, Betty Lee Sung developed the series *Chinese Activities*, six-minute broadcasts profiling Chinese Americans, which was broadcast by the Voice of America throughout Asia in several Chinese dialects.[96] Her goal was to combat negative stereotypes about Chinese Americans by portraying their accomplishments. Though she did not see her broadcasts as anti-communist—VOA was blocked in mainland China—her goals for the series supported the State Department's desire "to represent the United States as a free, democratic society where all peoples, including those of Chinese ancestry, could assimilate and thrive."[97]

Sung aimed to "portray Chinese Americans in a positive light to counter preexisting negative stereotypes, and that of the federal government, which aimed to represent the United States as a free, democratic society where all peoples, including those of Chinese ancestry, could assimilate and thrive." Toy Len Goon's VOA story ended with the words "America, declared Mrs. Goon, is a land of opportunity. . . . Mrs. Goon has honored America. She has set an outstanding example of honesty, industry, and motherly care; and Mrs. Goon has given to her adopted country eight outstanding young American citizens."[98]

Chinese American Exceptionalism, Racial Positioning, and Marginal Inclusion

However, Toy Len Goon's story was not a straightforward tale of assimilation and being a "good American," as her Chinese origins also served a strategic purpose in that political moment. The President's Committee on Civil Rights, in a 1947 report, saw Japanese internment as a scar on the US civil rights record, and proposed to allow Japanese Americans to become naturalized citizens along with other Asian American groups.[99] Their underlying motive was to rebut the Soviet Union's accusations that racism in the United States undermined the legitimacy of US democracy, and to remove a barrier to creating a sense of trust with non-Western nations, thus linking the concept of democracy to national security.[100]

> The committee looked to establish the importance of civil rights reforms to advancing the nation's Cold War policies of internationalism and communist containment. It maintained that racialized minority integration was critical to reclaiming the legitimacy of American democracy and that this restoration could help contain the influence of communist ideologies and foster trust and cooperation between the United States and non-Western countries.[101]

Cindy I-Fen Cheng argues that the positioning of Chinese Americans as both included and excluded within US society shaped their racialization, and that the state played an active role in creating specific narratives that were designed not only to back its Cold War strategy, but also "for influencing the efforts by Asian Americans to secure their social and political legitimacy in Cold War America and the stories they told about race in the United States."[102] While some of these state narratives emphasized the extent to which Asian Americans had assimilated to US society, others portrayed them as potentially disloyal to the United States and as requiring increased scrutiny because of this concern. While Asian Americans were positioned in between whites and Blacks, at times closer to one group than the other, they were simultaneously treated as perpetual foreigners with continued ties to Asia.[103] In highlighting the strategic positioning of Asian Americans by the media and the state, Cheng asks us to consider that democracy has not produced racial equality. Rather, ideas about racial equality, and about race in the United States more broadly, have been produced by the state.[104] Using this framing, we can view the media's manufacturing of a model Chinese American family to bolster the country's image as a democracy as having helped create the ideal of possible racial equality and opportunity in the United States rather than being a product of it.

Furthermore, as Ellen Wu observes, the shaping of Asian American identities between World War II and the Cold War and civil rights period cannot be separated from the larger context of the Black-white racial structure of the United States.[105] According to Wu,

> The model minority is a wonderfully telling example demonstrating that racial categories are never static or omnipresent, that they change over time and vary across space, and that they pivot on the contemporaneous making and remaking of other racial categories. It also vividly illustrates how productions of race are crucially determined by confluences with other axes of identification—in this case, gender, sexuality, class, and nation.[106]

Images of Asian American success were promulgated through the US media, with the accompanying message that these improvements were enabled by US democracy and freedom. Wu asks, How did "the Asian American success story itself become a success story—literally front page news—edging out other possibilities for understanding their place in the nation?"[107] As Wu notes, it was significant that Asian Americans were neither Black nor white, occupying a middle ground within the US racial structure that enabled them to be held up as an example of minority success and integration, while still skirting the pressing issues facing other minority groups. But Wu also emphasizes that the context of this "race making" process also resulted in Asian Americans being subject to new forms of exclusion as perpetual foreigners. The focus on cultural explanations for Asian American success meant that culture remained a marker of Asian American difference.[108] In a similar vein, culture of poverty and cultural deficiency arguments would later be used to explain the lack of success of other minority groups such as African Americans.[109]

While not diminishing Toy Len Goon's struggles or accomplishments, analyzing the above historical, political, and social contexts of her award helps explain why she was such a strategic selection for the American Mothers Committee. She represented a "good," nonthreatening Chinese American citizen who embodied the values of hard work, resilience, and opportunity that seemed representative of American democracy and the potential it offered immigrants. Her children benefited from higher education and were deemed "successful" in mainstream US society, and thus stood as perfect models of assimilation and upward mobility. And her Chinese immigrant origins, in the opinion of politicians and the media, made her a perfect proxy to be used to counter communist critiques of US democracy—a woman who escaped the oppression she would have experienced in China had she not emigrated to the United States.

Connections between the United States and China have historically been marked by tensions in which Chinese Americans have been variously included and excluded from the US imaginary, simultaneously domesticized and "othered," assimilated as model minorities and feared as foreigners. Crafted through official legislation and backed by discourses circulating in the media and popular culture, these contradictory notions of belonging are further complicated by the multistranded and often imagined connections to the Chinese homeland that are constructed for Chinese Americans. These relationships are more abstract than concrete, but nevertheless make the possibility of achieving full US cultural citizenship questionable.[110]

Chinese American/Asian American exceptionalism—the idea that Asian Americans were high-achieving "good" minorities—enabled Chinese Americans to be "accepted" as model minorities in ways that have not been possible for other US minorities.[111] However, Chinese Americans have historically been contradictorily positioned sometimes as perpetual foreigners and at other times as honorary whites who face little if any discrimination. In the United States, Chinese American difference from mainstream society has often been framed as primarily cultural, rather than racial, such as in the context of Chinese transracial adoption.[112] However, Chinese immigrants have also been racialized historically, and more recently during the twin pandemic of COVID-19 and anti-Asian hate. Those subscribing to the assimilationist rhetoric in the early twentieth century that emphasized the cultural malleability of new immigrants saw Chinese Americans as capable of becoming part of US society. This framing of Toy Len Goon's story as one of patriotism to the United States reflects efforts toward the inclusion of Chinese Americans as a corrective to earlier forms of exclusion.[113] However, the more inclusive framing represents a form of marginal inclusion, obfuscated within the model minority idea and the sense of belonging it implies. Ellen Wu discusses how the "global imaginary of integration" was brought in to soften the focus on the containment of communism. Chinese Americans were viewed as good potential subjects for these efforts at cultural exchange and integration. Citing Christina Klein, she notes, "It was precisely the dual identity—the foreignness—of Chinese Americans that gave them value as Americans in the 1940s and 1950s," arguing that integration led to "new modes of exclusion" by "re-marking them as 'not-white' and indelibly foreign, even after the ending of the legal regime of Asiatic exclusion."[114]

Discussing how the story of Toy Len Goon was shaped by the politics of containment during the Cold War provides a historical backdrop from which to consider the shifting terms through which Chinese Americans have been conditionally included within the US imaginary, as this imaginary, and the position of Chinese Americans within it, continues to shape the experiences of Chinese Americans in current contexts.

The media's emphasis on Toy Len Goon's motherhood and her production of American children/citizens enabled her to be seen as a "domesticated" minority whose example could be used to symbolically counter the perceived threat posed by Chinese communism in the US public imagination.[115] Her story was celebrated within the specific confines of domesticity, as a working mother who ran a laundry business, and who therefore did not veer too radically from "traditional" roles occupied by women of color, but also as a mother who produced successful, productive, patriotic US citizens. Her Chinese origins facilitated her being viewed as a representative of how the Chinese people could be transformed through the democratic practices of a liberal US state. Her media portrayal as an assimilated model minority served to erase the complexity of her multiple roles, her connections to China and the Chinese American community, and the challenges that she faced with the state as an immigrant and woman of color.

Some of Toy Len Goon's descendants have remained invested in a version of the narrative that reflects the media's main message about the exceptionalism of Toy Len Goon and her family and are perhaps reluctant to think about the broader historical and political framings of her selection for the award. They feel that further analysis of how the event was framed by the media or used for political purposes detracts from a focus on her achievements, and the hard work and other exceptional qualities that led to them. They are hesitant to depart from the narrative of immigrant success that the story supports. Throughout my discussion of her story, I aim to bring theirs and others' perspectives into dialogue, with the hope that it will result in a more nuanced yet also more robust version of these events.

6

"One Lifetime Is like Other People's Working Four"

Toy Len Goon's Story as Told by Herself and Others

ANDREA: So you, you worked very hard?
TOY LEN GOON: *Work hard.*
A: Yeah.
TLG: *Work* ngit saai jo, *not work* thli saai waa [literally: I worked one life, not four lives (but it's like I worked four lives)].[1]
DORIS: [*Laughs.*]
JANET: She says one lifetime is like other people's working four.[2]

Later in the interview, Toy Len Goon expands on this when talking about Dogan for a few minutes, fully in Hoisanese (a dialect spoken by people in Toisan):

> The people in Hong Hau know/knew how much I've had to endure.[3] He married me and brought me over here. They all said, "Bringing Dogan's wife over there to the US, tomorrow [inaudible]." They said it would be difficult for me to live [in the United States]. At home [in the village] everything I, I had on my own. I had wheat, I had rice, sometimes, I had sweet potatoes and taro to eat. I had all of this. That's why people said that life was difficult for me. When I was here in the United States I was also very scared! Did you think that him being like this, that people didn't know what he was like? People said, "When he was alive, you worked [hard] like this, when he was dead, you worked [just as hard] like this!" What's the difference?[4]

This chapter focuses on the multiple ways Toy Len Goon's Mother of the Year award story has been told in both past and present, by the mainstream media, in popular accounts, and in her own words. As discussed in the previous chapter, while the mainstream media of that time presented her story through frameworks of domesticity and containment, including conflicting portrayals of her as either a traditional or a modern woman, her story was also represented in other sources, including in her own words. Each of these portrayals creates a different narrative, including inaccuracies that, whether intentional or not, shift the mythology surrounding her story. To counter the omissions and biases in the media coverage, this chapter brings Toy Len Goon's own voice and perspectives to the fore, as she discusses the hard work she had to endure both in China and in the United States, challenges in her relationship with Dogan, and the stresses associated with being Mother of the Year.

She told her own life story in different ways to different people at different times. Some of what she said in the version of her life story she entrusted to Amy Guen differs from what she said in the interview I did with her in 1992, with my mother and aunt translating and adding their own editorial comments. However, it is important not to take one version of her life story as a more legitimate version of the "truth" than another version. Rather, the various renditions can be analyzed for what and how she chooses to share about her life and perhaps what she doesn't share in certain circumstances. All versions of her life story are mediated, whether through translators and the lens of reporters, authors (both academic and non-academic), or her family members telling her story in particular ways. This book represents another mediated version of her story that, while not striving for objectivity, aims to bring together a wider variety of narratives, more fully contextualize them within the historical and political climates in which they were written, and place them into dialogue with one another. In the next chapter I examine what effect the narratives have on her descendants as they continue to craft them.

Media Coverage

As part of her sudden emergence as a public figure in the national eye, the telling of her story in the media became a means through which journalists and policy makers could promulgate the visions for women and minorities that they hoped would be associated with US democracy for audiences both at home and abroad. The standard narrative that was used to describe her—as the widow of a US World War I veteran who raised eight successful American children—became a canvas onto which these various visions were painted. These media portrayals often contrasted with her actual experiences and her own perspective on her story.

As discussed previously, savvy reporters such as Portland-based White House correspondent May Craig used Toy Len Goon's selection as Mother of the Year and her visit to the White House as an opportunity to editorialize about strategies of Cold War containment, which included getting messages about the success of Chinese American immigrants such as Toy Len Goon behind the Iron Curtain. In the 1952 article cited in the previous chapter, Craig comments,

> This Chinese lady who came here as a girl, married happily, became a US citizen, raised her children well, with good educations, was chosen the Mother of the Year, from among all others, and honored in the White House and Capital. You just can't laugh that off, or bury it with lies, as the Communists do.[5]

Craig realized how compelling the Goon family's success story was, as well as its potential political implications. However, while she gets many details about the Goon children's accomplishments correct, her portrayal of Toy Len Goon's early life is grossly inaccurate. As we know from the many details of her early life that she entrusted Amy Guen with recording, her immigration records, and even from her interview with me in 1992, she did not come to the United States as a girl, but rather when she was twenty-nine, after having been previously married and widowed. Nor was she happily married. She worked extremely hard both in China and after coming to the United States; her arrival in the United States did not free her from the intense manual labor she did in China, but rather shifted it to a new kind of labor.

In the 1992 interview, I asked my grandmother about her early life. She said she raised pigs and vegetables and would go to the market to sell them. "Was the market far away?" I asked. She said it was around three miles away. My mother asked her whether she walked there, and my grandmother responded in English, "Walk, always walk. Walk so much. Everything walk. No car. No ride horse. No car." My aunt Doris asked where else she would walk, and my grandmother continued in Chinese, describing how she would walk to get water to store in a big trough, replenishing it when it was depleted. Switching to English, and likely referencing the fact that many people try to exercise to keep in shape, she said, "Nobody exercise. Just work exercise. Hard work."[6]

As highlighted in the opening quote for this chapter, I asked, "So you worked very hard?" She replied in English, "Work hard," and then switching to Chinese, said, "One lifetime is like other people's working four."[7] Switching back to English, she said, "I operation," referring to the procedure she had to fix her varicose veins. She described getting up at "half past six" for "cooking for my children eat breakfast."[8]

The narrative that May Craig hoped to spin about Toy Len Goon's life was that it was happy and successful due to her emigration to the United States. But as Toy Len Goon recounts, she had to work hard her whole life, whether as a young girl living with her parents and siblings, carrying out household and childcare duties for her foster family, fulfilling the role of stepmother and caretaker for her first husband's wife and daughter, or raising her children while running the laundry while in the United States. At the age of one hundred, Toy Len Goon did say that she felt that life in America was good. During the interview, I asked,

ANDREA: Ask, . . . what does she like about America? What does she like about China? What does she not like?

DORIS: [*Translates question.*]

TOY LEN GOON: O Faa Ki *everything* ho.

D: Everything is good here.

TLG: *Everything* ho, mot ho o Faa Ki aa? [Everything is good, what is there that is better than America?]

D: Hong Saan ne, Ma? [What about China?]

TLG: Hong Saan hai tlim fu du, diu jiu hek. [In China, it is with hard work that you get to eat.]

D: Just work, work too hard.

TLG: Yeah. Jiu mot ok geng aa *everything* e. Ngoi luk sui diu hoi em hi sin gim zi si waa. Hoi ne zi si du, du naai zaa waa. [Yeah. What (isn't) hard work. Everything. When I was six, I started. When I woke up, I had to pick up pigs' poo. Took the pigs' poo for fertilizer.]

D: Six years old. She had to pick up pigs' droppings for fertilizer. That was her job. So when you start, when you were six years old.

JANET: I thought it was bad when I had to take care of the customers' [inaudible] laundry bills.

D: We'd do that when we were—

TLG: Ngoi go maa jeng zi je, jeng zi naa. [My mom had raised pigs, raised sows.]

D: Yeah?

TLG: Cut sip gi e zi doi je. Jeng aai ne zi doi jiu maai e, jiu hu ne ngaan ne, hu lai maai sung ne ko ne. Jeng e zi maai, jeng aai jiu maai jiu, hu ne ngaan loi, hai ko la. [She gave birth to over ten piglets. We raised the piglets and sold them, and took the money to buy groceries and such. Raising pigs to sell, raising again to sell, using the money, it was like that (in China).]

D: She's not saying China's bad. It's just that it's a tough life, that she prefers this country.

A: But she worked hard in this country too.

J: Yes, but she has something to show for it.

D: Kui waa ni o Hong Saan jiu du lo, loi koi jek du lo. [She (Andrea) said, in China you worked hard, you came here and you worked hard.]

TLG: Yeah.

D: *So*, ni, ni zung ji Faa Ki u go Hong Saan maa? [So, you, do you like America more than China?]

TLG: GAANG! Gaang hai, gong kui, gong nek, hai e, Faa Ki haai du lo, jek, jek ho wong saang je! [Of course! Tell her, I told you, yes, America. It's hard work (in America) but it's also very prosperous, too.]

D: Haai ni ne doi nui naa, hai maa, ni ne doi nui du aak gong, hui Hong Saan m du ak. [Look at your kids, right, your kids can do work (here). If they went to China they couldn't do (what they did here).]

TLG: Ho, ja. [Right!]

D: It gave us the opportunity to, better ourselves, you know. Of course we could be—

J: She's trying to say—

D: In China you could save money and buy a little house in China, really, but here she could even do that!

J: The opportunity is definitely . . .

TLG: Ni gu sieng loi aak loi ji mo? Ni du koi bein faan hui hu ngoi lai ji mo. [You think you can come just because you want to come? (Your father) lived over there and came back to take me (to America).]
D: She said not everybody can come. She was lucky to come and it was only because it was her husband was a veteran of World War I did she get the chance. That he married her did she get a chance to come.[9]

Toy Len Goon's comments imply that the difference between her hard work in China and in the United States was that the hard work in America seemed to pay off, as she had seen her children benefit from opportunities in the United States that would not have been available to them in China. Her daughters' opinions about the opportunities they saw growing up in the United States, inserted throughout the conversation, also clearly reflected this idea. However, her statement about working the equivalent of four lifetimes during her own life was a powerful commentary on the hardships she had faced. May Craig's narrative also glosses over just how difficult it was for Toy Len Goon to come to the United States and become a citizen. Craig would have likely been unaware of Dogan Goon's illegal entry into the United States and the difficulties she had in her marriage, which would have vastly complicated the celebratory tenor of the story.

Marginal Success

Thus, while the media framing of her story creates a tale of immigrant success and assimilation, Toy Len Goon's "success" might to some extent be better seen as having occurred in the context of overcoming the conditions she lived under in the United States. Racism and xenophobia produced the social and legal marginalization of Chinese immigrants in America that excluded them from legal entry into the United States and forced those who were able to enter into labor-intensive occupations such as laundry work. For women, the conditions of isolation were even more dire. Judy Yung's groundbreaking study on the history of Chinese women, *Unbound Feet*, was driven by her desire to create a new conceptualization for the study of social history that took into account race, gender, and class in an integrative manner, something that scholars at the time were starting to do, but mainly within a Black/white binary.[10] She was concerned with questions of oppression versus liberation, the "segregation of their paid and unpaid labor to their private (domestic) sphere" as it related to their position within the family, as well as issues of agency, gender conflict, and class and generational variation in women's experiences.[11] She concludes that "their experiences have been as much a response to economic, social, and political developments in China as in the United States."[12] According to Yung, women who emigrated to the United States were freed from filial duties to their mother-in-law and father-in-law, and their labor was more valued due to its essential contribution to family income.[13] Yung argues that in the US context, while the family remained a "site of oppression" for Chinese women due to the demands of housework and childcare, and potential for abuse, it was also a "source of empowerment."[14] While there is no singular story for immigrant Chinese women, Toy Len Goon's was characterized by several challenges that required her to exercise her agency and resourcefulness.

Omissions and Silences

At one point in my interview with her in 1992, I asked about where she lived in Portland. She remembered that I had been to her house at 615 Forest Avenue, recollecting, "That house I buy . . . you see that house. house . . . Large house. I Mother of the Year I live that house." As noted previously, she tricked Dogan into thinking that the majority of the $500 down payment was in the form of loans, when she had actually stashed it away herself. She did this because she thought this was the only way she would be able to save that amount of money. I quote the interview, translated by Genevieve Leung, extensively here as an illustration of how she retells this important event in a mix of Chinese and English.

> TOY LEN GOON: I live old house. First place I live, I lived old house. Gonna tear down, make a gasoline station. 640 Forest Avenue, next move Deering Avenue, you know? 615 Forest Avenue. Ngoi m gi aak e ne [I don't remember]. That's the [first] house I buy.
>
> ANDREA: This was the, after, after Grandpa died?
>
> JANET: Before.[15]

At this point in the interview, Toy Len continued on for a few minutes solely in Hoisanese, with my mother and Aunt Doris for the most part remaining silent. There was emotion in her voice, which sounded like exasperation and possibly anger. It sounded like she repeated herself several times. Based on the little Hoisanese I knew, I could make out a few words here and there, including the phrase *mouh yung* (H) (useless), which she used to describe my grandfather. At one point she said the word "nothing" in English. My mother's translation after she finished was succinct: "She said she worked hard all her life before and after she was married and before and after my father died, because he didn't help much." I knew she had gone into more detail than this, but since she spoke mostly in Chinese, and my mother and aunt chose not to go into more detail in their translation, I figured that those words weren't intended for my ears.[16]

As part of my research for this book, I asked my mother to listen to the tape again to provide a more complete translation. However, the quality of the cassette tape that had been converted to a digital audio file was not clear, and my mother's hearing was not as good as it used to be. Though my father speaks a slightly different dialect (Hoksan [C], Heshan [M]), he was able to make out more of what my grandmother was saying on the audio file, either because his hearing is better or because he remembers more Chinese. I considered asking my parents to try to work together to translate this portion of the interview but knew that it would be a difficult process.

As I continued to work on this book, I wondered whether I should pursue obtaining a more complete and precise translation. I contacted Genevieve Leung, a linguist at University of San Francisco specializing in Toisanese (also known as Hoisanese), and she initially suggested a couple of people I could contact to have the whole interview translated, and later generously offered to do it herself. But I worried that translating the untranslated portions would be airing dirty family laundry, so to speak.

How would I decide what to do with the silence and awkwardness around my grandmother's opinion about my grandfather in the context of my research? Was it my responsibility as a researcher to find out exactly what she said to fully document and communicate her feelings on the matter? Or was her choice to speak solely in Chinese? Were the partial translations made by my mother and aunt an indication that her comments were effectively off the record, and not meant to be fully translated? Perhaps these dynamics between my grandmother and her daughters around the omission of her full comments are more telling than the specifics of what she shared in Chinese. Should I have honored her choice to speak in Chinese and my mother and aunt's decision to not translate it then and there?

After discussion with some historian colleagues and with the permission of my mother, I took Genevieve up on her offer to translate the interview, the contents of which have provided valuable insights into Toy Len Goon's thoughts throughout this manuscript. The excerpts below are from an extensive section that was not originally translated by my mother and aunt. They involve my grandmother complaining about my grandfather's gambling problem, which made it impossible for her to save money, and how she was forced to save money behind his back for the down payment. I have included the transcription of the original audio that reflects when Chinese was used and when English was used, along with the translation.

TOY LEN GOON: Nek e u bok u u thli. Mo goi thlen. *Down payment* mo, mo ngaan waa. Mo ngaan. Ngoi waa gi hek [inaudible] tiu nit e ngaan. Ngoi ning si aai ngi waan saang waa. Koi ngoi, mm baak ngaan, mm tein ngaan maai nin gaan uk ge ne. [Your father/grandfather gambled himself to death. He didn't have a penny. We didn't didn't even have money for a down payment. No money. I said, "How can we (inaudible). . . . saved a little bit of money." At that time "Aai ngi" was still alive. So I, $500, $5,000 to buy this house.]

JANET: That's a lot of money!

TLG: Ei. Mm tein ngaan nin si ho. [Yes, $5,000 at that time was very (a lot of money).]

J: $5,000, that's a lot of money then.

ANDREA: How did you get so much money? How did she get the money?

DORIS: You kind of have to ask—

J: She's telling you right now, she kind of put it away out of the earnings from the laundry.

TLG: Gong ni, mm tein ngaan maai, i mm baak ngaan *down*, kui mo ngaan waa. [Let me tell you, $5,000 to buy, $500 as down payment, he didn't have any money.]

D: 10 percent down payment.

TLG: Waa mm baak ngaan down kui mo ngaan waa. *Nothing*! [Waah, $500 down and he didn't have the money. Nothing!]

D: Her husband, my father, didn't have it.

TLG: Maai ngoi, maai ngoi mo uk waa. [Otherwise I, otherwise I would not have a house.]

D: So she, she had it [*laughs*].

A: How did she do that?

J: She saved it.

A: By herself?

J: Well, you know, there's a laundry, so the money came in cold cash [*laughs*].

D: But she saved it.

J: She saved it because he gambled so she knew how to [save].

TLG: Kui hu 500 ngaan down. Kui kui oi *nothing*. Ngoi diu gong aai waa, ngoi waa kui hu 300 ngaan. Ngoi diu gong deng waa, ngoi wa, ngoi waa i e 100 ngaan. Haam, haam aai ngi de 200. Ni cut e 200. Kui diu 200 ngaan kui mo waa. Cut e Boston hui haam a Bon Lam Baak eh, Bo Si Bon Lam Baak de 200 ngaan. Ngoi diu zek haak haam aai ngi de 200. Waa gi baak. Ko i *down payment* waa. [They were asking for $500 down. He (her husband) had nothing in his pocket. So I told a lie and said, "They're asking for $300." Then I told the truth and I said, I said, "I put up $100 and I asked 'Aai Ngi' to borrow $200. You contribute 200." He didn't even have 200. So he went to Boston to ask "Bon Lam Baak," eh, Boss Bon Lam Baak, to borrow 200. Then I went immediately to "Aai Ngi" to borrow 200. Wah, a few hundred dollars. This is how I paid for the down payment.]

J: That's why the . . .

TLG: Mhai ngo mo uk di ne 500 ngaan dau mo! [Otherwise I'd have no house to live in! I wouldn't have the 500 dollars!][17]

May Craig's political agenda was best served by portraying Toy Len Goon as a happily married woman and ignoring the challenges she faced. The silencing of Toy Len Goon's struggles with Dogan in the official story told by the media does not seem to do full justice to the whole of her life experiences and challenges. But for their purposes, Dogan's story best serves the narrative as a veteran and doting father who gained citizenship by somehow convincing the commissioner to rule not guilty in his immigration hearing and made the wise choice of going back to China to marry Toy Len.

Curated Images

Toy Len Goon's public image as a nonthreatening, maternal model minority character served the purpose of symbolizing the successful integration of Chinese American families into US democracy in the context of Cold War containment. Media coverage presents her as quite assimilated, quoting her as speaking fluent English, and as an unthreatening model minority who has raised good citizens, despite being small, unassuming, and shy. Toy Len Goon was routinely described in news articles as "shy," "frail," "tiny," "slight," and "gray haired." While at the age of fifty-seven, she was certainly graying, and at 5 feet, ½ inch was not a large person, the media's emphasis on those physical characteristics served to portray her as unassuming and nonthreatening. Most articles, and Soule's nomination letter, also mention that she did not have a formal education, but emphasize that she made sure that her children were able to receive strong educations. An article titled "Chinese Launderer 1952 Ideal Mother: Portland Widow Worked, Raised 8" in the *Portland Press Herald* notes, "She had no formal education, but has encouraged her children in their studies in their participation in civic affairs." She was described as a woman "who lives by the golden rule and has taught her children to do so." Most of the news articles portray her as being fluent in English, and also imply that she was comfortable with the attention and the festivities. The above article quotes her as saying, "I feel like there are other mothers who are much more deserving" and "All I have done is train my children to the best of my ability. I've tried to show them the difference between right and wrong. The credit is really theirs."[18] In rendering her as more fluent in English than she was, the media presented her as more assimilated, more "American," and more comfortable in her newfound public role than she really was. However, Toy Len Goon's own perspective is glaringly absent. Her recollections were notably devoid of the rhetoric of Cold War containment, yet more complicated than the portrayal provided in the media.

Nerva

In the *Portland Press Herald* editorial mentioned earlier, May Craig describes Toy Len Goon as "serene":

> I was fascinated by the serenity with which she received all of the honors, the famous people, the famous places. She was pleased, you could tell—and she said so, but she was never visibly nervous, not even when she met Mrs. Truman, who was breezily cordial, or the Ambassador, or the Assistant Secretary of State. I thought Representative Judd spoke only the truth when he said she represented the best of both countries, the melting of cultures which make the United States what it is.[19]

But though the award was a high point in her life, it also came with anxieties and stress. Toy Len Goon often used the word "nerva," her version of the word "nervous," to describe situations in which she felt nervous or anxious. Her children could not remember whether she used the term to describe her experiences in Washington, DC, but they do recall that the newfound attention she received as Mother of the Year was also a source of stress for her. In an interview with Gary Libby and Fenggang Yang, her son Edward recalled that she was extremely nervous having to speak in public as Mother of the Year, and she believed that the stress led to some long-term medical problems.

> She was very, very nervous. . . . She wasn't too comfortable being put in that position because she couldn't express herself to the American public. In fact, she said, later on . . . that some of her medical problems were because of all that stress, becoming Mother of the Year. It was a big honor and she had a lot of responsibility, but she's the type of person to say, "Well, I'm in this position now, I'll do as much as I can," but she was very uneasy about it.[20]

In a 2017 interview with me, Amy said that Toy Len had told her she had to take Librium to calm her nerves before accepting the award. The award brought other expectations of Toy Len and her family. As previously discussed, Amy and Helen's wedding plans to the Goon brothers Edward and Richard were revised to be befitting of the family's higher status in the Chinese American community resulting from her award.[21]

When asked what her mother thought of the experience, my mother, Janet, who was fifteen at the time and had been at her mother's side for all the festivities, shared,

> She was overwhelmed, but she welcomed that. I think she knew that it was a nice thing to do, that she looked nice. It was part of the award that she would be presented in a nice way to the public. Because from that point on, she wasn't the same. She was very self-conscious. We always felt that she was more nervous, a more nervous person, a little anxious. I think she made sure, wanted to make sure she lived up to the hype that had gone on because . . . she was Mother of the Year, and then China got involved. She got all these awards from China [Taiwan], and [in] the village, her picture was up and all that.[22]

Similarly, in a scene from the PBS documentary series *Asian Americans* in which my mother, my Aunt Amy, my Aunt Doris, and I are looking at my grandmother's awards, my mother recalls that her mother was never the same after the award, as she felt that she had to live up to the title:

> She was very compliant, but she was a little overwhelmed. [Doris added: "She was."] In fact she was never the same after all of this. She always felt like she had to live up to the name of being American mother. [Doris: "Yes."] And I think as her kids, didn't we also feel a bit of pressure that way?[23]

The Chinese-language coverage in the *Chinese-American Weekly* also illustrates her nerves:

> After Mrs. Millegan's speech, the officials announced Mrs. Toy Len Chin Goon as the Mother of the Year of 1952. Everyone stood up and applauded for her. They clapped non-stop for 23 minutes. When Mrs. Toy Len Chin Goon was asked to stand and give a speech, she stood there for a while,

> in what seemed like a sad mood, before speaking. She said, "I have five sons and three daughters. The only reason why I am living my life is for my children." Then she could not continue speaking. During the time, there were many female VIPs who were crying. The host asked Mrs. Toy Len Chin Goon's son Carroll/子富 to speak on his mother's behalf. After his speech, the whole audience started applauding again. You could feel fraternity in every corner of Starlight Hall.[24]

There are some exceptions. While a *New York Times* article emphasizes her shyness, it also conveys her lack of fluency in English. "There the shy little woman, who has not learned much English since she left her native China several years ago, heard Gov. Frederick Payne read a certificate naming her mother of the year." It quotes her as saying, "I am very glad," in "a halting voice," and also as saying, "I am very nervous," with "a shaky laugh."[25]

Public Symbolic Performance

The pageantry surrounding her celebrations and honors as Mother of the Year and its reporting in the media can be seen as a series of public symbolic performances helping to convey the transformation of a Chinese immigrant woman and her family into Americans through the power of strong mothering and the freedom allowed by US democracy.[26]

Media descriptions by May Craig of the visit of Toy Len Goon and her successful American children to Washington, DC, the nation's capital and seat of power, highlighted details, including the dressy outfits worn by her and her children, and being the guest of honor of Bess Truman and Ambassador Koo. Craig describes the Capitol luncheon hosted by Representative Hale, around a T-shaped table under large, gilded mirrors, with Hale seated next to the wife of Wellington Koo, the Taiwanese ambassador, and Senator Margaret Smith of Maine. Mrs. Hale was seated next to Ambassador Koo, who was seated next to Toy Len Goon. Other representatives from Maine, Minnesota, New York, and Ohio were also in attendance. Craig also detailed Toy Len Goon's visit to the White House, accompanied by Mrs. Hale, Clara Soule, two representatives of the Golden Rule Foundation, and some of Toy Len's children. They received a tour of the first floor of the White House, and then were greeted by Bess Truman in the Red Room and proceeded to pose for photos on the North Portico.[27]

Mrs. Hale and Soule also accompanied Toy Len to the Chinese embassy reception. This visit with the Taiwanese ambassador would have been particularly symbolic during the Cold War era, when the United States had cut diplomatic relations with mainland China and established them with Taiwan, where the Nationalist Party it supported was in exile. She was also given a series of official documents from the Republic of China government, which indicate that the significance of her award was appreciated by that body, which drew upon traditional poems about child-rearing in extolling her virtues. In the process, the ROC was also claiming Toy Len Goon as one of its own, even though she had been born in Toisan County, Guangdong Province, in what was, by 1952, the People's Republic of China, the communist rival of the ROC. The second letter (starting on page 3) was written by an ROC official named Deng Hui Fang, who had originally come from Guangdong Province. In her letter, she uses honorific language to show her respect for Toy Len Goon, referring to her as a "virtuous older sister," while also proclaiming her award as an honor for the ROC. She refers to the ROC as "our mother country" and in addition remarks on the pride she feels as a fellow Yue/Cantonese woman, drawing upon their shared native place in mainland China as the root of their connection. The use of both native place/ethnic origins and claims to shared national identities was not surprising, as the ROC saw Toy Len Goon's award, in the context of the Cold War, as an opportunity to improve its relations with the United States. I reproduce the letters from the ROC officials and from Deng Hui Fang below, with translations and context in square brackets, provided by Liyi Tien and Genevieve Leung:

> Dear Mrs. Goon Chin Toy Len [using the honorific 惠鑒, which is used when the writer is the same age/status of the person receiving the letter], or whomever will first read this letter, the news of Mrs. Goon receiving in Mother of the Year of 1952 came to us, and we rejoice in/are so happy about this wonderful honor [曷勝慶幸].
>
> Mrs. Goon laboriously raised her children under difficult conditions [鞠育劬勞] and as a result received triumphant success [碩果], and in winning this honor, it has carried forward how virtuous the women in my country [我國] are to the rest of the people overseas. Mrs. Goon

receiving this award is also a triumph for all women in my country, and we use these four words: 懿德遠昭 [Esteemed virtue (used for women) that shines forever] on a scroll [with calligraphy] as a sign of sincere respect for you. This letter was written specifically for this reason [of Toy Len Goon's receiving the award]. We wish you health and peace.

Ma Shu Cheng 馬書城
Liu Pu Ren 劉譜人
Xia Jing Ru 夏景如
Wu Zhi Mei 伍智梅
Lu Yun Zhang 呂雲章
Sun Ji Xu 孫繼緒
Ren Pei Dao 任培道
Li Xiang Heng 李薌蘅
Wang Xiao Ying 王孝英
Zhao Shu Jia 趙淑嘉
Wang Hua Min 王化民
Wang Dong Zhen 王冬珍

To my virtuous older sister Mrs. Goon Chin Toy Len [two honorifics used here: 賢姐惠鑒, which is used when the writer is the age/status of the person receiving the letter, but the writer is still younger than the recipient].

This time, Mrs. Goon being selected US Mother of the Year of 1952 is really our country's highest honor for my country's [吾國] women. And also because of the fact that under bitter hardship [of raising your children and working in the laundry], you competed against all other women in the US and were still ultimately selected, when I heard about this, I felt extremely glad and thankful. I hope that your future generations will positively serve/contribute to the virtue of our mother country [祖國], so that the many hundreds of Yue/Cantonese women can also distinguish themselves with extraordinary splendor, and also their ancestors past [忝屬鄉末] can feel the same pride from it [the Cantonese women distinguishing themselves]. Sending my sincerest and timely well wishes. I offer humbly [敬祝],

Health,
Written by Deng Hui Fang 鄧蕙芳
May 16 [1952][28]

Toy Len Goon also received an engraved silver tray and a number of other gifts from various Chinese American organizations. Coverage of the parades given in her honor in New York, Boston, and Philadelphia Chinatowns shows the streets lined with admirers and Toy Len dressed in a formal outfit, a smile on her face, waving to the crowd with what her daughter Doris calls "the royal wave." The media images described above were curated within media reports—articles, newsreels, and photographs—as a selective collection of images and actions to communicate the evolution of this Chinese immigrant and her family into an exemplary American one. Though the White House visit was not presented as a formal ritual, the media's rhetorical framing of the event could be used to powerfully convey the idea of this transformation and its seeming permanence.

Her successful Americanization was illustrated through her recognition of portraits of the Founding Fathers during a tour of the White House:

> Mrs. Goon spotted George and Martha Washington immediately in a portrait in the East Room and though he was bare of his beard, easily recognized a picture of Lincoln in the State dining room.
>
> Miss Soule, a retired Americanization teacher [and] a close friend of Mrs. Goon, said the mother was thoroughly familiar with the main figures in American history.[29]

Interestingly, Toy Len Goon was not a naturalized US citizen during the festivities celebrating her as US Mother of the Year. In fact, she would not become a naturalized citizen until February 1968.

Toy Len Goon's Politics

Though it is unclear to what extent Toy Len Goon understood the political implications of her award, she was somewhat informed about US politics and had expressed great admiration for Franklin D. Roosevelt. Janet remembers that in her later years, she would often ask her children what was going on politically:

> Democrats, Republicans, current events. She was a very big Roosevelt admirer. I remember she was crying in the kitchen when his death was

> announced. And I think she appreciated the New Deal and all of the help that he gave to the disadvantaged. She understood that he was the person who oversaw that.[30]

She remembers her mother listening to Roosevelt's speeches and fireside chats, "huddled around the radio" along with her children. It's likely that the children helped explain what was being said, but "all of us would be interested in what he had to say." Toy Len respected Roosevelt:

> She just felt that he helped the people who needed it. That would include herself. Even though she didn't accept welfare or anything like that, she knew he was trying to help people like herself. And also the fact that he was the wartime president, that he was the commander in chief, that he would deal with Winston Churchill. I remember she would ask about Winston Churchill and what was going on with some meetings. I remember her being engaged, that's the important thing.[31]

Toy Len Goon seemed to be either unaware of or unconcerned about Roosevelt's incarceration of Japanese Americans, as her children do not remember her mentioning this issue. A photo found in the Maine Historical Center archives shows Doris and Janet holding an issue of the *Portland Evening Express* that bore the headline "Japs Offer Surrender if Hirohito Spared."[32] The photo shows both girls sticking their tongues out while looking down at the headline, with Doris thumbing her nose at it. This photo was likely taken to show "good" Chinese Americans participating in anti-Japanese wartime sentiment. I asked my mother whether she remembers why the photo was taken, and she did not.

While her meeting with Wellington Koo, ambassador from Taiwan, mentioned above would have been symbolic of the United States' recognition of Taiwan, it likely did not involve any substantive discussions. A May 14 editorial by May Craig describes a luncheon given by Representative Hale, during which she met Wellington Koo, the Chinese (Taiwanese) ambassador to the United States, and "chatted in her native tongue" with Ambassador Koo and Congressman Judd, who also spoke Mandarin Chinese.[33] However, it was highly unlikely that the ambassador and congressman spoke the rural dialect of Hoisanese, which is unintelligible to Mandarin and even Cantonese speakers. However, while the symbolism of this meeting was potentially powerful, it did not reflect Toy Len Goon's own politics. Doris, who was in attendance, later confirmed that they only shook hands and had their picture taken together.

While the Goon children did not remember their mother talking about politics frequently, she did share her opinions on the head of the regime, Chiang Kai-shek, and his wife, Madame Chiang, with my mother, noting that she did not like them, finding them to be corrupt and elitist. In response to my question about whether her mother followed politics in China, my mother shared,

> She did not like Chiang Kai-shek and Madame Chiang because their reputation was that they were exploiting their office and the masses. I remember that she really didn't like them. I remember they visited the US and that is when she volunteered that she did not look favorably upon them.[34]

President Chiang had invited her to visit Taiwan, in a move to capitalize on this opportunity to build relations between the United States and Taiwan in the context of Cold War tensions with the PRC.[35] Chiou-Ling Yeh observes that the popularity of Madame Chiang in the United States helped promote Taiwan as the "good China." According to a 1951 poll by the American Institute of Public Opinion, Chiang was the third most "admired" woman by the American public. Yeh writes,

> For its battle against Communist China, Taiwan manipulated the Cold War political climate in the hope of winning more support from Washington. It launched numerous propagandist and subversive activities against the PRC, often aimed at strengthening Sino-American relations. Policymakers perceived Goon's achievement, among other strategies, as useful to distinguish Taiwan from Red China and to bond with the United States. . . . The Goon awards illustrated that the American people and "Free China" shared the same gender ideology, while Communist China was the enemy of both because communists denied mothers a domestic role; this elevated Taiwan as an ally of the United States in the fight to contain communism and to safeguard motherhood.[36]

Closing the Laundry for the Festivities

On a more practical level, to attend the festivities, Toy Len Goon was forced to close the laundry. A letter from Walter L. Spallholz from the Universal Laundry in Portland congratulates her and offers to take care of her laundry work free of charge so that she can enjoy her trip, as recognition of the honor she has brought to the region.[37] Interestingly, this large, mechanized laundry would have been a competitor to Toy Len's modest hand laundry in the broader context of an ongoing struggle in New York in which Chinese hand laundries were being threatened by ordinances that would have driven them out of business.[38] However, she was still faced with the reality of maintaining her business, which could not run in her absence.

When I asked Josephine whether she thought that there had been any downsides to the experience for her mother, she reflected,

> The only stressful part, I think, was that she had to leave her work. That bothered her. If it weren't for that, I think she would have had even a better time. She didn't like closing the laundry or having people take care of her business when she was gone. She didn't like that part. But while she was doing the activities, she seemed to enjoy herself. She had responsibilities at home. She didn't like leaving it.[39]

Despite the awards and accolades, the Mother of the Year honor did not provide her with more financial security. In fact, she sold the laundry and moved to Massachusetts to live with her son Richard not long after becoming Mother of the Year, because all of the children had left home except for Janet, who was still in high school.

Various Tellings of Toy Len Goon's Story

Toy Len Goon's story has not only captured the imagination of historians interested in the evolution of the model minority myth, it has also been retold in public venues such as museum exhibits and popular writings.[40] She was featured in Maine Historical Society exhibits (2003 and 2021) and the New York Historical Society's *Chinese American: Exclusion/Inclusion* exhibit (September 26, 2014—April 19, 2015).[41]

The New York Historical Society's exhibit consisted of five parts, including "United States and China, 1783–1905"; "The Machinery of Exclusion, 1882–1943"; "Journeys in America: 1882–Today"; and "What Makes an American." Toy Len's story fit within part 3, which focuses on how "Chinese Americans challenged Exclusion and discrimination even while they struggled within its limits to build lives for themselves and support relatives in China." This period includes both World Wars and the repeal of Exclusion (1943), in addition to the Cold War and immigration reform in 1965. In the online overview of the exhibit highlights, Toy Len Goon's story, sandwiched between a feature asking Americans to write to their congressman to ask for the repeal of the Exclusion and a portrait of the Low family, who encountered difficulties in bringing over their youngest daughter, reads,

> When Toy Len Goon immigrated to Portland, Maine to join her husband in 1921, she spoke no English. After her husband's death, Goon took over their laundry business and raised eight children. In 1952, the American Mothers Committee awarded Goon "American Mother of the Year," calling her success a tribute to the "saga of democracy." She was honored with a parade in New York's Chinatown and invited to visit the White House where she met First Lady Bess Truman. Here she is pictured with her children and the ambassador from the Republic of China, V. K. Wellington Koo.[42]

Though there are no glaring factual errors in the text, it focuses solely on the positives of Toy Len Goon's accomplishments following the passing of her unnamed husband. It does not fully recognize the integral role that she played in running the laundry business prior to Dogan's death, and it glosses over the specifics of her struggles while focusing on her triumphs. Unlike the feature on the Low family that follows, which details the challenges faced by a World War II veteran who was able to bring over his wife and two younger children but not his daughter due to inadequate papers, Toy Len Goon's story seems to focus on her success, seemingly marking the transition of Chinese Americans from exclusion to inclusion. However, as is the focus of this book, her migration story, daily life in the laundry, relationship to Dogan, connections back to China, and other aspects of her life reflect a much more complex picture. While it is not my intention to critique this groundbreaking exhibit, which does acknowledge the challenges faced by both newer migrants and their descendants, what I find interesting is how Toy Len Goon's story is often inserted into broader historical narratives in ways that signal the acceptance of Chinese Americans, thus silencing other aspects of her story. The exhibit's description for that period does acknowledge that "[From] increasing divergent bases of historical experience and perspective, Chinese Americans continued to navigate their relationship to and identities as Americans."[43] However, the use of Toy Len Goon's story does not portray the nuances or complexities of this process of navigation and negotiation.

Other renditions of her story, such as the piece that appeared in *Mothers of Men*, a publication of the American Mothers Committee, contain a significant number of factual inaccuracies that reflect an investment in a particular narrative of her life. In the *Mothers of Men* piece, the predominant narrative focuses on how different Toy Len Goon was from the wealthy white Americans who are usually selected as Mother of the Year. As with the news media coverage, it characterized her as a "serene, small gray haired woman" without education, who had produced educated children. Some inaccuracies are rather inconsequential. She is said to have come over at the age of nineteen, when she was actually twenty-nine, and had been previously married and widowed when she came over. She was described as having taken over the business after Dogan died, but had actually started working in the laundry as soon as she had arrived in the United States, while pregnant with her first child, Carroll. The family was said to have attended the First Baptist Church, though Toy Len never attended, and Janet, the youngest, remembers refusing to go. The article put the purchasing of the laundry long after Dogan's death, when in reality, she had arranged to purchase 615 Forest Avenue before his death. The article also gets some important details correct, such as Dogan's purchasing of war bonds (noting, "They believe in America"), the children working in the laundry, Toy Len's taking on the bulk of the laundry work, and her emphasis on the children's education.[44]

However, the overall tenor of the story told here, aided by the omissions and factual errors, is one of an assimilated Chinese American family, made successful by a woman who stepped in to fill her late husband's shoes. While this narrative may be to some extent true, it also does not give Toy Len Goon full credit for her central role in managing both family and laundry both prior to and after Dogan's death, and reproduces the idea of a patriarchal household as the norm.

An article on the mud silk garments that Toy Len Goon brought with her to the United States, likely made with material purchased for her by her foster family, narrates another interesting version of her life story. Jacqueline Field, a textiles expert in mud silk, saw the pieces that had been donated to the Maine Historical Society and wrote a carefully researched article linking the material artifacts to Toy Len Goon's life story. The article, titled "Mud Silk and the Chinese Laundress: From the South China Silk Industry to Mud Silk Suits in Maine," both contextualizes the production of mud silk within the specific sociohistorical conditions of the region of Guangdong in which it was produced, and speculates on how Toy Len Goon must have sewn those suits for her trousseau as she waited for Dogan to return from the United States to marry her, only to store them in a box when she migrated to the United States.[45] The article provides an in-depth textile analysis of the special mud silk that Toy Len Goon's three suits were made from, as well as a history of the silk industry in Guangdong and the single women who comprised the labor force.[46] But though carefully researched, including interviews of some of the Goon siblings, and an important contribution to the literature, her attempts to weave together the materiality of the mud silks with Toy Len Goon's own story sometimes resulted in misinterpretations or improper assumptions regarding Toy Len Goon's life. Perhaps due to her focus on the silk industry, Field assumes that Toy Len chose to work as a domestic helper over going into the silk industry after becoming widowed when her first husband passed away.[47] However, Toy Len never mentioned to Amy or her children that this was an option that she had considered. When I asked Amy whether she had heard of any Toisanese women entering the silk industry when she had lived there in the 1930s, she shared her own narrative of Toisanese survival strategies, and of Field's assumption that Toy Len would have considered this as an option:

> I think she had a lot of fictional thinking into it. China had a history. . . . Many area of China silk growing, weaving was an industry, but not Taishan. We are a bunch of people who came down from northern part of

> China. We are surrounding by a few hilly part for the whole county. The first thing we did was how to get out of that to southeast Asia, . . . US. Most people wanted to get out.[48]

Field's article also mentions that Toy Len "found employment with" the Goon family, when in actuality, she married into the family in a proxy ceremony, an arrangement made by her mother. Her mother proposed to Dogan's mother that Toy Len might marry into the family to take care of the newborn baby girl that Dogan's former wife had given birth to and left with Dogan's mother when she left the family. Field also discusses how Toy Len prepared her trousseau while waiting to marry Dogan, but the mud silk fabric was actually given to her by her foster family for her first marriage. Amy Guen had kept the box of Toy Len's clothing after Toy Len offered it to her daughter Terry when she was getting ready to study in Taiwan after college and had thus had a chance to examine the garments. She believes that the foster family would have been the only ones who could have afforded to give her such fine quality of mud silk. Amy recalls wearing a lower-grade mud silk during the summer while living in Toisan in her youth. Her family was able to afford to have silk outfits made by a tailor in Toisan City. Though it was standard practice for young girls to learn how to sew using cotton fabrics, she and her sisters never learned how to sew mud silk. Upon inspecting Toy Len Goon's mud silk outfits, Amy could tell that the stitching was excellent and surmised that she must have had very good eyesight.[49]

In the conclusion of her article, Field writes that Toy Len "put her mud silks—vestiges of her heritage—aside and embraced American dress, culture and the opportunities afforded to her and her children."[50] However, while the putting aside of her traditional Chinese clothing might be a tempting analogy for Field to make for Americanization, assimilation, and its associated opportunities, Toy Len's story is more complicated. During a conversation I had with Field at the unveiling of the historic marker at 615 Forest Avenue in October 2021, I shared some of Amy's comments, and she admitted she may have jumped to conclusions, but had done the best she could. As was discussed in a previous chapter, while Toy Len's children were busy gaining a foothold in mainstream US society, she maintained ties to the Chinese American community and back to China, fulfilling obligations and building on social capital within these networks.

A chapter published by Kate Kennedy in her book titled *Maine's Remarkable Women* profiles Toy Len Goon, calling her "an amazing woman" who "carried water on her shoulder as a young child." She discusses how Toy Len Goon was "married twice by proxy," with her groom being "represented by a rooster."[51] She accurately portrays other facts, such as the fact that Dogan has been in the United States illegally during the Chinese Exclusion Era, but eventually obtained citizenship, as well as the fact that the family of eight children and two parents supported themselves by running a hand laundry, and that Toy Len Goon continued to support the children after Dogan's death by continuing to run the laundry. She also relates how all of the children attended Deering High and then went on to higher education.

While happy that Toy Len Goon's story has been getting national attention and that she is being discussed alongside other prominent women, family members have also expressed concerns about the way her story has been told. During my interview with Doris, she asked,

> Do you have that book that Kathy Kennedy wrote? I think she did that a year or two ago. She worked closely with me on that, but that is pretty factually correct. There was something at the end that I thought was a little bit off. I think the very last paragraph. Something about . . . that she just threw in to make it more Hollywoodish. Something she just threw in. She sent it to me. I edited it; she's good about that. The ending was a little bit off. I bought all these books and I gave them to my family and I'm looking for my own copy.[52]

Amy, in speaking with me about how she went about writing Toy Len Goon's story, said that she was very careful not to insert her own opinion, and that her husband, Ed, was especially concerned that the story be accurate. She recalls, "But Ed doesn't want me to put my opinion. He says, 'Where did you find that?' I said, 'You ask Rose.'" She compared her husband's concern to those shared by her, her son Leo, and Doris regarding Kennedy's write-up of Toy Len Goon's story, saying that they had felt that "a lot of things were too fictionalized or dramatized."[53] In particular, Amy felt that in learning that Toy Len Goon had been raised by a foster family, Kennedy had thought that "it was torturous or laborious life that she had. But Grandma didn't. She really felt that she learned a lot from . . . It was so privileged to have a family [that] wanted her to be her daughter." She had heard this directly from Toy Len Goon when asked to record her life story.

While Doris felt that Jacqueline Field's article on Toy Len Goon's mud silk included "a few things that weren't right," she was appreciative that Field arranged for the donation of one of Toy Len Goon's outfits to the Smithsonian Museum:

> They wanted something cotton or wool, something peasanty. So they took that. But this woman who knows her silks remembered seeing it, and after all those years she said, "Do they still have those silks?" So I said, "Amy, they asked about the silk," and she brought it over. She said, "I will submit it to a couple museums." I had to sign off. "If they don't want it, I'll give it back to you." Turns out the Smithsonian wanted it. So I went to see it. [The dress was exhibited for] twenty-four months. I took some pictures, and other people took pictures. They put it on a figure.[54]

Many people have tried to tell Toy Len Goon's story, each with their own framings and motivations for those framings. This chapter's aim was to present and contextualize these public versions of her story and contrast them with how she told her own story. While those close to her felt that there were some inaccuracies in the various renderings of her story, the interview I conducted with her in 1992 provides additional insights into how even the way she told her own story was mediated and situational, depending on whom she was telling it to. The story that she asked Amy Guen to write contains many points of contrast to what she shared in her interview with me, particularly surrounding Dogan's place of birth. However, while some of her narrative is guarded, the interview I conducted with her also reveals her uncensored thoughts about her husband, Dogan, emphasizing the lengths to which she had to go to ensure the financial stability of the family because of his gambling problem and inability to save money. She also shares in the interview some of the moments that she was most proud of, such as when she realized that there were scholarships available for Carroll to go to college. While newspaper coverage and biographical pieces written about her imply an almost magical transformation of the family from laundry workers to solidly middle-class through hard work and good behavior, her interview reveals the uncertainties, complexities, and challenges she faced as she raised her children.

7

Dirty Laundry (or Keeping Clean Laundry Clean)

The Legacy of the Model Minority Myth

More Than a Model Minority

This chapter discusses how the Goon grandchildren view the family legacy as shaping their own status as aspiring model minorities, or perhaps as not-so-model minorities. My interviews with Toy Len Goon's grandchildren illuminate how they saw the family story and their upbringings as shaping their ideas of success and upward mobility, and where they saw their own accomplishments as fitting into that larger framework.[1] The interview process also played a role in shaping or reshaping individual cousins' understandings of the family story, elucidating how processes of memory-making and revision, including conceptions about the family's exceptionalism, both influenced and were reshaped by the research and interview process itself.

The Goon grandchildren's reflections about the family story occurred in the context of societal ideas about Asian Americans as model minorities and associated expectations regarding accomplishments. While the Goon grandchildren did not necessarily subscribe to this myth, they understood their own success and formed their perceptions about successful family members in relation to both of these broader ideas. At the same time, Toy Len Goon's grandchildren invoked the Mother of the Year story and their parents' role as hardworking and devoted children who balanced laundry work and school in constructing understandings of their own family's story that differentiated them from other tales of Chinese American success. They viewed their grandmother as a moral center, a guiding presence, who seemed to embody wisdom that stemmed from her hard work, perseverance, and sacrifice. In contrast to stereotypes of hyper-educated, overachieving model minorities such as Amy Chua's Tiger Mom, who demanded perfection from her children from her privileged position as a Yale law professor, Toy Len Goon's grandchildren saw her as a source of positive encouragement who was instrumental in helping them build confidence in their own abilities.[2] They recalled how well she understood the strengths and weaknesses of each of her twenty-four grandchildren, her open-mindedness regarding their career paths and life choices, and her expressions of unquestionable love for each of them. Their respect and affection for her as the family matriarch came from their recognition of the above qualities, an appreciation of her charismatic personality, and her wonderful sense of humor. She was not perfect, nor did she expect perfection, only that they try their best and be "good." Her grandchildren marveled at her ability to express approval or disapproval with just a look or tone of voice and recall that they respected her so much that they wanted to please her. Rather than expecting each of her grandchildren to fit into a single success model, she only asked that they try their best, and had confidence in them that they could and would do so.

Dirty Laundry (or Airing Dirty Laundry?)

The transformational mythology surrounding the Goon family's upward mobility is captured by the metaphor of dirty, unsorted laundry being processed into clean, pressed, and packed laundry through the Goon family's arduous manual labor. Dirty laundry came in and clean laundry went out, cleansed by the labor of the Goon family and guided by the strong yet motherly and unassuming figure of Toy Len Goon. The Goon family could be seen as transitioning from Chinese to American, from uneducated to educated, from under-resourced to comfortably middle-class.

But while Toy Len Goon's children seemingly made great strides toward successful economic and social integration into US society, there was no guarantee that this would be maintained by following generations. As Jennifer Lee and Min Zhou observe, perhaps a more accurate measure of the success of the children of educated immigrants may be in terms of "how much progress a child of immigrants or refugees makes from the position already achieved by his or her parents."[3] Having gone on to further education and middle-class status, the Goon children appeared to have attained educational and economic success. The next generation would have a hard time improving on the accomplishments of their parents.

Just as clean laundry can become soiled again, it was not guaranteed that Toy Len Goon's grandchildren would maintain the same level of economic and social comfort. The same is true for her great-grandchildren. After all, the stakes were different for her grandchildren and great-grandchildren, as they were raised in comfortably middle-class homes and did not have the same incentive to invest in education to escape doing laundry work the rest of their lives.

But what tools did the Goon children have to ensure the success of their own children? While economic security attained by Toy Len Goon's children meant that educational and social opportunities could be facilitated for Toy Len Goon's grandchildren, how was success measured, and what type of success could they be expected to achieve? And how did Toy Len Goon's grandchildren view her legacy as having affected their parents' expectations of them, and in turn, their expectations of themselves and their own children?

Several factors could play into this. Did they choose practical, lucrative professions, as their parents had? Were they able to perform well at school, or were they challenged by learning differences, lack of educational opportunity, or mental health issues? What types of support systems did they have access to for guiding them through challenges they may have faced? What structural barriers, including both everyday and institutionalized forms of discrimination, did they face? How did current manifestations of anti-Asian rhetoric affect how they saw their place in the world?

I discuss many of these questions in my interviews, but first I address the model minority myth and how it has changed over the years since Toy Len Goon's story was used to help establish it. Key to this discussion is how the myth, along with various theories about it, takes on different implications for Asian Americans depending on their ethnic background, social class, generation, and migration history.

The Myth

The version of the model minority myth prevalent when my cousins and I were growing up holds that "Asian" family values, particularly an emphasis on education, hard work, being "good," and conforming to the rules, leads to middle-class (or above) economic stability and the American Dream. However, my interviews show that like the scholars who critique the model minority myth, Toy Len Goon's grandchildren had problems with the myth. Lee and Zhou discuss the 2012 Pew report titled "The Rise of Asian Americans," which highlights the comparatively high college education rates for Asian Americans through data that show that "Asian Americans place more value on hard work, career success, marriage, and parenthood than other Americans and are also more satisfied with their lives, their finances, and the direction of the country."[4] However, they also observe that the report drew criticism from the Asian American community for implying causation—that Asian American attitudes about hard work as a way to attain success resulted in their high achievement levels.[5] Instead, Lee and Zhou argue for a more nuanced understanding of the combination of elements, including cultural values, that factor into the apparent success of Asian Americans. Beyond acknowledging the usual critiques of the myth—that not all Asians are successful and that the myth of hard work leading to success can be used to view less successful minority groups as deficient in culture and work ethic—they hope to unpack and contextualize the complexity of and cultural frameworks for success without reinforcing the myth. As such, they "place culture front and center in our analyses but do not lose sight of the structural circumstances that affect the formation of cultural institutions, frames, stereotypes, and mind-sets."[6] They assert that while explanations of Asian success that focus on essentialized ideas about Asian cultural values as a means to achievement are not helpful, examinations of culture and assimilation do have a place in discussing Asian American (specifically Chinese American and Vietnamese American) success. They define the "success frame" as attending a prestigious university and obtaining a job in a highly respected profession.

Lee and Zhou highlight the role that the hyper-selectivity of Asian migrants plays in perceptions of Asian American success, meaning that within the groups of Chinese and Vietnamese immigrants they examined, there is "a higher percentage of college graduates among immigrants compared to non-migrants from their country of origin, and a higher percentage of college graduates compared to the host country."[7] They note that while stereotypes that have arisen in the aftermath of the migration of these highly educated migrants perpetuate ideas about their apparent success, these migrants also continue to work toward success by creating social, community-based supports to enhance educational opportunities for their children, and these mechanisms are effective in facilitating their achievements. However, Lee and Zhou also ask, “How would the narrative change if Asian immigrants had the socioeconomic profile of their counterparts who migrated at the turn of the twentieth century?”[8]

A Different Myth

Toy Len and Dogan Goon fit the socioeconomic profile of the turn-of-the-century migrants to which Lee and Zhou refer. As poor villagers from rural China with little or no education, they were far from the hyper-selected educated Asian migrants that Lee and Zhou describe as bringing with them “success frames” of attending an Ivy League university and entering a high-prestige profession. Rather, their aim in coming to the United States was survival—to make a living and feed their families, both in the United States and back home. Roseanne Len recalls overhearing an interview of her grandmother conducted by Ed and Amy Guen.

> Did Auntie Amy tell you about the interview she and Uncle Eddie had with Ngin about her trip from China to the US? I don’t know how I was so lucky. I was an adult by this time, but I don’t remember if I was on the phone or in person at Ngin’s and Auntie Doris’ condo. I do remember listening and concentrating very hard because the whole discussion was in Toisanese. Auntie Amy and Uncle Eddie meant to bring a tape recorder and forgot it.
>
> Ngin and our grandfather, Dogan, entered the US via Canada. There was an especially tense moment when they entered Canada, I believe, when Dogan forgot who he was supposed to be (something to do with Dogan’s uncle and the paperwork) and Ngin saved the day. This showed Ngin to be very quick-thinking. . . .
>
> During that same interview, Ngin got very, very sad—which I had never experienced before. Auntie Amy told me later on that Ngin was recalling leaving China knowing that her siblings were going to starve to death.[9]

Rose's memory speaks to the family's tenuous entry into the United States and also what Toy Len was feeling as she departed China and likely during her long journey to North America. Toy Len Goon's immigration journey differentiates the family from more privileged migrants who came over after 1965 under occupational preference categories, whom Lee and Zhou associate with the "success frame."[10] Far from expecting her children to attend prestigious universities, she did not initially even realize that a college education was a possibility for her children.

While many of her children ended up fulfilling the criteria of the "success frame," their achievements were not the product of the "success frame" that Lee and Zhou describe. Toy Len Goon believed that if you bring up the eldest child correctly, the rest would follow. But she initially did not have a clear conception of what success could look like for her oldest son, Carroll, nor how he would achieve it. In the interview I did with her in 1992, she said, "Carroll was first, obedient/well-behaved, very obedient/well-behaved. He had a pin, that the school gave him." My mother added that there was a Chinese saying that says "Raise the first one right and the rest will follow." Toy Len continued, "He had a pin, he was still wearing it, he was so obedient/well-behaved." Though she could not recall what the pin signified, more than fifty years after the fact, she took pride in the fact that that pin was given to him. In discussing the pin, she then remembered how Carroll had to "temporarily pause two years of high school" after Dogan became unable to work, and the teachers would come to the house to ask him to come back and finish his last two years of high school. She said that while Carroll had hoped to return to school after one year, and brought his books home to study, at the end of the first year, she told him, "'Carroll [子富], you haven't finished school, and he [husband] can't work yet,' and he helped us a second year." She continued to explain that the school let Carroll skip one grade, and that

> he would say, "I am studying at Maine College. I'm going to college! I know they have no money." [I asked,] "You, you, why would you say that [we have no money], Carroll [子富]? If you have no money, of course, how can you go to college?" Like that. He said that people said that if children like to study, there is also money to be had![11]

She had told this story before to Amy Guen and to my cousin Rose. Rose asked me,

> Did you hear the story about Uncle Carroll telling a customer when asked that he was going to college after he graduated from high school? Ngin told me she lost a lot of sleep over that. After the customer left, she scolded Uncle Carroll for lying. Why did you tell that customer a lie?! The thought of any of her children going on to college was unimaginable to Ngin. She told me that she had no concept of scholarships, and they had no money, so why was Uncle Carroll repeatedly lying to people?! Of course, once she understood, she couldn't have been prouder.[12]

Toy Len Goon had thought it presumptuous that he would strive for such lofty goals and mention his desire to go to college to the customer, when the family clearly did not have enough money to send him. But as she recalled the events during her 1992 interview,

> I did not know there was a thing called "scholarship." Why was there something like this [I asked]? It was because if you liked to study, there was money to be had! To help him go to school. The scholarships. Mother Ka Ni Sian. Your [inaudible] class Mother Ka Ni Sian gave, gave, $400, gave, all together gave $2,000, all together gave thousand dollars in scholarship money.[13]

She proceeded to detail the various scholarships he received, including one from the Woman's Club (Fu x woi, nai jiu i) and some "clubs" in Boston that she had interacted with when she became Mother of the Year. In relating this story, she used the "reported speech" of several different people, including herself, Carroll, and others, which was evidenced by her use of different pronouns and speech conventions such as "ko" (like this/like that).[14] This indicates that she had reflected on these events and told the story several times. It may also show how she understood the perspectives of the multiple parties involved and how they shifted over time—for example, when she went from being unsure how he could afford college to discovering that there were school leader and civic organizations that could help arrange for scholarships.

While Toy Len Goon had always emphasized the importance of schoolwork, it was only after Carroll achieved his goal of attending college on a scholarship to Syracuse that Principal Wiggins helped him obtain, that she realized this might be a possible goal for all her sons. Her daughters were not encouraged to attend college but did seek further education, with Josephine attending secretarial school and Doris becoming a court reporter. Janet, the youngest, went to Simmons College after her guidance counselor in Lynn, Massachusetts, urged her to apply.

Rethinking the Model Minority Idea

Though the Goon family may seem to embody model minority myth success, this myth, just like the mythical American Dream, is an amorphous, ever-changing set of discourses. Rather than being static, it takes new shapes in different contexts and time periods, has different impacts on different individuals, and is the result of a process of subject formation.[15] In this sense, it is defined by a central set of societal ideas that are filtered through the lens of family histories, accomplishments, and associated expectations, and may be interpreted differently by different generations and individuals within them.

Toy Len Goon's story, among others highlighting high-achieving Chinese and Japanese Americans, was a precursor to current ideas about the model minority myth.[16] The highly educated and elite Chinese immigrants entering the United States in the 1950s and 1960s that Madeline Hsu discusses in her work helped shape public perceptions of Chinese Americans as highly intellectual and achieving.[17] The Immigration and Nationality (Hart-Celler) Act of 1965 resulted in the selection of educated, professional immigrants from all over the world, including Asia, who came in through the occupational preferences system. William Petersen's article "Success Story, Japanese American Style" was published in the *New York Times* in 1966, and David Brand's "Education: The New Whiz Kids" was published in 1987 in *Time* magazine.[18] Amy Chua's *Battle Hymn of the Tiger Mother* was published in 2011, and immediately spurred debate both within and outside the Asian American community for her account of strict Tiger parenting, in which she demanded perfection from her daughters, restricted their social activities, and doled out punishments for not meeting her standards. While not the only source of discourse on the model minority idea, Chua's book was published during a time when many of Toy Len Goon's grandchildren were raising their own children and represents a version of the model minority idea.

Toy Len Goon's grandchildren interpret the model minority myth through the multiple discourses discussed above, but also through the family story and legacy of the successes of their parents' generation. As they think about their own life paths, as well as that of their own children, they craft narratives that depart from the stereotype of the driven, overachieving Asian American family fueled by parental pressure that has come to dominate the model minority discourse in recent years. Since Toy Len Goon came from a Chinese peasant background focused on survival, the version of the model minority that she was seen as exemplifying is viewed by most of her descendants as contrasting with current model minority discourses. Contrary to Amy Chua's Tiger Mom, Toy Len Goon's success was not seen as being rooted in elite Asian cultural values but rather in her ability to adapt to American society and prepare her children to be well-behaved and hardworking, qualities that would position them for upward mobility. Her grandchildren were not totally free of parental expectations, even if they were not pressured to attend an Ivy League school. Nor did they escape the model minority discourses circulating within popular media and in various forms within their nuclear and extended families.

Asian American Playbook?

Recent academic works discuss Asian Americans and their attempts to attain educational success and upward mobility. *Stuck*, by Margaret Chin, focuses on the challenges that Ivy League-educated children of post-1965 immigrant Asian Americans face in gaining upward mobility in the workplace. *Race at the Top*, by Natasha Warikoo, discusses Asian American and white parents in elite suburbs who are trying to position their children to gain admission to top colleges. And *Hyper Education*, by Pawan Dhingra, examines what he calls "an education arms race" to excel in the American public education system through participating in extracurricular academic enrichment activities and competitions.[19]

Toy Len Goon's grandchildren and great-grandchildren grew up during the periods discussed in these books, and while it may be tempting to apply some of the above frameworks to them, there are some crucial differences in generation, immigration history, and class origins that make this comparison inaccurate. The second-generation children of immigrants profiled in Chin's *Stuck* attended Ivy League schools in the 1980s and 1990s. In contrast, Toy Len Goon's second-generation children went to college in the 1940s and 1950s, and as discussed, she initially did not encourage them to pursue college educations because she did not know about scholarships. Toy Len Goon's grandchildren, the third generation, attended college around the same time as the second generation profiled in Chin's *Stuck*, but they were not told to strive to attend Ivy League schools and didn't focus on the competitive extracurricular academic enrichment activities discussed by Chin, Warikoo, and Dhingra to build a competitive portfolio. Though a few of Toy Len Goon's grandchildren attended prestigious colleges or universities such as Cornell and Rensselaer Polytechnic Institute, many others attended schools that were not considered elite at the time, including Tufts University, Bowdoin College, Northeastern University, Boston University, University of Lowell, University of Massachusetts, and Salem State Community College. As my interviews show, while they were expected to study and be well-behaved, many discussed not getting exceptional grades and being involved in extracurricular activities that interested them rather than to build a portfolio.

Toy Len Goon encouraged her children and grandchildren to be well-behaved and work hard to achieve. However, this is where the similarity stops. Though it is tempting to compare the upwardly mobile trajectory of the Goon children with the ambitious families discussed by Warikoo, Dhingra, and Chin, my interviews show that they did not follow the "Asian American playbook," which is defined by Chin as

> a set of maxims forming an ever-shifting collection of oral advice handed down from generation to generation among Asian Americans. This advice, an essential if unspoken element of handed down precepts for living one generation to the next, is designed to instruct young people as to the best way to make their way in the world, whether by compiling an impressive academic record or achieving in various extracurricular activities designed to enhance their portfolio when it comes time to apply for college (which it is assumed they will attend, graduate from, and perform well in). And it is this playbook that in many respects lies at the heart of

> the dilemmas and challenges that second generation Asian Americans face when they enter the world of work.[20]

My interviews show that while each of her children could be seen as successful in their careers, they did not follow a prescribed playbook like the one that Chin discusses. Rather, Toy Len Goon improvised as she went along. Chin's playbook was created within a very specific historical period—in the 1960s and 1970s—and focused on children of post-1965 immigrants. Because of occupational preference provisions in the Immigration and Nationality Act of 1965, post-1965 immigrants represented a more educated demographic than most earlier immigrants such as Dogan and Toy Len Goon. In addition, Toy Len Goon's children went to college prior to this period.

Chin's research focuses on how second-generation Asian Americans used the playbook in their efforts to achieve success in the workplace—specifically, gaining access to the "C suites."[21] She then asks why these Asian Americans with elite educations do not succeed in reaching those positions in high numbers. In contrast, the Goon family's approach was informed by their turn-of-the-century working-class roots, with a focus on escaping economic precarity and reaching and maintaining middle-class status. Their goal was to not have to do laundry work the rest of their lives, to support their mother, and to provide economic stability for their own families.

My interview data with Toy Len Goon's grandchildren focused on her legacy as it affected their conceptions of themselves and of others. I found that ideas about hard work, success, and achievement that they saw Toy Len Goon as modeling were interpreted differently both across generations and within them. While I asked about upward mobility and financial security in my interviews, I found that their educational experiences and challenges growing up differed based on expectations placed on them by their parents, which were not uniform. Their attitudes toward the model minority myth, anti-Asian hate, and immigration were also diverse. One common theme was a disidentification with contemporary forms of the model minority myth that focused on elite immigrants and elite education.

However, Toy Len Goon's grandchildren and the children of immigrants discussed in the three books do share some general similarities.

These include dealing with parental expectations, experiences with racism, and for some, navigating a white-collar workplace. Both the second generation discussed by Chin, Warikoo, and Dhingra and Toy Len Goon's grandchildren (the third generation) grew up during or after the 1980s under the shifting shadows of the model minority myth. Despite being of different generations, both interpreted and, in some cases, modified the advice given to them by previous generations. They grappled with ideas surrounding affirmative action and the shifting racialization of Asian Americans over time. As seen in my interviews, the family immigration history impacted their engagement with the model minority myth, though not in uniform ways. Asian American experiences are marked by diversity across generations, but also vary within specific historical periods, elucidating the complexity of the model minority myth as it has evolved over time.

Emotion Work

Angie Chung views the family as "the site for both the production and the enactment of emotion work."[22] She examines "how emotions are managed and expressed in adaptation to family roles and structural constraints, the way they are conveyed across generational and cultural differences, and how they condition the ethnic worldviews of the second generation."[23] Chung describes two facets of the model minority myth presented in the literature. One "praises Asian families for upholding the traditional heteronormative structure and ideal of the 'normal (white) American family' based on a hardworking male breadwinner and a family-devoted wife/mother who raises obedient children with proper family values."[24] This version of the model minority myth echoes the ways that Toy Len Goon's life was presented by the media, except that she carried out the roles of both breadwinner and devoted mother. The other aspect of this myth focuses on the overbearing and usually gendered ("oppressive," "patriarchal" father and "education-obsessed" mother) parenting practices of Asian Americans that result in the educational and career success of their children, but at the expense of personal autonomy. Chung points out that both models place Asian American families outside the "normative" white middle-class family.[25]

Chung aims to go beyond this paradox by examining the "emotion work" that the children of Korean and Chinese immigrants and their children perform to "save face," including regulating how they act in front of others and stifling emotions such as "anger, shame, and disappointment" to avoid embarrassment.[26] She emphasizes that beyond these internal psychological motivations for saving face, it is also important to consider how this emotion work is also shaped by structural factors, including dealing with the family's "racial difference," and doing one's part within a larger family strategy to make ends meet. Chung argues that this emotion work continues to affect how later generations view their ethnic identities and family cultures, and also plays out differently within the family according to factors such as gender and birth order.[27] Finally, she discusses how the children of immigrants present a sense of self that sometimes employs the very ideas that are often used by others to describe them, including a focus on "family values," Asians as model minorities, essentialized ideas about differences between "Eastern" and "Western" values, and the American Dream.[28] However, this vocabulary obscures their feelings about the sacrifices and emotional labor of their parents and themselves, issues that often reemerge as the children of immigrants go on to pursue their careers and raise their own families.

I discuss Chung's work here because it provides a sociologically rooted framework, drawn from ethnographic interviews conducted in the early 2000s in the New York and New Jersey metro areas, for understanding the ways that the second generation narrates their family histories of immigrant struggle in relation to their own identity formation as children of immigrants. Though not addressing that specific historical period, Chung provides a framework for understanding how the Goon children and grandchildren may employ ideas of familial sacrifice and the American Dream in ways that differ based on birth order, family role, and gender, and that also derive from the emotion work that they perform(ed) as the children of Chinese immigrants. While the children of immigrants in Chung's study were influenced by the very specific discourses surrounding immigrants and upward mobility in the early 2000s when she conducted her research, so were the Goon grandchildren, with their parents' views having been shaped by the World War II and Cold War eras in which they were raised. I am also interested in how current discourses and debates on immigration and upward mobility may both reflect and influence how the children and grandchildren of immigrants see and recollect their family stories.

Is the Model Minority Idea Actually a Myth?

While there have been many compelling arguments about why the model minority idea is harmful, there is also a body of academic literature that argues for the importance of recognizing the very real effects of this idea for families who subscribe to it. The idea of model minority success is communicated through parents and embedded in societal expectations, so much so that it becomes ingrained in the worldview of the next generation. In her essay "The Model Minority," erin Khuê Ninh asks Asian American studies scholars to rethink the ways we teach about the model minority myth:

> We train our students to retort that the model minority is a figment of the white imagination. We tell them statistics lie; Asians are not doing nearly so well; look after all at the Southeast Asians, they are in gangs. But it is a red herring and, moreover, a disingenuous case to make. The heart of the issue is not whether Asian immigrant families currently meet the measures of the model minority; the issue is whether they aspire to, whether they apply those metrics. And they do. The racial ideologies, the economic infrastructures, the educational paradigms of Asianness do not circle the immigrant home like vampires, held at bay by bulbs of garlic; they are invited in to dine, made part of the nuclear family. Which is to say that the immigrant nuclear family is not only busy grappling with, fending off, and challenging certain structural racisms; it is also busily reinforcing, perpetuating, and living up to certain other aspects of racist structures.[29]

In her book *Passing for Perfect*, Ninh focuses on "outlier" examples to explore the lengths to which many go to fulfill the model minority idea due to family pressures. Rather than being merely a myth that can be disproven, she argues, the pressure to be a model minority comes at high costs for many. In one example she details the story of Jennifer Pan, a Chinese Canadian student who failed her high school calculus class and lost early admission to university. Rather than telling her parents she had to retake the class, she chose to pretend she was at university for four years. When they found out she was not telling the truth, she hired a hit man to kill them. Khuê uses these extreme examples to illustrate the pressures felt by Asian Americans, for whom the model minority idea is quite real.[30]

My Interviews

My interviews with Toy Len Goon's grandchildren show that Goon family members hold complex relationships to the ever-changing model minority myth, and that they in various ways invoked the Mother of the Year mythology surrounding Toy Len Goon to reappropriate ideas about their family's exceptionalism in ways that go beyond the standard rendering of the myth. Toy Len is attributed the wisdom of knowing how to raise her children to work hard, study hard, and lead the family toward upward mobility, despite not having had the advantages of education herself and having overcome many obstacles during her own lifetime. Her children came to see their own success as a product of US opportunity and the fulfillment of the American Dream based on their ability to assimilate, in contrast to the assumptions about Chinese cultural values that are often viewed as fueling Asian American ambitions.

Toy Len Goon's grandchildren found themselves at the intersection of societal discourses about Asian Americans as model minorities, expectations placed upon them by their parents, who had their own ideas about success, and comparisons to other more successful friends and relatives. When I asked about the model minority myth, most cousins had heard of the idea. However, most did not see themselves as embodying this stereotype, or as having endeavored to do so. But they did reference other cousins who they felt did fit the criteria of the model minority, and to whom they remember being compared when they were growing up. While Toy Len Goon's grandchildren were accomplished in their own ways and were confident in the exceptionalism of their family's story, they also did not view themselves as model minorities, associating the idea with more elite and accomplished individuals who attended Ivy League universities or held prestigious professions.

Uncle Carroll's Story of Exceptionalism

Toy Len and Dogan Goon's oldest son Carroll's story has taken on almost mythic proportions within the extended Goon family. His story is one of exceptionalism, as the oldest son who sacrificed his schooling when he took time off after his father's death, but through hard work and perseverance fulfilled his dream of becoming a doctor. However, in examining his and his family's story, we can see that there were also challenges and tensions that add complexity to the idea of exceptionalism and how this manifests in expectations of success for the next generation.

After attending Syracuse University, Carroll became a surgeon, receiving his degree from Johns Hopkins Medical School, where he met his wife, Marguerite, a surgical nurse. He was respected by all his siblings and held a special place in Toy Len Goon's heart as her devoted son who would fly back to Boston from Utah whenever she needed medical help.

Carroll worked most of his career and raised his family in the small, predominantly Mormon town of Monticello, Utah. According to his son Jonathan, he had moved to the small uranium mining town expecting it to grow quickly, but stayed, as the only doctor in the town. As non-Mormons, and the descendants of Chinese immigrants on Carroll's side and Greek immigrants on Marguerite's side, the Carroll Goon family never fit into Monticello. However, he was highly respected and trusted by the townspeople, for whom he worked daily to provide cutting-edge medical care as a Johns Hopkins–trained surgeon. Marguerite would assist him with surgical procedures.

His children participated in activities such as Boy Scouts alongside their classmates, while also excelling at their schoolwork. His son Jonathan remembers knowing that he wanted to pursue a PhD from the time he was in first grade. All were strong students and went on to higher education outside Monticello. The younger three went into science and technical fields, following in their parents' footsteps. Kathy became a nurse, Jimmy an engineer, and Jonathan a mathematician. But while his other children followed their parents' footsteps into STEM fields, his eldest daughter, Carroll Ann, was interested in the humanities and has struggled with the idea that she has not lived up to his expectations.[31]

Carroll Ann is the oldest of the Goon cousins. She was named after her father, and chooses to go by Carroll, as opposed to Carroll Ann, because it is her father's name. She remembers him being a legend in their small town, describing his hands as "beautiful, strong, capable, sensitive," and recalling that "when he sewed someone up, it was a work of art."[32]

However, while she felt pride in her father, she also felt pressure to prove that she was successful according to his conception of what was a valid achievement. During our discussion of the model minority idea, she wondered whether our grandmother would have been chosen as Mother of the Year if the children had not been employed in "successful occupations." I replied that she likely would not have been selected, and Carroll quickly added that if the children had not been successful, their story "would not have spoken to the American Dream." She told me that she feels that "she has experienced the darker side of that," referring to the model minority idea. Unlike her STEM-oriented parents and siblings, she has always "tended toward English literature, theater history, and classics." She remembers her father asking her, "Why would you study that? Sounds like studying spooky houses." She elaborated that "in my family it was medical." Her sister Kathy was a nurse, and her brothers were EMTs before Jim became an engineer and Jonathan a mathematician. She was "the odd man out" and felt that "what I was working on was not good enough." I asked whether she thinks that medical and technical careers were more valued because of the influence of Chinese culture on the family, or because of their parents' focus on the medical profession. In response, she shared an example of when her sister Kathy was inducted into Phi Beta Kappa. Her father had found the notice and said he wanted to attend the ceremony. He laminated the newspaper clipping and kept it in his wallet. Hoping to receive similar approval, Carroll also applied and was accepted to Phi Beta Kappa, but remembers feeling that she did not get the same reaction from her father that her sister did. From this and her other interactions with her father, she "got the message about what was worthwhile work and what wasn't." I offered that perhaps the humanities were just not "on his radar," and she agreed, repeating his comment about "spooky houses," something that "you can't touch."[33]

Not fitting into her family's conception of success has had a long-term impact on Carroll's confidence. Now in her sixties, she has settled into a fulfilling career in adult education in theology for laypeople. She also has honed the craft of storytelling, which she views as a survival tool to help her find meaning in difficult experiences. As we reflected further on the model minority idea, she once again brought up "the darker side of the model minority, people who get trampled because for whatever reason could not make it as a model minority." As she understands it, the idea of the model minority is used to send "a message to other minorities who are not model minorities," and that it is often attached to ideas about the "deserving and undeserving poor." While she believes that many Chinese Americans "have done well for themselves," she also thinks that they "are now the measuring stick for all immigrants, all minorities." She also believes that despite being "high achieving" they were not "political" and did not speak out about social injustices.[34]

Despite fitting her father's conceptions of success, Carroll's sister Kathy, a nurse, also found fault with the model minority idea, which she feels has been "twisted' to "beat up on other minorities." She also observes that the idea of hard work leading to immigrant success is not just for Asians, sharing that her mother's family's story with immigrant parents from Croatia and Greece was also remarkable.[35]

Feeling Uncomfortable with the Myth

Most of the cousins I interviewed expressed a degree of discomfort and sometimes active disidentification with the model minority idea for a variety of reasons. They recall not feeling pressure to succeed from their grandmother, but rather an acceptance that each person had their strengths and weaknesses, coupled with the expectation that they be "good" and try hard in school. Connie, the third-oldest of Toy Len Goon's grandchildren, said that the term "model minority" made her "feel uncomfortable." "Yes, we're hard workers, but a lot of people are," she commented. For her, the model minority term brings up the Tiger Mom stereotype, where "you have to be perfect, get straight A's." While she believes that "as a whole, our race doesn't commit crimes, works hard, get ahead, [get a] good job, provide for our families, live the American Dream," she also emphasizes that this is true for many people, and that "we're not perfect, we're not above everybody." She admits that she does not want to draw attention to herself, or for others to think she is a "model citizen." She is "just like everybody else." Connie worked for

Aunt Doris's court reporting firm, starting as a reporter and eventually becoming vice president of operations.[36]

Connie believes that Toy Len Goon knew that everyone had their own strengths and weaknesses. When her son, Jay, now in his thirties and a successful folk singer-songwriter who has opened for nationally famous music acts, decided to leave college after his second year, she remembers receiving pressure from others to make him stay in college. Connie thinks that Toy Len Goon would have understood her decision to support her son's choice—that because she had so many grandchildren, she knew that "one path won't fit everybody." She believed that our grandmother knew that "we aren't all good at everything," recalling a story she heard from her mother overhearing our grandmother telling one of her sons, "There's always going to be someone better than you." Connie believes that people with a variety of skills are needed in society, including "roofers, plumbers, people who build bridges," and thinks that our grandmother understood this. When Connie was first dating her husband, who is non-Chinese, she was conscious of the fact that he came from a "completely different background, . . . a blue-collar guy, rough childhood." However, she recalls that our grandmother "had no problem with it," trusting Connie's judgment, welcoming him, and making her feel confident in her decision. "Grandma always had something positive to say about all of us," she remarked.[37]

Connie recalls our grandmother telling her, "You so see-mart," drawing out the *s* into more of a *see* sound. Many other grandchildren echoed similar sentiments regarding her ability to see her grandchildren for their individual strengths and weaknesses, and to find ways to encourage them through positive reinforcement.[38]

Tim, the third child of Edward and Amy, saw Toy Len Goon's words as both expectation and praise. He recalls her asking in her limited English whether he was being a good boy and checking in on how he was doing in school, and in response he recalls trying to do "as well as you could in school."[39] Terry, the youngest of the four siblings, saw Toy Len Goon's approach toward her grandchildren as one of optimism, recalling, "When you were with her, it was optimistic." She would remind them to be good, and would tell them that they were special, reassuring all of them that they had "a place." She remarks, "As a child we all felt that if you were with grandma, you could do things too" because of the positive, direct attention she paid to her grandchildren. However, she does not remember feeling pressure to succeed, contrasting that with her mother Amy's experiences. The eldest of four children who had lost both their mother and father, Amy had been sent to China to be raised by their father's first wife. Amy was sent back to the United States and given the task of paving the way for the other siblings to resettle in Boston Chinatown.[40]

Varied Expectations

Like her cousins, Janine, second daughter of Richard and Helen, had a complicated relationship to the model minority idea, while also feeling that Toy Len Goon understood and supported each of the grandchildren individually. As she reflected on her own education journey and the variety of experiences and expectations she observed being placed on her siblings and cousins, she thought about her own views as an educator and how they were informed by her upbringing. She saw her parents' emphasis on education as having been born of the expectations that Toy Len Goon placed on her children to go on to higher education as a means of upward mobility, and that the aunts and uncles in turn placed on their children. She viewed these messages about striving toward educational goals as being ingrained in her parents' and her own generation, perhaps on a subliminal level. Her father wanted all his children to pursue higher education, though Janine also thought he had different expectations for each. Her oldest sister, Roseanne, was "a great student," eventually earning an engineering degree at Rensselaer Polytechnic Institute, but Janine didn't think that her father had the same expectations for her, as she had struggled in school. She now believes that she had undiagnosed ADHD, which made it hard for her to focus. Her two younger sisters went to secretarial school, though Ilene, the third of the five children, told me that she had been admitted to the University of Hawaii. As discussed later, her brother Richard, the youngest in the family and the only son, recalls that because he was a male, his parents expected him to excel in school and go on to a good college.[41]

Janine differentiated her own childhood experiences from those of many of her cousins. Growing up in Lynn, Massachusetts, in a working-class environment, she felt that she and her siblings did not have the same exposure to higher learning that many of her cousins did. She mentioned Uncle Albert and Aunt Rose, who brought their children on college tours, and Edward and Amy Guen (parents of Leo, Michael, Tim, and Terry mentioned above), who sent their children to Chinese school and brought them on college tours. Uncle Albert kept file folders of articles of interest for each child to read, while Edward was head of the PTA and created a library at a local school. In contrast, her parents, Richard and Helen, were busy running a television and electronics business, and did not emphasize education for their daughters as much as the importance of marrying a man who could support them. Helen, a straight-A student studying chemistry at Regis College, had dropped out of college at Richard's request, after having had to temporarily withdraw after contracting tuberculosis. Richard told her, "I don't need a chemist, I need a bookkeeper," a skill that Helen mastered quickly.[42]

Janine joked about being on the eighteen-year plan, as she did not complete her teaching degree at Salem State College in Massachusetts until she was thirty-five years old. She first went to art school to study to be a fashion designer, then to the University of Massachusetts, Amherst. However, she thinks that she was "too immature to handle living away from home." Later she was married, then divorced, and worked at Eastern Airlines, eventually remarrying.[43]

Janine recalls that her "Nginny," her term of affection for her grandmother based on the word "Ngin," which all of Toy Len Goon's sons' children used to refer to their paternal grandmother, would call her a "sweet girl," while calling others "smart." She realizes that she was a "late bloomer" in terms of her educational development. Despite her early challenges in school, and knowing her grandmother's emphasis on education, she felt understood and loved by her. Moreover, she sees it as a blessing that she was able to live with her Nginny for a time while finishing her degree in her mid-thirties. Toy Len Goon was one hundred years old and needed someone to stay with her while her daughter Doris, with whom she lived, was away on a trip. Janine reflected that spending time with her Nginny as an adult helped her more fully appreciate her sense of humor, warmth, and wisdom. She believes that because Toy Len Goon did not know how to read and write, she spent time thinking and observing, recalling that she would sit in her "golden chair"—actually a gold-colored upholstered chair—in the condominium in Swampscott that she shared with Aunt Doris, look out at the trees, and be able to discern that it was the right season to find delicious apples at the grocery store.[44]

She admits that as an elementary education teacher, she was a "Tiger teacher," with high expectations of her students that she believes came from her family upbringing. She expected the children to be respectful to one another and to her as their teacher. She shared that when she met the parents of her students who were facing challenges raising their children as single parents, she would sometimes wonder why these parents were not doing a better job of raising responsible, well-behaved children. In the back of her mind, she knew that she should be more tolerant and that it was not good for her to judge these parents in that way, but she would always think of how Toy Len Goon had been a single mother who had raised "outstanding citizens."[45]

Janine remembers that her parents often compared her and her siblings to a more successful family that their mother went to school with in China and who her parents sponsored to the United States, who were fictive kin to the Goon and Chin families. The wife had been a schoolteacher in China and the husband worked at a restaurant. Their three children went to Harvard, Vassar, and Dartmouth, respectively, and became successful businesspeople. She also remembers being compared to their younger cousins whom her parents deemed successful, including siblings Pamela and Stephen, children of Arthur, Toy Len Goon's fifth son, and his wife, Dottie. Pamela went to Tufts and later went to medical school to become a doctor, and Stephen went to Cornell and became an engineer.

At times, it seemed that Janine did not feel that she lived up to the myth, while at other times she saw herself as reinforcing it as a "Tiger teacher," thus putting her on both the sending and receiving ends of the model minority myth. Her internalized expectations of others and of herself were based on her understanding of her family's exceptionalism—the ability of Toy Len Goon to grind through circumstances of poverty and single motherhood to produce successful children. However, she did not subscribe to the myth as an undifferentiated whole. Though her daughters excelled in school, she does not see them as model minorities because they "don't feel that Asian pressure." Given that her children have an Italian American father and a Chinese American mother, she thinks that they are "totally Americanized" and do not practice Chinese American culture, particularly because they grew up in Florida, far from the rest of the extended Chinese American family in Boston. She associated model minority expectations with Asian and Asian American cultural pressures more specifically, but did not necessarily see these pressures as involving the end goal of excelling academically and going to a prestigious university.[46]

Model Minority Myth as Discourse and Stereotype

Other cousins describe having grappled with the model minority myth as both a set of expectations and a stereotype in relation to their own and their children's experiences. They discuss pressure they felt to perform academically, to be well-behaved, and to assimilate. Their drive to assimilate coexisted with navigating positive stereotypes and expectations associated with being Chinese American.

I mentioned that I would discuss the idea of the model minority myth in the email I sent requesting interviews and in my interview questions. In response to my recruitment email, my cousin Marie texted me back while camping in the Everglades, "Myth, I think not," but when I asked her to explain further during our call, she said that when her son, who is half-Chinese and half-white, attended Phillips Academy, an elite private prep school in Andover, Massachusetts, he was not one of the "smartest" students. The strongest students were 100 percent Asian or Asian American. Or perhaps she was thinking about herself, she wondered, as she does not have the stereotypical characteristics associated with the model minority myth, such as excelling in music and math.[47]

Tim, brother of Leo, Michael, and Terry and son of Edward and Amy, recalls that when he was growing up in Needham, a suburb of Boston that was primarily white, with a 40 percent Jewish population and few Chinese families, people "knew the Chinese kids were smart." He "always had a sense that more was expected of him" in school, given his assumed capabilities. He recalls that his mother would check his report card to make sure that his grades were good, and as noted earlier, he would receive similar messages from Toy Len Goon about "being a good boy" and doing well in school, so he strived to please her. His friends also assumed that he was a good student, though like his siblings, he was also very active in extracurricular activities, including sports. He believes that the focus on academic achievement was "a paradigm in his life" that was not shared by his non-Chinese friends.[48]

Tim said that he felt some pride in being Chinese, and that being Chinese at times benefited him, feeling that there is a "cultural advantage of having history and heritage of being Chinese." He also saw being Chinese as an asset that made him special, noting that it was particularly "nice to have a celebrated grandmother," which "contributed to the idea that being Chinese was a positive differentiator." His first job after graduating from Bowdoin College in the early 1980s was at Proctor & Gamble. He remembers going back to the Bowdoin campus with members of the management team to recruit students and recalling his boss saying that one of their goals was to break out of the white male–dominated culture. However, in a somewhat awkward moment, he recalls that his boss forgot that Tim himself was a minority. Tim describes his boss's oversight in not seeing him as a minority as a "weird moment." He believed that the fact that his boss did not see him as Chinese meant that Tim had "successfully assimilated into white male culture—testimony to being a chameleon," as a sign that he had been able to use his "interpersonal abilities to fit in and say the right thing." His boss mentioned that Tim would be part of a management training program, and that people like him would be a "future general manager" of the company. Tim saw this recognition from his boss as a reflection of "the skills he brought and people saying this Asian guy has the smarts and intellectual firepower to do more important things." He recalls that for the following two years, his image appeared on the company's recruiting brochure.[49]

While Tim believes that he has benefited from the positive stereotypes and expectations related to his being Chinese American, he also saw himself as having developed the skills to navigate and assimilate to the mainstream corporate world. Still, he recognized the impact that his Chinese upbringing had on how he navigated the corporate world. In a blog post, he quips, "I have been in sales and marketing my entire professional life, and I have been Chinese-American for even longer. So I feel qualified to suggest that Chinese people have done a pretty lousy job marketing themselves in the Western world. And that we could really benefit from some re-branding." He continues by describing "an unofficial brand re-positioning campaign for Chinese-Americans back in the

1950s" in which his family played a "central role." He explains further the Eisenhower administration's effort toward "assimilating immigrants to become Americans by being law-abiding, hard-working, and patriotic," noting that his grandmother emigrated to the United States and raised eight successful children while running a hand laundry, making her a convenient example of a "Model Minority" image that the United States wanted to communicate to the rest of the world. As he observes, many Chinese Americans viewed her award as a sign of having been "accepted in America's melting pot." However, he argues that due to "Chinese cultural values" that discourage drawing attention to oneself and letting one's accomplishments speak for themselves, Chinese Americans are not well understood. He concludes that because there is no brand manager for Chinese Americans, it is up to individuals to "unpack the myths and bring new meaning to the brand, one placemat and one fortune cookie at a time" by representing the brand "by what you think, say, and do." His take on the model minority idea sees being Chinese as both a positive asset and something—in its emphasis on humility—that holds one back from fully participating in the business world, thus requiring a re-branding. Overall, he emphasizes the importance of assimilation to a white, male mainstream business world by working hard and honing one's skills.[50] When, during the interview, I raised the critique of the model minority myth as using Asians as an exemplar to drive a wedge between the white-dominant culture and other minority groups, he admitted that he hadn't thought about it in that way, and that "we didn't sign up to be" part of what he saw as the "politicization of racism."[51]

Tim's reflections on his career and the family story focus on the need to assimilate to the white male-dominated corporate world, and the exceptionalism of his and other Chinese Americans' performances based on hard work and the cultivation of skills, but also drawing on his "intellectual firepower." He views his Chinese background as something that cultivated a focus on education, but also produced stereotypes that he has had to navigate. Interestingly, he still felt that he did not "measure up" to other cousins, commenting that neither he nor his siblings was Pam, naming a cousin younger than he who became a doctor.[52]

Tim's sister Terry also emphasized the importance of fitting in and assimilating, noting, "We knew that Grandma's goal was to have American citizens." She remembers being "focused on fitting into Needham," the town where they grew up. While her mother, Amy Guen, was fluent in Chinese, having grown up in Chinatown and in the village in Toisan, China, she remembers her father being the "Americanized one," remarking that he "seemed to fit in everywhere—he ran track, played tennis," and that as children she and her siblings felt "grateful that we had our dad who fit in." She wondered whether her grandfather Dogan had been similar in his ability to assimilate. Reflecting on Dogan's trial with Commissioner McCabe, she concluded that if Dogan had not been bright, we would not be here now, as Dogan would have been deemed illegal in the United States and sent back to China, and thus would not have been able to bring Toy Len Goon here to start a family. Tunney Lee, a well-known community historian in Boston, told her that there was an inspector who "just let people in." But she thinks that "if you look at the photos, [Dogan is a] good-looking guy, speaks some English," was strategic by choosing to live away from Chinatown in a non-Chinese population, and had developed "skill sets and personality" that enabled him to fit in.[53]

Terry owns her own landscape architect firm in Chicago and has worked on high-profile projects, including Millenium Park. In 2011 she was appointed by the Obama White House to the Advisory Council on Historic Preservation and was reappointed in 2016. But she says that the model minority stereotype did not resonate with her and "seemed separated from my reality." Unlike her parents, who had to find a way to make ends meet, she did not feel any pressure to accomplish anything specific.[54]

In contrast to his siblings Leo, Tim, and Terry, Michael remembers not being a strong student growing up. However, he remembers his grandmother praising him for continuing to work hard despite not achieving good grades. Michael would later go on to earn a PhD in psychology and become a doctor of traditional Chinese medicine, as well as a master martial artist, studying with a prominent Ba Gua lineage.[55]

Gendered and Birth Order Expectations in a Chinese American Context

In this section I discuss how gender and birth order factored into the expectations and roles of specific cousins. I discuss two male cousins—Leo, who is the oldest male cousin, and Richard, who is the youngest child and only son of Dick, Toy Len Goon's second son. Both recall specific pressures and expectations associated with being sons. I also discuss Rose's experiences as the second-oldest cousin, older than Leo, and her relationship with her youngest brother, Richard. Each cousin discusses their relationship with Toy Len Goon, parental expectations, the model minority myth, and anti-Asian hate. I group these interviews together because of the centrality that gender played in how they saw themselves and their relationships.

As Toy Len Goon's oldest male grandchild, Leo, brother of Michael, Tim, and Terry, felt a different set of pressures than his younger siblings did. His role was defined based on Toy Len Goon's traditional expectations for her oldest male grandchild and reinforced by his parents. Since his mother, Amy, had grown up in Chinatown and in Toisan, China, she was familiar with the role the oldest grandson usually played and could also converse easily with Toy Len Goon about her expectations.

At the time I interviewed Leo in 2021, he was product manager and developer for JP Morgan Chase and at the age of sixty-seven was planning to transition to part-time work as a step toward retirement. As one of the youngest cousins, I had never realized the responsibility that Leo felt, as the eldest grandson, to "lead the clan." As noted previously, his mother had shared that Toy Len Goon had seen the birth of her first grandson as an important milestone in transitioning the leadership of the Goon clan to the next generation, marked by the donation of incense money by his parents and the red egg party in his honor.[56]

Leo admits that he took the role of being the oldest grandson and its accompanying responsibilities seriously, but also felt that it was a position that he needed to earn by developing the qualities needed to carry out those responsibilities:

> I bought into the . . . idea that I was the eldest grandson, and so therefore, I should be leading the clan. . . . Understanding that it's not just, you don't just get the position, you also have to have the character and behavior and respect of your, mutual respect and relationships with your, with your cousins, and relatives. But I was in a position to do that. So . . . I always thought about the expectation of, well, I have to be a role model.[57]

He had believed that he should move back to Boston upon retiring and continue the civic work that his parents and maternal uncles had been doing in Boston Chinatown for the past sixty-plus years. His parents had been involved in building South Cove Manor Nursing Home and in activism to preserve local ownership of Chinatown real estate. His maternal uncles were local business owners and involved in both Chinatown and Boston city politics. However, his mother recently reminded him that "you'll never be able to replicate what we have done in our generation, because circumstances are different now. As far as like, trying to establish the nursing home, it would be so much more difficult today to do it than it was back in the day. So you should just find your own things that you're passionate about."[58]

Hearing that he didn't have to repeat his parents' accomplishments was a relief. From a very young age, he had felt compelled to represent his extended family. He had learned that there was "an idea in Chinese culture, that society and the emperor or the government or whoever, especially other families, are watching" and that in that sense, "there's like a performance of representing." Even though he realizes that nobody was watching him or the family, he remembers being told by his mother when he was going into first grade that it was important that he do well because, he recalls her saying, "'You're not just representing our family, you're representing all Chinese.' . . . Gosh. So yeah, a little bit of pressure."[59]

Leo was motivated to perform well academically, athletically, and socially as a way to combat the racism and bullying he experienced growing up in Needham, a suburb of Boston with a small Chinese population, figuring "the best defense against being picked on . . . that if you could be one of the smarter kids at school and the more athletic at school, then people would pick you on their teams and give you respect." He recalls experiencing a couple of racist incidents growing up. When he was in first grade, a fourth grader at his bus stop called him a "rice bug." He remembers coming home crying that afternoon and telling his mother about the incident. She told him to call the fourth grader a "potato bug," but he recalls that that strategy was not effective. He also thinks that his parents modeled strong social skills for him that he used to get along with others and not be bullied. He remembers being hurt when another student called him a goon (based on his last name) in high school, but now realizes that the student came from a troubled home background. Interestingly, he thinks that "the biggest discrimination I had was actually from other Asians, from other Chinese in Chinatown" whom he encountered when working in his uncle's restaurant while in high school and college. He was told by the immigrant Chinese waiters that because he didn't speak Chinese and was not born in Hong Kong or mainland China, he wasn't really Chinese. He termed this feeling "the pain of being an ABC [American-born Chinese], . . . a different pain than people who are immigrants who come to this country. . . . It all has to do with being an outsider . . . but in a different way."[60]

In contrast to the emphasis that many of Toy Len Goon's descendants and media coverage placed on her ability to assimilate to US society, Leo articulates a different dynamic, of feeling in-between cultures, not "Chinese" enough but also not "American" enough—an "outsider" to both. His observation encourages us to think beyond a linear model of assimilation, and question wholesale assimilation to mainstream US society as an overall goal, while also acknowledging that it might not be possible or desirable. His desire to be seen as "Chinese" and to represent his Chinese family also illustrates the complexity of Chinese American identities. In discussing how he grew up with the feeling of not being "Chinese" or "American" enough in various contexts, he explains that his underlying motivation for excelling academically and athletically, and developing social skills and connections, was to prevent being bullied. These unspoken and unwritten rules helped guide Leo to a college education at Bowdoin College, where his father had attended, and into a successful career, one in which he feels his colleagues didn't see him as "Chinese" in a way that differentiated him from his coworkers.[61]

In many ways, Leo appears to fit the model minority profile. During our conversation I asked him what he thought about the model minority myth in terms of his own and his family's experiences. Leo clarified that while he never studied the idea of the model minority, he believes that "the word 'model' means that the values are aligned with the majority," such as being "honest" and able to "work hard." However, he notes that it also includes not causing trouble, an approach that left Chinese workers with little recourse when they were faced with violence in the context of European labor competition in the past and had to "take [their] lumps." He saw not being able to "fight back" and lacking "representation" as major shortcomings of what he saw as the Chinese strategy of working hard and trying to align with the majority. The strategy of upward mobility through education by getting into "elite colleges and get[ing] advanced degrees" was another part of this adaptation, and a way of "working within the system" to gain acceptance.[62]

However, Leo does not see himself as fitting this definition of a model minority. He recalls being a B+ (not an A) student, which he sees as an indication that he was "not as smart or hardworking" as his father; he thinks that he got into Bowdoin College as a beneficiary of his father's legacy. However, he believes that his ability to be "on the edges of many groups" allows him to be a "bridge"—for example, serving as a class agent for the past thirty-five years.[63]

Leo's understanding of his family story informed the expectations he created for himself. He recalls having an original copy of a book containing our grandmother's story on the bookshelf of his family home growing up, and that having the story "in black and white" made him "proud and privileged to be part of this family." His mother Amy's side of the family had an extraordinary history as well and were very prominent in Boston Chinatown and in Boston politics. He saw himself as being "in the confluence of . . . these two streams. I thought very lucky and felt I had a lot to live up to."[64]

However, part of Toy Len Goon's influence very early in Leo's life took the form of inspiring him to be better behaved, despite also emphasizing his importance as the eldest male grandchild. He would stay with her for a couple of weeks during the summer when he was four or five years old and, as discussed earlier, he remembers her being "very clever, but always very kind" in telling him he was a good boy, even when, as he now admits, he would relentlessly tease his other cousins around his age, Rose, Connie, Janine, all female, in an effort to get attention. Leo recalls experiencing his grandmother's words, always spoken in English, as "an inspiration and praise" due to their positivity, and he didn't want to let her down. She was also skilled in redirecting him toward more positive behaviors, and willing to discipline him, despite his privileged position as the eldest grandson and future leader of the Goon clan. Leo reflects,

> Yeah, you have to give her a real credit for wanting to bring me up right, as opposed to wanting to just please me. That probably came from, you

> know, her, her whole life story, you know, having been the servant girl and immigrating, and all the difficulty, and she just realized she had to stick to her principles more than try to please anybody. Just like, when she was being asked by . . . when Dogan died, she was being asked to give up her Woodfords [Corner] Forest Avenue building, [they] said, "Well, you have to give this building up. So then you can . . . get welfare, . . . take payments from welfare." Nope. We've sacrificed and bought this building and my husband, I got it. Now own it, we're not going to give it up. And we'll take our chances and see if we can try to earn the money and not just take from the state.[65]

Leo sees Toy Len Goon's strength and perseverance as having shaped her life story both while in China and as an immigrant to the United States. In our discussion of anti-Asian hate, he says that he doesn't remember anybody reporting that our grandmother ever experienced discrimination, nor do his parents remember being targeted. However, he does acknowledge that Asian Americans are currently experiencing anti-Asian hate. In the long run, he hopes for a progression from Asian Americans achieving success in the workplace, to being accepted and no longer being considered outsiders. The final step would be achieving "diversity," in which people of various backgrounds, including minorities, could become part of the "inner circle." He doesn't yet feel compelled to act against anti-Asian hate but believes in karma and feels he will know when he is meant to get involved. Still, he emphasizes the importance of Asian Americans viewing themselves as part of a larger community affected by these issues, even if they have not experienced them personally.

As the youngest child and only son of Dick and Helen, Richard Len, whose nickname growing up was Doi (Hoisanese for "boy"), had experiences that were quite different from those of his four older sisters, but share some similarities with those of Leo in terms of gendered expectations. He admits to having been very spoiled growing up, not because he was the youngest, but because he was the son his parents had been waiting for. He was doted on as a child; his older sister Rose said that he would always be in someone's arms when he was a baby. And he described how every year he would receive an "over the top" gift from Aunt Emily and Uncle Stanley Ng, whom his parents helped sponsor to the

United States from Hong Kong. One gift that he remembers distinctly was an air hockey table: "a big real, like, super-nice one." He reflects on this moment as one that drove home how differently he was being treated in comparison to his older sisters. He also understood that the gifts were one way that Uncle Stanley and Aunt Emily were expressing their gratitude for being sponsored to the United States by his parents. The gifts being showered upon him, he realized, were not about him, but an extension of the relationship between his parents and the Ng family, which was expressed through culturally rooted forms of reciprocation. Like Leo, who was the oldest male grandchild, Richard realized that he, as the male descendant of one of Toy Len Goon's sons, occupied a special role within his family. He was the only one of his five siblings who was given a red egg party.[66]

When I asked him about pressures and expectations that came with being the only son, he said that he "did feel just pressure to get good grades. That was pretty much the only stress in my life . . . , but I felt it as pretty intense." He wasn't sure whether or not his older sisters had felt the same pressure, remarking, "Again, I was so spoiled. It was all about me. . . . I was pretty clueless, I think, to their stuff." But he also reflects that perhaps one reason his parents focused on his educational success, sending him to a private Catholic school, St. John's Preparatory School, instead of Lynn public schools was because by the time he was born, his parents already had their hands full parenting his four older sisters.[67]

Despite his upbringing being largely defined by his position as the youngest of five siblings and the only son, Richard discussed other experiences that resonated with what other cousins had shared. He felt that even though our grandmother had so many grandchildren, he felt a gentle calm every time he visited her, remembering "just every time leaving feeling so good . . . special." He believes that he was one of her favorite grandchildren, even signing his text to me "Ngin's favorite grandchild." He said that the subject came up on a recent family Zoom call with his sisters, in which each of them said that they thought they were her favorite, remarking, "That's the amazing part. . . . Everyone felt like they were her favorite." However, he reminded them that Aunt Doris would always tell him, "You're her favorite" when he would leave after visiting them at her condo. He admitted that he had "an advantage" as his father's only and long-awaited son. He would see her often, as he would drop things off frequently. Like the other grandchildren, he remembers Toy Len Goon telling him to "study hard. Get good grades. Go to college. Get a good job," which added to the pressure that he felt because he didn't want to let her down. He attended Northeastern University and became a department store buyer, and believes that being Asian may have benefited him. More specifically, he believes that the idea that Asians are smart may have "come in handy," since being a buyer involved some use of computers and working with numbers, but also required the ability to work with salespeople and marketing people who might be more versed in fashion trends than in numbers.[68]

The importance of working hard was a message that he would later share with his own children, but he also tried to ensure that his children knew that he only expected them to try their best, and did not expect perfection from them—he was never a straight-A student himself. He felt pressure from his own parents when they would remind him that cousin Pam was number one in her school and would hear which cousin was going to which college, recalling that he heard these comments from his mother more often than from his father.

Regarding the recent rise in anti-Asian hate incidents, he feels that he was "totally clueless" about the experiences of Asian Americans who were working in factories and not successful in a stereotypical manner, whom he describes as having been "left behind." He notes that he has been living "in a bubble," as his kids "never faced racism or faced people making fun of them" while growing up in Georgia. Reflecting on his own childhood, he does not recall experiencing racism or being singled out growing up in Lynn, even at St. John's Prep, where he was one of a handful of Asian American students. However, he does remember feeling out of place during college when he started hanging around with his cousin on his mother's side, Mark Chin, and his Chinese American friends. Unlike this group, Richard could not speak Cantonese and started to feel self-conscious "amongst Chinese people" because "I wasn't the Boston street kid. I was the Lynn . . . not redneck, but you know, basically, like, they could tell, like, I was not one of them."[69]

Rose Len is Richard's older sister, and the eldest of the five siblings. Despite their twelve-year age difference, she and Richard were quite close growing up. While she remembers spoiling him when he was a young child, she also hung out with him when he got older, along with their cousin Mark Chin and their circle of friends. They would go to Celtics games and to Chinese martial arts movies, sometimes just Rose and Richard.

Rose reflects that prior to Richard's birth, she "tried to be a boy. You know what I mean? Like, . . . I tried to fill that role. You know, as well as I could." Her parents valued having a son to carry on the family name. Rose recalls that prior to her mother giving birth to Richard, her parents had boys' names picked out for each of her mother's four pregnancies, all of which produced girls—Rose, Janine, Ilene, and Marie.[70]

Despite marrying her high school sweetheart, Larry, and having her first child right after high school, Rose eventually finished college with a BS in mechanical engineering at Rensselaer Polytechnic Institute, and at the time of the interview was still working as an aerospace engineer at age sixty-eight. She had asked for my interview questions in advance, and provided thoughtful, extensive written responses, including the one that follows, in which she details her long path toward her college degree while working full-time as a young mother with two children.

> Because I had my first child right after high school, I had a lot of time to think about "what I wanted to be when I grew up." I initially settled on architecture because it was both technical and project-oriented, something that had a beginning and an end. I wanted to be a traditional stay-at-home mother, which I was until necessity interceded. Working at General Electric Company in various non-professional jobs steered me to Mechanical Engineering—they would pay 80% of my tuition. Before that though, I discovered that there were no accredited architecture schools in Boston with classes at night. I also did some research and talked to an architect. He told me that after studying all those years and taking that 8-hour exam, you end up drafting for the more prestigious architects and making less money than I was making as a technician at GE. I went to Northeastern University while I was working full time, then went to the University of Vermont for a year, and then finished my undergraduate degree as a full-time student at Rensselaer Polytechnic Institute . . . where my father got his undergraduate degree in physics. My plan worked! My father's buttons were bursting from pride for his daughter who "was just going to get married and have kids anyway."[71]

Despite having overcome numerous obstacles throughout her life to raise her children and establish her career, Rose does not consider herself to be a model minority. She does recall being treated differently as a female engineer working at General Electric, once being hired for a position that she was not qualified for because her boss assumed she would be smart, capable, and easy to work with, and another time being told that she counted twice, as both a woman and a racial minority. However, a work incident she shared supported her claim that she was not a model minority:

> But, if Ngin was a "model minority," I am not. Have you ever had a dream in which you are yelling and yelling, but it feels like no sound is coming out? Maybe not, but I had an episode like that at work with a coworker, where I was screaming as loud as I could in his face, and it wasn't loud enough. He was not making the correct safety decisions, and I had had enough. Afterward, we had a meeting with several people in my manager's office, and everyone sided with me! She asked him, "Who has put this monkey on your back, because I did not."[72]

She admits to not having heard of the model minority idea until she watched the PBS documentary *Asian Americans*, in which our grandmother's story was featured in episode 3, "The Good Americans." She reflects, "The program described it as not making waves, and living a life representative of the American Way. But historically, haven't Americans always made waves? The first white people to arrive were dissenters of sorts of the values that they left behind."[73]

She thinks that Toy Len Goon's children may be considered model minorities because they were able to go on to higher education and achieve financial stability and have "all worked very hard for what they achieved." She acknowledges that she too has worked hard, "almost to the point that if things aren't really difficult, something must not be right!" Her children have also had to work hard but faced different sets of challenges; her daughter Amy has two autistic children. Yet Rose mentioned some Vietnamese families she knows in Seattle whom she believes are

> clearer examples to me of the model minority, as they have been so purposeful in seeking and achieving the American Dream, and in how they

> continue to pursue the Golden Ring via their children and their children's education. They are all younger than me, and when I think about what they have been through. . . . They are first-generation immigrants who have lived through a war. Do you think that maybe our generation are not model minorities due to how Americanized we have become? I remember getting a job at GE because I was attributed with having more education and knowledge than I actually had because I was Chinese. I don't know if we are all model minorities, but we seem to have that strong work ethic. It does seem that a strong work ethic is common among Asian Americans.[74]

She wonders whether there is a "cultural characteristic" that has made Asian Americans strive to be successful, musing, "Is it insecurity from being displaced from the native land? Is it because we look different? Are we partially driven by fear to be successful? Those are things that all ethnicities must have experienced when they came to this country."[75]

Rose is aware of the recent rise in anti-Asian hate that coincided with the COVID-19 pandemic. However, while she acknowledged that it was a real issue, she said that she was tired of living in fear. She reflects that coming from Lynn, Massachusetts, a working-class city with a large immigrant and lower-income population, she has "heard too many stories of young children whose only daily meal is in school." But she believes that

> whatever hand you have been dealt, it is up to you to make the most of that hand. If we continue to be victims in any way, that is on us. Whatever has been deeply ingrained in us—whether it be for centuries, or only during our own lifetime, it is now up to us what we do with our lives. I have not walked in everyone's shoes, and I have had a lot of support in my life—often from complete strangers whom I encountered for just that moment of critical need, but this is the only way I can see to approach this issue of inequity.[76]

At the same time, she believes that the anti-Asian hatred that we are now seeing, fueled by Trump's rhetoric, "was there all the time . . . and it was just waiting for an excuse to come out."[77]

Being an American

Another theme expressed in numerous interviews was the importance of being seen as an American, which encompassed a variety of meanings, from having a rightful place in the United States, to admiring Toy Len Goon's open-mindedness and ability to fit in, to being able to defend against anti-Asian hate by claiming belonging in America. Linda, daughter of Josephine and sister of Connie (mentioned earlier), also had tremendous respect for her grandmother, remembering her as being "so smart," despite not having a formal education. She also emphasized Toy Len Goon's ability to adapt, to "fit in," and also how open she was to new ideas. Linda says that growing up, she knew that her grandmother was "special" and possessed so much wisdom, and that "she understood so much" and "had so much to give to us." When she had to write a report when she was in elementary school about someone she admired, she recalled that instead of picking an actor or actress, she chose her grandmother, citing her "generous spirit" and "kindness." Linda also remembers being told, "You so see-mart" and being encouraged by her to do well at school. Like other cousins, Linda remembers how Toy Len Goon "gave us all time with her, encouraged us," "got us . . . what we were all about," and "knew what everyone was doing." One example of her wisdom that Linda cited, likely heard via her mother, was how she handled Uncle Carroll's marriage to Aunt Marguerite, whose family had emigrated from Greece. When Carroll announced that he wanted to marry Marguerite, she first had to let go of her expectation that he would marry a Chinese woman, but eventually decided that if she did not approve of the marriage, she would risk compromising her relationship with her son. In the end, she decided that she would "either lose a son or gain a daughter-in-law," and once she had the opportunity to get to know Marguerite, they got along very well. I heard this story repeated by other relatives as a testament to her open-mindedness, adaptability, and practical thinking. For most immigrant Chinese women of that generation, having one's child marry a non-Chinese would have been a significant departure from tradition.[78]

Linda reflected that our grandmother would be pleased and happy with how her kids, grandkids, and great-grandkids were doing. Toy Len Goon had gotten to meet Linda's daughter Samantha when she was just a baby. I asked what Linda thought our grandmother would think about Samantha's marriage to her longtime girlfriend, which had occurred a few months before my interview with her, a small wedding due to the pandemic. She believed that she would have been okay with the marriage and would have seen her daughter and her wife as being "a good match."[79]

Toy Len Goon's open-mindedness was reflected in her desire to keep tabs on "what the Americans do" and adopt similar practices. Linda heard from her mother, who helped with most of the cooking, that Toy Len Goon would try to replicate the meals that the Americans made, such as Prince spaghetti, or beans and franks. According to Linda, she "felt that being in America," you should try to "fit in." In contrast, other friends did not move out of Chinatown, and "those families missed out."[80] Amy Guen similarly remarked that Toy Len told her that she would periodically get together with other neighbors, some of whom were immigrants from Syria and other places, to taste one another's baked beans. However, her goal during these tastings was to make sure that hers were the best![81]

For Linda, being an American is an important part of her identity, which created conflicting feelings for her when she first heard Donald Trump, whom she supported in the 2016 presidential election, use the term "China virus" to describe COVID-19. She believes that his remarks have been a driving force behind the rise in anti-Chinese sentiment, remarking that her father, Tony, a World War II US Navy veteran, took "great umbrage" at the fact that Trump had to implicate the entire Asian community in making this association. She emphasizes that she has never even been to China and is "American through and through." Having supported Trump for his first term because of the promises he made to build the economy, she was at first not sure whether she wanted to vote for him again in 2020. She wonders about the Chinese immigrants who have lived here all their lives but still have a Chinese accent—are they safe from ignorant people who will now associate them with the virus and take it out on them? Her sister Connie takes the "T" (MBTA) to work and once had to switch trains because a man approached her and was staring at her. Linda believes that these ignorant people need to "take it out on somebody else" and that they "need an excuse." Trump provided that excuse. Connecting her thoughts on current Chinese immigrants to the family story, she reflected, "Thinking about Por, she wanted kids to fit in, don't create any waves, go under the radar. You are different [but] we don't want you to be perceived as different."[82] She reflected that "a lot of people look at Asians [as being] smart. [They] follow the rules, work hard, but [are] hated because you are taking an opportunity away." She also understands that things are difficult for non-Asian immigrants and minorities. She has friends who work with minority families whose parents "are working so hard to survive." One friend teaches kindergarten in a school where there are twenty-two different languages spoken at home. These families work hard. However, now she sees "a big split" in terms of who gets privileges. However, while she recognizes that "it's not that people don't want to do better, they don't have opportunities to do better," she also believes that "people need help, but don't need to be enabled," remarking that some people are "waiting for a handout.... You owe me this." She heard from a colleague who works as a court reporter that if he were on welfare he would make more than his current salary, and she believes that welfare "shouldn't be a lifestyle."[83]

Others saw their family history, as encapsulated in Toy Len Goon's national recognition as US Mother of the Year, as something that validated their place as Americans in the context of anti-Asian hate. Marie, sister of Rose, Janine, Ilene, and Richard, shared this thought:

> Well, if you look at current events right now, and the concerns about the Asian Americans and being safe and careful, you know, how do you protect yourself? I'm ready, Andrea, for someone to come at me. And for me to say with my finger, "Do you know who my grandmother is? We are more American than you are. Don't you . . . dare, you know?" Yeah.
>
> Was your grandmother American Mother of the Year? Yeah, it takes . . . it takes her . . . her title. Fast forward. You know, how much more proud can we be in this day and age in this culture? You know, to be proud Americans.[84]

Stephen Len, son of Arthur and Dottie Len, saw the family story as something he could use to defend against the bullying and racism he experienced growing up. Growing up in Chelmsford, Massachusetts, an area where there weren't many Chinese people, Stephen recalls that he experienced racism. In one case, a fellow student wrote some scribbles in their notebook and asked Stephen if he could read them, and when

Stephen said he couldn't, the student proceeded to make random sounds to make fun of how Chinese sounds. He would occasionally be pushed by other children during phys ed. He never knew whether he was being treated in these ways because he was Chinese or because he was a self-described "nerdy kid," though these acts were often accompanied by racial slurs. Growing up, he was also aware of the anti-Asian sentiment in the 1980s directed against Japanese automakers but often carried out against other Asian Americans. He also recalls what he terms "the flip side" when in middle school he asked another student a question, and the student replied that Stephen should know the answer because he is Chinese and should be smart. He describes it as a "weird kind of racism. . . . Like, you're pointed out that you're racist, but then is that a bad thing, that they think that Chinese people are smart? I don't know how to interpret that."[85]

In response to the racism he experienced for being Chinese, he saw his grandmother's award as "kind of being validation to me that, you know, this shows that my family is American. And, you know, we're as American as anyone else who thinks that we're not." He adds that he remembers feeling this at a young age, and it gave him "courage" and was "reassuring." He emphasized that his pride stemmed from her being *American* (my emphasis) Mother of the Year, reinforcing that idea that "we belong here, and we've achieved things," but also that "this is something that you shouldn't take for granted. And we should definitely make the most of the opportunity that we have in the US."[86]

Kasey, Stephen's second daughter, a student at Columbia University when I spoke with her, put it slightly differently. Hearing that I was interviewing her father, aunt Pam, and other relatives, she reached out to chat with me about my research. I shared with her what Marie had said about just waiting for someone to question her Americanness. Kasey agreed, noting that knowing that your grandmother was Mother of the Year "anchors your indignation."[87]

Politics Surrounding Mother of the Year Award

While for many cousins, their grandmother's award helped validate their sense of belonging as Americans, many were also aware of the strategic importance of her award in the context of the Cold War United States.

Shortly after Chiou-Ling Yeh's *Pacific Historical Review* article was published in 2012, it was circulated to the family via email. While some relatives resented what they saw to be an over-analysis of Toy Len Goon's life story, Tim wrote an email in which he explained that investigating the historical context could add an important dimension to her accomplishments. In my interview with Terry as part of this book's research, Terry shared that she recalls Toy Len Goon making a comment to her when she was "really old" about how she was selected as Mother of the Year because of the Cold War situation. Terry, who admittedly is not a history or politics buff, remembers not understanding what she meant by the Cold War, which makes her confident that she heard her grandmother make this politically aware statement about the context for the selection of her award. She also recalls her saying during the same conversation that after she became Mother of the Year she had a "nervous affliction" because she had to uphold the public image associated with that title throughout the festivities, but with her limited language skills. Because Terry does not speak or understand Toisanese, the conversation would have taken place in English.[88]

Changing Economic and Historical Context

Just as it was important to understand that Toy Len Goon's award did not occur in a political or historical vacuum, it was also essential to consider that the rapid upward mobility that Toy Len Goon helped her children achieve was also historically situated and could not necessarily be replicated by later generations. Nancy, daughter of Albert and Rose, provided an economically and historically contextualized explanation for why the model minority idea is problematic. She believes that economic circumstances are different now compared to when our parents were growing up, so it is now possible to work hard and not get ahead in the same way that previous generations were able to make strides in upward mobility. She recalls that her father "was always conscious about how precarious it is financially for households." Though she did not fully understand why when she was younger, she now realizes that it was important to him that his children be financially independent because he lacked a reliable source of income growing up. He was supportive of whatever careers they wanted to pursue, and they all went to school for different things, Nancy studying accounting, her brother Ted working as an engineer, sister Sharon as a broker, and Susan as court reporter. However, he continued to emphasize that they needed to be able to earn enough to support themselves, at one point sharing that it was difficult to live hand to mouth so that you barely have enough to cover the bills. She realized that "there wasn't an overabundance when he was growing up" and that he did not want his children to experience that situation. She emphasizes that he did not want them to be wealthy and was not pressuring them to be successful. He just wanted them to not have to worry about covering basic living expenses. And though he never said that his emphasis on financial stability stemmed from his own upbringing, which he did not talk about often, she assumed that it might have been related.[89]

She also believes that part of her father's urgency was that he realized that the "economic landscape is a lot different than generations ago." In the past, people would not necessarily have needed a college degree to get a job that paid enough to help them put food on the table. Now there is a "disparity of wages and income." People now are working just as hard, but "the fruits of their labor would not convert" to money to pay for what they need, including healthcare. She remembers that her father once shared a discussion he'd had at work with a colleague about how kids aren't working hard enough because they have already "made it." Some of the kids were renting an apartment or living at home instead of owning a house. However, he interjected, reminding them that "the cost of housing took off in the '80s and '90s, increasing beyond the increase in wage," which made it difficult for people to afford homes, even with two incomes. She took this as an indication of his deep understanding of how unreasonable it was for people to expect their kids to do what they had been able to—work hard and buy a home. She reflects that for her own children, "things are more acute today" because "housing and wage inequality has gotten worse."[90]

In spotlighting Nancy's perspectives, I am not implying that she is the only cousin who holds such opinions. However, in sharing her own and her father's perspectives, she provides insight into how the Goon family's upbringing affects later generations' understanding of financial priorities and of success and security. She attributes her father's practical focus on financial stability not as a form of model minority striving or pressure to attend a particular college or enter a specific profession, but rather as a means to avoid financial precarity. He understood "success" as being a relative term in the context of a shifting economic landscape that made it increasingly difficult to be self-sufficient.

Nancy was familiar with the model minority idea from having been involved with "a lot of Asian groups at work" that were working to "help Asians succeed in the workforce," including one called ASCEND. She said that she thinks that the idea of a model minority is a myth because "for immigrants today it feels more challenging to create the same success stories because of the economics to get over the hurdle and be self-sufficient," noting that it is "so much harder to come here with nothing regardless of what country" and that there are "more barriers, hurdles for housing and health insurance, insurmountable as a percentage of income."[91]

Nancy's understanding of the systemic barriers to upward mobility are also reflected in her attitudes toward immigration. I tried to address immigration in most of my interviews if the conversation led in that direction. She noted that many people have strong opinions on immigration, and that she has heard that six out of ten businesses are founded by immigrants. "The notion that it is a bad thing is a tougher argument," adding, "the notion that if you came here and can't make it and are on public assistance is a reflection of how little wages they are making. . . . It's not unwillingness to work hard. For a good number, they are required to work harder."[92]

Nancy and her husband, Billy, purchased a house in Newton, an affluent suburb just outside Boston, in 1990, on the advice of a relative who knew the real estate market. Nancy's experiences raising her children in Newton gave her additional insights into the sometimes invisible systems that those with resources used to maintain or improve their social and economic status. Though the price of the house seemed almost out of reach at the time, they managed to afford it, and now realize that it was a good investment, and that they would never be able to "buy into the community" now. Having grown up outside Boston, I knew that Newton has a reputation for having an excellent school system. I mentioned to Nancy that it was great that her children were able to take advantage of the Newton schools, but Nancy's response surprised me:

> We found after our kids had been in the public school system for a number of years, . . . one of the revelations we had is that even though it's perceived to have a strong school system, because of the high MCAS [Massachusetts Comprehensive Assessment] scores, and the like, that an awful lot of students here in this community, their parents have private tutors for them. So it's supplemented a lot. So it's a little bit deceptive. . . . I guess everybody has tutors, for their kids, for the . . . subjects. So that's why it was just this, we—Billy and I—were just oblivious to this. I think that that was the norm for what was happening.[93]

Unbeknownst to Nancy and her husband, many parents in this affluent community had hired tutors for their children, something that they did not think to do. The hiring of tutors reflects an investment in education by members of a relatively privileged community who were trying to give their kids a competitive advantage to ensure their success within the public school system.[94] While Nancy made sure to emphasize that the school system was indeed strong, she also realizes that she and her husband were not connected to the social capital networks that many of their community tapped into to access strategies for school success, including hiring tutors for their children. Not having come from backgrounds where this was common, Nancy and Billy had been busy with their work and had not been aware that their children were not receiving the same extra resources that it seemed that many of their classmates had available to them. The "success frame" discussed by Lee and Zhou or the Asian American playbook discussed by Chin refers to a set of strategies that some Asian American communities, even those who are not well-resourced, invest in as a means for the attainment of success.[95] Nancy's experiences reinforce that she, like the rest of the Goon family, did not take part in this supplementary system. Instead, their approach reflected an earlier framing from the 1950s that Toy Len Goon and other Chinese and Japanese Americans exemplified, one based on hard work and good behavior, but working within the existing system, rather than creating alternative, supplemental ones. Ultimately, they decided not to get tutors for their children, as Nancy felt that "it just seemed like it would never end, like you would start supplementing the public schooling." "And it would just be school all the time," I interjected.[96]

Model Minority Cousins?

As noted above, Pamela Wang and Stephen Len were mentioned by many cousins as high-achieving and exemplary. Without any prompting from me, many cousins told me that their parents had compared them to these siblings, or when discussing the achievements of the family overall made note of them as examples of family members they considered more successful than themselves.[97] My individual interviews with Pam and Stephen elucidate how they each view the family legacy, their own achievements in relation to one another and the rest of the family, and those of their own children.

I interviewed Pam in two segments over a weekend, as she had scheduled a hike with friends, a regular part of her weekend routine. A busy doctor in private practice, she works hard and rarely takes time off. However, since her husband, Phil, passed away in 2020 at the age of fifty-five from an aggressive form of cancer, she has been finding solace in her Christian faith and in hiking with friends.

I asked Pam how Uncle Caroll being a physician affected her own decision to become a doctor. She remembers hearing about him when she was a young girl and being "in awe" of the fact that he was able to become a physician given his family background, noting that "especially in an Asian family, to be a physician, . . . that's just held in such high regard."[98]

While Pam felt a connection to Uncle Carroll as the only other physician in the family (until our cousin Sharon married Spiros, who is also a doctor), she did not feel that Uncle Carroll had directly influenced her to become a doctor because, like most of the family living on the East Coast, she did not have many opportunities to interact with him. He was the only doctor in Monticello, Utah, and was seldom able to take time off. However, Uncle Carroll had clearly made an impression on his siblings, who universally looked up to him, and these sentiments were passed on to the next generation. Pamela reflects, "I know that my father really admired him and thought so much about him and, you know, talked about him and in such . . . glowing, warm terms. And so, you know, I had that . . . impression that I had about Uncle Carroll. . . . Yeah, so I kind of felt like I was in, you know, nowhere near the level of him, but I was like, in this really special company."[99]

I shared with Pamela that other cousins had mentioned her as someone their parents held up as an example of success. I told her, "Your name has come up more than once, because you're a doctor." Pamela replied wryly, "Well, good thing that didn't get back to me, my head would be gigantic. None of that got back to me." She continues in a more serious tone,

> I just, I see the whole family as a unit being a giant success story, you know. When you, when you take it from, from the time of, of Ngin and see this success generation to generation, I mean, it's just, it keeps growing. And now we're talking about, you know, grandkids, great-grandkids and, and great-great-grandkids, you know, as, as the generations unfold, the success continues. . . . Yeah, I never, I never really thought about the family like that as little units, . . . but as more just, like, a lot of success stories within this larger, fascinating . . . story. So . . . the comparison thing is natural . . . in families.[100]

Pam's comment above shows that like other cousins, she views the family's success as stemming from the legacy created by our grandmother, who was able to overcome poverty and ensure that all her children received an education, without necessarily differentiating between different parts of the family. At the same time, she reflects that her parents never expressed to her directly how proud of her success they were. She observes,

> You know, my parents never—I mean, maybe it happened when they weren't around me and with the family, but they were typical Chinese parents— . . . I think they were proud of me. But it wasn't something they said to me a lot. Yeah, like, oh, you know, "Look where you are, you're doing so much, . . . you're a doctor, you have your kids, and you know, you have the stable [life]. . . . I get it, like, in a birthday card once a year: "Oh, we're so, you know, you are doing so well, Pam," . . . but they were very reserved about that . . . outward display [of] approval. And it's, it's like the typical thing where, you know, they love you, but they will never say it. . . . It's all understood, and they show it, but they won't typically say that to me verbally, and verbalize it.[101]

While Pam views her parents' conservative use of direct verbal praise as being consistent with Chinese/Chinese American parenting practices, she also knew from a young age that she was expected to go to college, and never questioned this path. She never felt pressure from her parents to become a doctor, but felt a calling from a young age, inspired by her pediatrician. She remembers being very ill with strep throat at the age of eight or nine, and going to her pediatrician's office. "He walked in, you know, he had his like, top hat. . . . And he had a cane, but he had no trouble walking. I think it was just like a fashion accessory." She was not necessarily responding to his bedside manner, as he was not "soft and fuzzy, warm." But she appreciated that "he knew how to make me better. . . . And he . . . exuded this confidence. . . . I remember that, and for me, I was like, 'Wow, I kind of want to be like that. I want to help people.'" She also remembers entering kindergarten not knowing how to speak English well, as she would speak Toisanese to her mother, a first-generation immigrant from Hong Kong, and her maternal grandmother, who lived with them. She surmises that perhaps she favored the sciences because in elementary school, "the language might still be a challenge. But knowing numbers and math, that's universal."[102]

Pam also recalls being motivated after hearing about the hardships that Toy Len Goon and her children endured. She remembers seeing how much her father and his siblings respected their mother for providing for them and creating opportunities for them, which put her "in awe" of her grandmother. She developed an appreciation of the privilege and opportunities that she had in comparison with her father's generation, who had to work in the laundry while going to school, and reflects, "So I felt, I wouldn't say an obligation to make something of myself, but certainly there was no excuse to not be the best that I could be at whatever I chose to do with myself. So, you know, going to school. Oh, it was really drilled into me that that was extremely important. And that the only way that Grandma's kids all became successful is they all went to school."[103]

She also observes that when our grandmother came to the United States and raised her children, that was a

> very different time to be Asian in America. And I think there were probably, from what I've read, many more barriers to success at that time than

> there are now. They didn't have the term . . . "model minority" back then, like they do now. You know, back then is when they were proving themselves. . . . Having known [Toy Len Goon's] journey with her family left a very deep impression on me as a child and definitely as I got older, and it basically kind of made me feel like there was no good reason why I couldn't be the best that I could be. I already had a good home, I had plenty of food, I had opportunities that, you know, my parents did not have and yet . . . they were able to be successful.[104]

The expectation to be "the best that I could be" given the resources she was provided at home echoes the theme of the cleansing of dirty laundry discussed at the beginning of the chapter, and the need to maintain or improve on this new status. It is consistent with what other cousins shared about how fortunate they were compared to their parents and grandparents, who had to work so hard to survive and were able to achieve upward mobility despite these challenges. But it also speaks to the pressure that this generation has placed on itself to maintain or surpass their parents' level of success, as well as the evolving nature of the model minority stereotype. Pam notes that she believed that the model minority stereotype was not present when our grandmother was raising our parents' generation, and in a sense she is correct. As discussed earlier, Toy Len Goon did not work within the "success frame" discussed by Lee and Zhou that has shaped more recent Asian American immigrants.[105] However, her children and grandchildren were exposed to evolving ideas of the model minority myth. I told Pam what I had learned through the process of researching my book and shared what historians had found that contextualized the rise of the model minority myth and ideas of Asian exceptionalism during the Cold War.

Pam's conception of the model minority was more consistent with Lee and Zhou's model, based on the idea of high achievement of Asian ethnic groups, including Indians, Chinese, and Koreans. As noted earlier, this model emerged in the wake of post-1965 immigration, which shifted the profile of the Asian immigrant community to encompass more educated and professional classes.[106] This coincided with the second and third generations of earlier immigrants such as the Goon family coming of age and becoming professionals themselves. While certainly not all Asian immigrants or children of immigrants were professionally successful, the attention focused on Asian immigrant success was pervasive in the news media in the 1980s, when the Goon grandchildren were coming of age, and clearly shaped their (and their parents') perceptions of what was considered successful.

Pam was also aware of some of the critiques of the model minority myth. She acknowledged that some Asian groups "get left out of it," though she also said that she knows many Vietnamese who "are incredible successes right now." However, she also acknowledges that while the model minority idea might be "flattering" to those given that label, she notes that it also "creates more division between groups" and puts pressure on Asians to succeed. She recognizes that not everyone will be able to do well in school:

> When you label a certain group like that, then I think people just kind of feel like, well, whoever's not in that group, obviously, is considered something else, than, you know, exceptional. . . . It's . . . unfortunate that we just have to have labels on groups, . . . and I think sometimes it backfires. There's such pressure on Asians to perform . . . , because there's a certain, you know, idea that all Asians are successful. When, Oh, guess what, my kid actually has . . . a normal-person average IQ and didn't get into Harvard. Oh, but they're considered a failure in the family, you know, and I think that is really terrible, because it's not good for all the Asians who don't make it to the top. . . . They could be considered just normal people, but because they're part of this model minority group, they're considered, you know, less than because they didn't achieve. So I think it can be very harmful for especially Asian students, like, in college, who aren't doing well, and to not feel like you can just be a normal person having normal struggles. . . . I'm sure it's a generational kind of a thing too, where there's a lot of pressure that Asian parents put on their children.[107]

She also acknowledges that Asians being compared to Blacks is problematic, observing that it is more than "an IQ issue." She points out that many Black people live in neighborhoods "where you're just hoping your kid doesn't get shot by accident." She also refers to the number of households run by "Black women raising children on their own in these sometimes very dangerous neighborhoods. . . . And then . . . there isn't food on the table."[108]

While Pam realizes that as a physician in a Chinese American family she may be seen as successful and as a model minority, she is also aware of the problems with this myth. Interestingly, in addition to not hearing direct praise from her parents due to what she understands to be a Chinese parenting style, she also felt that growing up, she was always compared to her brother, who is around four years younger, joking that he is "the golden child."

> I don't think my parents know that I feel that way. But it's, you know, he's definitely, he's really held up. And I know how they think about him. And you know, he's, they tell me all the time, he is so smart, and you work so hard. And maybe he's saying that on the other side to them, but about me, . . . but I hear about my brother all the time. So I . . . don't even tell my brother this. Because, you know, it doesn't really, it doesn't bother me. But it's just, it's . . . funny. It's really funny. So typical Chinese family. I just call him the golden child. He can't do any wrong. Not that he does do any wrong.[109]

Since her husband passed away, she has grown to appreciate her brother even further, as he has helped her with several matters that her husband normally would have taken care of and was able to explain them clearly and with ease. However, despite her appreciation of her brother's intellect, she notes that he has mentioned to her that his wife's family all have PhDs, and that he is the only one without one. "So my impression was he almost felt a little bit, like, less accomplished, because he just has an MBA."[110]

Echoing erin Khuê Ninh's observation that the model minority idea is ever-present in Asian American families, Pam's experiences show that even someone who is seen as epitomizing model minority success by others in the family does not feel like a model minority, nor does she agree with the implications of the stereotype. She recognized that even her brother, whom she jokingly refers to as "the golden child," may feel less accomplished in relation to his wife and her family, all of whom have PhDs. Her story also illustrates how the model minority idea is an amorphous, ever-changing, and relational idea that can make people feel like they are never fully living up to its standards of success.

Coincidentally, I had interviewed Stephen the day before I had talked with Pam. Our conversation, held over the phone while he attended his youngest daughter's softball game, spanned several topics that touched upon and linked together the family story, the model minority myth, the pressure to achieve that many Asian Americans may feel, and racism and discrimination. While he saw our grandmother's award as a form of validation for his family's Americanness, he is also critical of the model minority stereotype, particularly when it comes to the pressure it puts on young Asian Americans to excel in school and attend a prestigious university.

Stephen is the youngest of the Goon cousins. He and his wife, Minki, have three daughters. The oldest, Milani, attended MIT, and the second, Kasey, attended Columbia. However, Stephen is very adamant about not putting pressure on his youngest daughter, Sabina, who was a freshman in high school at the time of the interview, to go to an Ivy League school. Even though both he and his wife went to Cornell, it was not their plan to have his daughters attend Ivy League schools. Milani decided to apply to MIT her senior year, at the suggestion of someone who thought she would have a good chance of getting in, and Kasey really liked Columbia as a school, but "that was never her goal, just to get into an Ivy League. In fact, that was the only [Ivy] she applied to."[111]

He reflects that for their youngest daughter, "we're trying to remind her that . . . the bar is kind of unreasonably high. And that she, you know, that's not something that she needs to reach for." Regarding the model minority myth, Stephen observes that "it's a crazy amount of pressure that you, unless you achieve . . . a certain level, then, I mean, it kind of implies that the only reason why you would not be able to achieve is because of your own personal failures." He feels that it's implied that "all Chinese people have it in them to, you know, well, to get a PhD."

The family has traveled to India, where his wife's family is from, and are aware "what her family has left behind." His daughters are also aware and proud of their paternal great-grandmother's Mother of the Year award. He has shared news stories about the laundry with them, and anecdotes that his own father had related to him about living under conditions of relative scarcity. As in the case of other cousins, the Mother of the Year story impacted Stephen growing up. He remembers hearing about our grandmother's award starting when he was quite young, sometimes thumbing through a scrapbook full of news clippings covering her award.[112]

He observed that he grew up in very "matriarchal" families and thinks it's important to make his daughters aware of the hard work that both sides of their family put into where they are now. But he also realizes that "to say that . . . you know, that unless you achieve that same level of success, . . . you failed, I think is dangerous. It's a dangerous line." Ultimately, he sees the hard work of previous generations as having created opportunities for the next generations to be "able to pursue something that you're really interested in" and not necessarily solely defined in terms of financial gain. As an example, he cites his niece Alyssa, Pam's daughter, who has followed her passion for violin, composing, and conducting and created the Boston Festival Orchestra.[113]

Concluding Thoughts

My interviews show that the Goon family's positioning in relation to the model minority myth framed internalized expectations of success for my generation and shaped assessments of their own trajectories in relation to those they believed to be more accomplished, including other family members. But they also expressed resistance to the Tiger Mom idea of perfection and shared that they sometimes felt they didn't measure up to siblings or cousins against whom they were implicitly or explicitly compared.

They saw Toy Len Goon's legacy as having been filtered through their parents, who exercised a diversity of approaches, with some of the Goon siblings seeming to emphasize education—sometimes in particular disciplines—more than others. Toy Len Goon's grandchildren felt that they were expected to continue the success of their parents through hard work and education, a formula that had worked well for that generation. For most of Toy Len Goon's grandchildren, knowledge of the family's origins and struggles has created a legacy that brings the family pride and that has given them opportunities that should not be wasted. They have had to navigate the implications of this legacy in relation to pervasive ideas about Asian Americans as model minorities—ideas that have continued to evolve since the early 1950s.

Conclusion

Closing the Laundry, Later Life, and Legacy

The Unveiling

On October 3, 2021, I attended the unveiling of a historic marker at the site of the Goon laundry at 615 Forest Avenue in Portland. Gary Libby, who had been the driving force behind preserving the community's history, had spoken with the current owners of the building, who had heard about Toy Len Goon's story and were happy to have a historic marker placed on their property. The storefront on the first floor that had housed the laundry was empty, ever since Green Gnome Holistics Medical Marijuana Dispensary had closed its doors. Gary, working in his capacity as treasurer of the Chinese American Friendship Association of Maine (CAFAM), had been planning the event for months, working to secure local city councilors and representatives from Senator Susan Collins's office, as well as representatives from CAFAM and the Maine Historical Society to speak at the event.

My parents and I arrived to find Gary, my Aunt Doris, and some of my cousins standing on the sidewalk. Though there were still a few minutes before the event was supposed to start, Gary expressed concern that few people would attend. However, soon more people began arriving, including cousins Sharon and Ted (two of Albert's children) with some of their children, cousin Roseanne (daughter of Dick), and Amy Guen, for whom the crowd parted to clear her path, accompanied by her daughter Terry and son Tim. Members of CAFAM, representatives from the city council, and the news media were also in attendance. However, several guests we had not expected also showed up after reading about the unveiling in the *Portland Press Herald*, and soon a large crowd had gathered, filling the sidewalk in front of the building. These included some local Chinese American families,

Jacqueline Field, who had written the article on Toy Len Goon's mud silk, and (non-Chinese) former schoolmates of Janet and Doris, who had fond memories of the family. The program consisted of speeches given by Gary, followed by remarks by the president of CAFAM, the building's owners, members of the Goon family (Doris, Janet, and me), a short speech by Jonathan Sun, the director general of the Republic of China Boston consulate, the reading of a proclamation by a Portland City Council member, the introduction of a representative from the Maine Historical Society, and finally remarks from a member of the local Asian community.

The plaque read,

Site of the Home and Laundry
Of Toy Len Goon
The 1952 Maine and American
Mother of the Year
And her family
Building purchased for $5,000 in 1936
With money saved by Toy Len Goon
Sold in 1956
Chinese and American Friendship Association of Maine

A few months earlier, Gary had met with me, my parents, and Doris for lunch and had shared with us his proposed wording for the plaque:

Site of the Home and Laundry
of Toy Len Goon
The 1952 Maine and
American
Mother of the Year
and Her Family
Building Owned from 1936 to 1952
Sponsored by the Chinese and American
Friendship Association of Maine

The family thought it was important to include that the property was purchased with money saved by Toy Len Goon, and to include the purchase price of $5,000, since it was impressive that a Chinese immigrant woman had the foresight to buy such a large property. Notably, neither version mentioned Dogan Goon. Gary patiently complied, asking the company to make yet another revision to the draft text for the plaque.

For most in attendance, commemorating Toy Len Goon's accomplishments was a way of celebrating the hard work that led to immigrant success and upward mobility, enabled by US democracy and freedom. These sentiments were also reflected in media coverage of the event, with one comment in a September 30, 2021, *Portland Press Herald* article noting, "People are just people. How wonderful! Are we as accepting now of hard working people?" More specifically, it was a testament to the resourcefulness of an uneducated Chinese woman, and the resultant achievements of her American children.[1]

At the luncheon that followed, hosted at the Italian Heritage Center in Portland by my Aunt Doris (with contributions by my Uncle Arthur), I sat with Doris and the owners of the building. At one point, the conversation turned to politics, with both my aunt and the building owners lamenting that things have become so uncivil and asking why everyone couldn't just get along like we used to. During a previous conversation with me, Doris had talked about how her mother had refused welfare, and the family had worked together to keep the laundry running, with the high school principal helping the older boys get scholarships to attend college and how "those were the good old days" when things were less uncivil and less "driven by politics."

While everybody there was present to celebrate Toy Len Goon, those in attendance also had varying relationships to and understandings of her legacy and its implications. Hearing my aunt and the current owners of 615 Forest Avenue talk, I realized that Toy Len's story continued to have broad appeal to people at various ends of the political spectrum. The fact that her story can be read in multiple ways can serve as a Rorschach test for how people think of the United States and the opportunities it provides. For some, it might represent the greatness of America during the "good old days," when Chinese Americans as exemplary minorities worked hard to get ahead, in contrast to other immigrants who were not putting in the hard work. This perspective views the United States as a meritocracy where the "American Dream" can be achieved through assimilation, good behavior, and hard work, implying that those who do not succeed are not working hard enough. For others, her story illustrated the systemic discriminatory and oppressive legal regimes that Chinese Americans were forced to navigate and under which they labored and lived marginal lives. Many held views somewhere between.

The international political implications of her story were also interpreted differently. For example, for Gary Libby, inviting members of the Taiwanese consulate to speak was consistent with Toy Len Goon's interactions with Wellington Koo, the Taiwanese ambassador, in 1952 during her visit to Washington, DC. The Taiwanese consulate representatives, Consul General Jonathan Sun and First Secretary Eric Chao, no doubt saw this as an opportunity to honor this extraordinary Chinese woman who had previously been recognized by his government but seemed unaware of his government's historical involvement in bringing her story to a global political stage. Gary offered to help draft their remarks and asked me for ideas. I sent him the translations of the documents from the Taiwanese Legislative Yuan and Control Yuan and an article about the long life character given to her by the Taiwanese government when she was eighty, all of which had been originally provided to me by Amy Guen. I found the circularity of this dynamic to be interesting, with her story being told back to Taiwanese government representatives via materials provided by Toy Len Goon's family, with the help of an Irish American lawyer from Maine.

Gary had mentioned to me and Doris in an email during the planning process that members of the "Chinese Consulate" were going to be invited. I had responded to him and cc'd Doris to ask whether he meant the Taipei Economic and Cultural Office, as I did not see a PRC China consulate listed for Boston. Gary responded, "If the Taiwan Consulate won't attend, I'd reach out to the People's Republic Consulate in NYC." Doris replied, asking for clarification about whether the latter represented "Communist China," to which Gary responded that "the Peoples' Republic is Communist China which is where Toy Len came from." Doris asserts, "Regarding the PRC, I personally would not want them invited to the unveiling. Chang [*sic*] Kai Shek was the war lord overseer of China when Father left, later followed by Mother in the '20s. Their stories have nothing to do with Communist China and I am happy to keep it that way."[2]

For Gary, the significance of the PRC stemmed from its place as the territorial homeland of Dogan and Toy Len Goon. Doris felt strongly that her family story should not be associated with the Communist Chinese regime. Her opinion, likely shared by many, is not surprising, considering that she had grown up during the Cold War, and that her family's story had been employed to tout the strengths of US democracy in contrast to Chinese communism. There had also been some concern expressed by other relatives that the laundry site had most recently served as a marijuana dispensary, something that the family might not want to be associated with, though I pointed out that it had moved location, was for medical marijuana, and required a prescription.

Gary had asked me to focus my comments on the historical context and significance of my grandmother's award. I addressed the themes that I have discussed throughout this book: how Chinese Exclusion had shaped the immigration stories of Dogan and Toy Len Goon, how the Chinese laundry was an institution created out of the social marginalization of Chinese immigrants, how Toy Len Goon's story, which encapsulated mothering and domesticity, was part of broader efforts for the containment of communism in Asia, and how Clara Soule had demonstrated her awareness of the implications of Toy Len Goon's award for propaganda in a *Portland Press Herald* article. I concluded by saying that there was much more to Toy Len Goon's story than what was presented in the media.

I wondered what my fellow speakers and the audience thought about what I had shared, particularly the representatives from Taiwan, as I had highlighted the political implications of my grandmother's story in the context of the Cold War that directly involved Taiwan. I was also concerned about what my relatives thought, since many were invested in the version of Toy Len Goon's story focusing on hard work, good behavior, and upward mobility—on the "American Dream," and not a discussion of how Toy Len's story brings out complexities of that idea. However, other speakers discussed her hard work and the subsequent success of her children, so I elaborated on the context for her award as Gary had asked me to do.

Leaving the Laundry

Despite the fact that 615 Forest Avenue had not been a laundry for seventy years, the unveiling represented an opportunity to cement Toy Len

Goon's place in the history of Portland, to not only commemorate what she achieved, but also ensure that her story would continue to be shared publicly in the form of the plaque affixed to the building that she was so proud to have purchased, and in the media coverage of the event.

In 1952, at the age of fifty-seven, Toy Len Goon closed the laundry and moved to Lynn, Massachusetts, to live on the second floor of the house on Chatham Street above her son Richard and his family. Her children were on their own, and establishing their families, and there was nobody left to help with laundry work, so it was time for her to retire. Only Janet, the youngest and a high school student, remained with her, with Arthur moving to Chatham Street after getting out of the Navy, and Doris eventually moving in after a brief marriage.

Though she left the laundry behind, it remained a symbol of her legacy in Portland. As I learned from Gary Libby, while there were around thirty Chinese laundries in Portland around World War I, with all but the Goon laundry and one other located on the Portland peninsula, the laundries started to close after the end of World War II, with the Goon laundry being one of the last to shut its doors. The very last to close was Chin Kow's laundry, with his retirement in 1966 at age eighty-three.[3]

However, while 615 Forest Avenue remained a significant symbol of her legacy, and thus remained important to her children, grandchildren, and great-grandchildren, the rest of her life represented a new and exciting phase as she saw her children's families and careers grow. These memories were grounded in interactions at the house on Chatham Street and later in the condominium she shared with daughter Doris in Swampscott. Toy Len Goon remained the center of the family, entertaining every weekend. She helped with childcare when her grandchildren were young. She hosted weekend dinners, serving hot dogs and baked beans on Saturday, usually for Richard Len's family, who lived downstairs, and cooking Chinese food for other families on Sundays. The grandchildren who lived in proximity to her each have fond memories of visiting her at Chatham Street. Richard and Helen's four daughters remember going upstairs to visit her, oftentimes in hopes that she would offer them something from her candy jar. The older grandchildren also remember having gatherings at her place, watching *The Wizard of Oz* while she served them snacks. She made it her business to continue nurturing her growing family by helping care for her grandchildren and took great pride in their accomplishments. She kept close track of what each of her children and grandchildren were doing in their careers and in school, including details about how much they made and what grades they were receiving.

Special Moments

Her grandchildren each recalled special moments that they had with their grandmother, sometimes embodied in memories of aspects of her physical being—playing with the skin on her soft and wrinkled hands, how she stood with her hand clasped behind her back, her long gray hair kept neatly in a bun, and her infectious laugh. They also cherish memories of particular habits and behaviors that spoke to her personality and the strength of her character—her sense of humor, how mentally sharp she remained even in her later years, and as discussed in the previous chapter, how she was able to understand and appreciate the strengths of each grandchild. Their recollections bring to light a more humanized version of Toy Len Goon beyond the one-dimensional hardworking mother stereotype that was encapsulated by the model minority myth promulgated by the media. They also allow us to see a different side of her from that reported by her children in their memories of growing up, when she was totally consumed with work and raising her family. In sharing their fond memories of her with me, her grandchildren described her adaptability, open-mindedness, and resourcefulness with great respect and admiration. They did not see her as infallible, but rather as a human being with multiple dimensions. They also characterized her as a "control freak" with a wonderful sense of humor, a busybody who knew what everyone was up to, and a matriarch who could "rule with just a look."

Rose, daughter of Richard and Helen, had many fond memories of her grandmother, having spent her early years living downstairs from her in the three-story Chatham Street residence in Lynn, Massachusetts. She had asked for the questions I planned to ask in the interview and sent me detailed responses to each prior to our interview, eloquently describing her memories of Toy Len Goon's cooking and time spent with her:

> "Nginny! Nginny!" I would call as I stomped up the back staircase up to her landing. There was a child height doorbell right in the middle of

> her back door. Ring ring ring. Knock knock knock. Most of the time she would come open the door and let me in. On a very few occasions there was no answer. At a very young age, I knew Ngin loved me so much that if she didn't answer the door, she was either very busy doing something important, or she wasn't home.
>
> One of my favorite memories is staying overnight in the twin bed that was pushed up against Ngin's twin bed. With eight children, she learned that if she used safety pins to pin the sheets and blankets together where they folded over at the top after she put clean sheets on the bed, it was a lot easier to make the bed. I loved the peace and order of Ngin's home. . . .
>
> We would both go to bed at the same time even though I was so young and it must have been early, but we would talk about things. At some point, Ngin would say that we should go to sleep now, no more talking. Being the "good girl" that I was, I would say okay and stop talking. And here's the funny part: every time, after a pause, Ngin would say, "What do you want for breakfast?" and we would both laugh and laugh and plan what she was going to make me for breakfast.[4]

Rose's sister Janine chose to share with me memories from Toy Len Goon's later life. As mentioned in the previous chapter, Janine lived with her when Toy Len Goon was one hundred years old and Janine was in her thirties, finishing her teaching degree. Janine shared vivid memories of her time with her Ngin. Unlike her older sister Rose, she could not speak Toisanese, but could communicate easily with her grandmother.

One moment that stood out to Janine was when she asked Toy Len Goon about her mother in China.

> I don't know how it came up. And . . . her eyes got watery. And she said I . . . Oh, it was just heart wrenching. She was one hundred years old. . . . And "I miss my, I miss my mommy. I still miss, I'm still missing her. After all these years. I'm still missing my Mommy."[5]

Janine admired her Ngin's wisdom, despite her lack of formal education, including the ability to read and write. She remembers how particular she was, but that this specificity came from having observed and analyzed the world around her:

> She was sitting in her golden chair. And she would look out the window, and across the street was Star Market. "Go to Star Market and buy me some apples." And she was so, I don't know if you know how particular she was, oh, everything. Everything had to be big. She was amazing. "Go back, buy me some apples. Janine, make sure they have the speckles on the top where the stem is. Because that means it will be crunchy." . . . No, she can't read. You can't write. She has broken English. She watches the news. But she can look out at the trees and know what season it is. And this is the time of year to buy the apples. . . .
>
> Well, imagine, she . . . couldn't read. . . . All she did was sit there thinking, analyzing, observing everything . . . and in conversation, and she would listen to the news, but I don't think the news gave you that information. I think she was just so observant and then she retained everything year to year. She would sit there just thinking about . . . different things. But she was so precise, and everything . . . was intentional. Everything, her movements, everything.[6]

Janine also remembers how particular she was about her hair, clothing, and overall appearance, describing her in a joking manner as "very vain," with her hair "perfectly brushed in a bun with a net over the bun," using a headband to keep the hair off of her face when she grew older and had trouble lifting her arms to do her hair. She also remembers how "nice and neat" her clothing was, including the precision with which she tied her apron. "She thought of everything, and what she should do for everything." When it was time for dessert, she would tell Janine to get an apple or orange to cut up "and . . . everything was just so precise."[7]

Janine recalls being surprised when she took her to a doctor's appointment and she wanted to be weighed, wondering why she was so insistent on knowing how much she weighed. Janine shared with me that when they would have dinner together, there would be several dishes served family-style, with a serving spoon in each dish. However, Janine had not grown up using serving utensils and just dug her fork into each dish, recalling, "After a couple of days, she was sitting there and I was getting the look." Janine, with great affection, said, "Of course she was a control freak. You know." She described how "she would sit there and she would watch your every move, you know, demurely. And then if she had something to say about it, you could see that it was coming by the look on her face."[8]

Several cousins asked me to ask Uncle Albert's children about the "English muffin story," so when I interviewed one of his daughters, Nancy Hunt, I took the opportunity to ask her about the incident. She recalls that her father had spent a few days at his mother's condominium because Aunt Doris was traveling and came home exhausted. While he had enjoyed spending time with his mother—Nancy assumes that she was probably cooking for him and taking care of many of her own needs—he relayed that he was tired because Toy Len Goon "didn't miss a thing." She had wanted an English muffin, so Albert had made one for each of them in the toaster oven and then got out the plates and served them. He remembers her looking down at her plate but not saying anything. Finally, she told him that he had given her two pieces from two different muffins instead of a top and a bottom from one. In relaying this story, he made it clear how amusing he found it that she was "so on top of everything, . . . sharp as a tack." Nancy remembers thinking that she and the rest of the family "thought it was pretty funny, because I can only imagine him, you know, you almost can't stay in front of her, you know, you try to do everything right."[9]

Pam remembers being struck by how Toy Len Goon was always so "ladylike," always wearing a housecoat or housedress and pantyhose, and never pants. She also remembers that she always wore her long hair up in a bun, and "always looked very proper," joking that during our interview she was wearing sweatpants and had her hair in a ponytail, and that our grandmother would be "horrified" if she had to dress like that. She also remembers her "famous laugh," noting that she "can actually conjure that memory of her laugh . . . very easily," calling it "this pure joy laugh . . . and you just had to laugh at her laugh. . . . It was just infectious."[10]

Pamela also marveled at how Toy Len Goon knew what each of her grandchildren was doing, including whom they were dating, and who their children were, exclaiming, "I mean, I couldn't keep track of all that." Describing her as "gentle but strong," she recalls being frustrated at not being able to communicate with her due to Toy Len Goon's hearing impairment. Though she had hearing aids, they would not always function correctly, and her famous laugh would often set off a feedback loop of sound that would result in a high-pitched ringing audible to those around her.[11]

Pam also remembers Toy Len Goon's "perfect" skin, with no wrinkles. She describes it as "smooth . . . and like alabaster" and remembers how soft her hands were. I shared that another cousin had told me they liked playing with the skin on our grandmother's hands, and Pam recalled that she did that also, trying to create a tent with the loose skin on her hands. Surprised that our grandmother would be okay with her grandchildren playing with her skin, I asked whether she seemed to mind, noting that I would not have dared to try that. Pam remembers her just laughing when Pam would play with the wrinkles on her hand.[12]

Though he is the youngest of the Goon grandchildren, Stephen still has special memories of our grandmother. He remembers that she would sometimes stay with them for a few weeks during the summer, and that he "thought it was cute" when she would converse with his maternal grandmother in Toisanese "because they could speak totally, entirely comfortable with each other."[13]

He recalls that she really enjoyed a chicken dish that his mother would cook that had whiskey in it, and they brought it over when they visited her. "She ate a lot of it, and I think she was getting a little tipsy off of it because her face was all red. And then she was getting very giggly and she was like laughing and laughing and laughing, and we're . . . kind of getting worried, like, oh, what's going on?"[14]

When he was in college and Toy Len Goon was in her nineties, he visited her and cooked a meal for her. On the menu were lemon rolls and salmon napoleon (salmon layered with pastry with shallot butter and wine sauce on top), and she was very appreciative. Stephen reflects that he felt "no pressure or anything" and that she would have been happy even if he had made her spaghetti. He reflected that "she was always just very, very supportive. And you know, regardless of who you are and what you did, . . . she was . . . pretty good at . . . seeing people's individual strengths."[15]

That she enjoyed the gourmet meal that Stephen cooked also illustrated her diverse tastes in food. Stephen reflects that "she didn't just like Chinese food, . . . which is interesting for that generation," observing that many of his mother's siblings who are from China/Hong Kong only liked Chinese food. He notes that his father would tell him that his Ngin knew how to make excellent Boston baked beans, as evidence that "she was quite Americanized."[16]

Stephen shared a couple of other incidents that he found to be both memorable and humorous. One, which he heard from our Aunt Doris, involved Toy Len Goon sitting at the dinner table when she was in her nineties and commenting that she had never really liked chicken and asking whether they had to continue eating it. According to Stephen, Doris said she replied that she should have told them a long time ago and that nobody was making her eat chicken. Another "distinct" memory was from when he was around seven years old and she was visiting him, seated at the dinner table in the kitchen near the front door. Stephen had decided to try to play a trick on her by taking a slice of American cheese that was wrapped in clear plastic and pretending to accidentally drop it on the floor. He remembers her looking at the cheese and saying in Chinese that she could see the wrapper, that "you think I can't see anything, but my eyes are really good."[17]

Stephen also remembers that during family gatherings, everybody would rush to the front door when our grandmother arrived to say hello, "like the queen" had arrived, and he saw this as a sign of the great respect the family had for her.[18]

Sense of Humor

Many other family members commented on Toy Len Goon's sense of humor. While being in the kitchen as she watched your every move may have been intimidating, Janine also recalls one time when Toy Len Goon asked her to help reach a dish that was up high, then breaking into laughter, giggling, "I shrunk three inches." I heard many family members tell me they had heard stories growing up about how, when he was a teen, Toy Len Goon's son Edward would make fun of her strict manner by holding a comb above his mouth to mimic Hitler's mustache. Even though he was challenging her authority, she apparently found his actions to be humorous, so while her children had described her as a disciplinarian, this example also highlighted the fact that she was often able to see the humor in the situation.[19]

Open-Mindedness

Other family lore spoke to her adaptability and open-mindedness, including accepting that her oldest son, Caroll, married a non-Chinese woman. Many of her granddaughters recounted stories about how open she had been when meeting their non-Chinese boyfriends.

Despite never becoming fluent in English, Toy Len Goon certainly embraced parts of American culture. Her passion for ice hockey—she was an avid Bruins fan—was well known among family members, some of whom had made the mistake of calling or visiting during a hockey game, only to be ignored as she sat engrossed in the game. Many cousins, aunts, and uncles recalled times when they were visiting her at the condominium that she and Aunt Doris shared. As soon as the Bruins hockey game started, Aunt Doris would go turn on the television and everyone would watch the game. While she cherished visits from her family, she had clear priorities, rarely missing a hockey game or her favorite soap opera.

Creating Family Histories for the New Generation

My interviews reveal that though they believe that they share a set of memories about her that have been passed down and shared amongst them, Toy Len Goon's children, grandchildren, and great-grandchildren each held pieces of knowledge and fragments of memory based on their specific interactions with her, as well as their interpretations of these interactions. They each also navigated their own paths in connecting to the family's past, including to China and Chinese cultural traditions. Each cousin had their own understanding of family history, often reinforced by family memory books or other versions of her story their parents shared with them. Thus, there is not one family history but rather multiple narratives about family history that her descendants have created by piecing together memories, artifacts, and stories. These are all part of what they believe to be their shared understanding of the immigration story and of their parents' and grandparents' upbringings. The research insights I shared with each cousin as I engaged in each interview resulted in an iterative process in which they reflected upon their own recollections in the broader context of family historical knowledge that I had provided them.

My interviews also revealed that many felt they had tenuous connections to Chinese culture and to the family history and legacy, which they saw as being manifested in language, knowledge of the family history and traditions, and other practices that they deemed "Chinese." What they felt to be tenuous claims to Chineseness and the family legacy were strengthened and reassembled out of these fragments of memories, embodied and rooted in specific objects and foods that they associated with their grandmother. Despite many grandchildren feeling that they were distanced from knowledge about family history and Chinese traditions, many saw cooking her recipes for both Chinese and American food as a way of honoring her memory and crafting relationships to the family legacy. They continued cooking her special recipes, sometimes gathering with other relatives to cook *haam tee*, fried dumplings that required the laborious process of kneading the dough until it became smooth and elastic, and then filling them with pork, onion, and shrimp or brown sugar muffins (*faat go tee*) together, or making Chinese recipes for their own families.[20]

Linda, daughter of Josephine, remembers her grandmother making gizzards, periwinkles sauteed with ginger and soy sauce, bitter melon with beef, beef peppersteak, steamed fish, *nguk beng* (H) (steamed minced pork) and egg fu yung, and shrimp with lobster sauce. She remembers how "gentle" she was when she stirred her melon soup, and the meat was always perfect. She views cooking as part of her grandmother's legacy, and she carried on the family tradition by going into her children's school for Chinese New Year and sharing her cooking. Both of her children enjoy Chinese food. Like her mother and grandmother, she continues to mince black beans, ginger, and garlic and store them in big jars for use in her cooking. She sees food as an important way of spending time with friends—she invites them over and cooks Chinese food for them and sees it as "part of me being put on the table." She always makes sure to put a variety of meats and fish on the table and fill the bowls with rice. But she also cherishes her grandmother's meatloaf recipe, made with ground beef, peppers, and bread. In my interview with Josephine, Linda's mother, she told me that she had learned that recipe at school but that it was always more delicious when Toy Len Goon cooked it.[21]

In addition to carrying on food-based traditions, many cousins I spoke with treasured specific objects associated with Toy Len Goon. In my cousin Ilene's interview with me, she showed me a familiar candy jar, the one her grandchildren remember eyeing when they visited. My cousin Marie excitedly showed me a traditional silk hand-stitched baby carrier that our grandmother had brought over with her from China. Other cousins kept items given to her by various parties as part of her Mother of the Year honors. She had also left specific items from those festivities to each of her children in her will.[22]

Language

Though Toy Len Goon could understand quite a bit of English, many cousins experienced their lack of proficiency in Chinese as a barrier to communication with their grandmother. A consistent theme expressed by many was that they wished they had been able to learn to speak or had retained the ability to speak Toisanese. Because her Toisanese-speaking maternal grandmother sometimes lived with her, Pam primarily spoke Toisanese prior to entering kindergarten. However, she now has "no memory" of herself speaking Chinese, though she remembers for a brief time being able to understand what people were saying in Toisanese. She laments,

> I lost grasp of the language really quickly, unfortunately. And I really tried so hard to relearn it. I remember, during the summers, for a few years, I would try to have my mom teach me some Chinese because . . . it really bothered me that I could not communicate with my grandmothers. But . . . it never really took off and I never had a grasp. And yeah, that's probably one of my greatest regrets in my life is not holding on to that ability to speak Chinese. I mean, I don't care about being able to read it or anything like that. But yeah, . . . I wish I could speak it fluently.[23]

I shared with Pam that I had heard from other cousins who also lost the ability to speak Chinese. Janine had told me that when she got to kindergarten, her teachers told her parents to stop speaking to her in Chinese because she was having trouble transitioning to English. In contrast, Roseanne, Janine's older sister and the oldest cousin in the Goon family, had adapted to public school while also retaining her Chinese-language abilities, making her the only cousin able to communicate with our grandmother in her native tongue. Connie, the second-oldest cousin, could also speak Toisanese before she started school. She remembers trying to speak with the neighborhood kids as they played outside in the street and realizing they could not understand her. She learned to speak with them in English and eventually forgot her Chinese.

Leo's recollections of being told by Chinese immigrant workers in his maternal uncles' restaurants that he was not Chinese because he could not speak the language continued to shape when and where he tried to speak Chinese. He described trying to speak Chinese as "traumatic for me," resulting in "different mental blocks of panic" when he would go up to a meat counter in Chinatown and order a pound of meat. He admits to feeling "this pressure": if he hears restaurant workers speaking with his mother in Cantonese or Toisanese/Hoisanese (the dialect spoken by Toy Len Goon and his mother's family and historically spoken in US Chinatowns), he feels that he should try to speak the "little bit of Toisanese" he knows. He did speak some Toisanese as a young child, but eventually realized that it is okay to try to speak to them in English or Mandarin. He had learned some Mandarin while attending Chinese school growing up and has continued to work on it over the last ten years that he has been with his wife, who is from Taiwan and is a native Mandarin speaker.[24]

However, despite their lack of fluency in Toisanese, Toy Len Goon's grandchildren felt that they had internalized messages from their grandmother about the importance of being devoted to family and working hard. Their understandings and interpretations of family history were constructed through making food and sharing stories and memories honoring their grandmother. These ideas shifted over time as they formed their own families and reflected on both their parents' and the next generation's success, and as they gained insight into familial emotional patterns and pressures.

Toy Len Goon passed away at home in Swampscott in 1993 at the age of 101. She was survived by her eight children, twenty-four grandchildren, and a growing group of great-grandchildren. Like many Asian Americans impacted by the model minority myth, Toy Len Goon's descendants continue to try to make sense of what this idea (along with their family legacy, which is enmeshed in this myth) means for themselves. They do this in relation to their own life experiences, perceived expectations, and reflections on their own parenting practices, amidst changing meanings of the myth. Their experiences reflect a dynamic between their own lived experiences and the discourses that continue to support the model minority myth—circulating not only within society but also within the family—that Chinese/Asian Americans are smarter, harder-working, and have strong family systems.

Aware that Toy Len Goon's generation came to the United States with very little and worked hard so that their children could achieve middle-class status, her grandchildren received a variety of messages about what was expected of their generation. The laundry, and laundry work, becomes a character in this story, standing in as metaphor for, and a vehicle by which, a Chinese immigrant family was able to be cleansed and emerge as successful Americans. However, while the message that Toy Len Goon gave to her children about the importance of hard work and participating in US educational institutions as the key to fitting in was clear, what were the expectations for her grandchildren? My interviews show that many of them resisted being identified as model minorities while being shaped by the myth and family legacy. These ideas were entangled with their views on what it means to be American, and also what it means to be Chinese in the United States, ideas that continue to shift in the context of discourses about immigration, race, and more recent attention called toward anti-Asian hate in the United States in the context of COVID-19 and the Trump administration.

Ultimately, a family that was held up as one of the early national examples of a model minority found itself grappling with the aftereffects of this evolving myth. Because it is a myth, it is impossible to pin down and therefore takes many forms in the imaginations of those it is imposed upon, and those who internalized it. As the family story is narrated and re-narrated to family members and others, the myth both changes and solidifies aspects of the story and its perceived significance.

My spatial analysis of the Chinese laundry serves as a critique of the ways that American and Chinese spaces and cultures have been seen in dichotomous ways within US discourses of citizenship and belonging. Chineseness was historically equated with exclusion from citizenship. However, in the 1950s, Chinese went from being unassimilable to assimilated, from bachelor society to families. That chapter discusses how sociologist Paul Siu, following Robert Park's assimilation cycle, saw Chinese as crossing from Chinese spaces to American ones through the process of assimilation. It also argues that the mixed-use space of the laundry and the social relations created around the laundry created a cultural contact zone that reflected the multistranded social relationships both within and outside the family that were defined and created through their everyday interactions.[25] This spatial argument moves away from viewing Chinese and American cultures as demarcated, essentialized wholes to consider a multiplicity of experiences, social relations, and identities that occurred both within and between them.

Toy Len Goon and her family were part of local and transnational Chinese immigrant networks that were created in part out of the necessity to band together in the context of a discriminatory US society. Therefore, while she was celebrated as a model US mother—an assimilated, industrious widow and homemaker—her story is much more than this. Her experiences speak back against stereotypes of gender and domesticity and the model minority myth. Yes, she was exemplary, but she was not Americanized and assimilated in the ways that the media portrayed her as being. While the Goon family in many ways bought into these ideas of Americanization and assimilation, Toy Len Goon and to varying extents her children have also remained connected to Chinese and Chinese American kinship and community networks and practices and conceptions of Chinese American tradition and heritage. These complex and multilayered connections to both mainstream US culture and Chinese American culture (which are not clearly demarcated) complicate the overly simplified ideas of what it means to be American and Chinese upon which ideas of assimilation and the model minority rely.

The Goon-Chin family reunion was held on June 24, 2023, at the Marriott Courtyard Boston in Norwood, Massachusetts. Four generations of Toy Len Goon and Ming Mow Chin's descendants gathered, linked by the marriages of three of Toy Len Goon's sons and three of Ming Mow Chin's daughters. As part of the festivities for the day, my cousin Terry, daughter of Amy Guen, presented documents focusing on the Chin family history and immigration, and I was asked to talk about

Toy Len Goon's story. I adapted slides from a presentation I had done for the Maine Historical Society two years earlier, but due to lack of time, I was unable to present the whole slide deck. I decided to present the following questions on a slide, noting that I only had time to answer the first three questions, and that they would have to wait for the book to learn more about the rest:

1. How did Dogan and Toy Len Goon end up in Portland, Maine, during Chinese Exclusion?
2. Why did they run a laundry?
3. What is the US Mother of the Year Award and how did Toy Len Goon become US Mother of the Year?
4. What was the significance of her award? What did her award mean to her, her family, and the American public?
5. How does her story relate to the model minority myth?
6. What other ways can her story be told? What is left out of the public narratives?

After the presentation, many people came up to me saying they enjoyed what I had shared with them, which included a discussion of how Dogan Goon ended up in the United States during Chinese Exclusion, and how he was able to go back to China to marry Toy Len Goon. I also talked about how the laundry that they ran was a product of the marginalization of Chinese immigrants, and how hard the family worked, particularly after Dogan became ill and passed away. I then talked about Toy Len Goon winning the US Mother of the Year award, and included an audio clip from the interview I did with her when she was one hundred years old, in which she talks about how people liked her children, after which some teared up at hearing her voice. I didn't get into the last three questions, and some people said they were interested in finding out more. However, over the course of the day, as I spent time with my aunts, cousins, cousins' children, and cousins' grandchildren and the family friends who had gathered for the occasion, I realized that the question of what her story and legacy mean to the family is still being written and will not be fully captured within the covers of this book. For this project, I was not able to systematically interview Toy Len Goon's great-grandchildren, who are further removed from the family history yet continue to be influenced by contemporary ideas about Chinese Americans and the model minority myth. While not being able to include these perspectives is a limitation of this research, I am also excited to potentially pursue these questions in the future.

ACKNOWLEDGMENTS

I could not have written this book without the help of so many generous people who have also been invested in Toy Len Goon's story in various ways.

Thank you to my editor, Ilene Kalish, for being patient while this project came together, and to Priyanka Ray for your guidance in putting together the manuscript for final submission.

While this book is about my grandmother's life, it is also about her legacy. I thank my aunts and uncles and their spouses for sharing their memories of Toy Len and Dogan Goon. Conducting research during the pandemic over Zoom with my cousins provided a valuable opportunity to reconnect with them during a stressful and isolating time.

I am indebted to Gary W. Libby, lawyer, former trustee of the Maine Historical Society, and current treasurer of the Chinese and American Friendship Society of Maine (CAFAM), for his dedication to researching and preserving information on the Chinese community in Maine. An amateur historian, Gary has spent countless hours gathering information for the Maine Chinese Archive, housed at the Maine Historical Society, and is working on his own book on the Chinese in Maine. Years ago, he conducted interviews with family members who have since passed away, and he has scoured eBay for photos and memorabilia related to Toy Len and Dogan Goon. I would not have the resources for this project without him.

The Maine Historical Society has played an essential role in educating the community about the Goon family and other Chinese in Maine. I have interacted with many staff members over the years, including Tilly Laskey, Sofia Yalouris, Tiffany Link, Jamie Rice, Kathleen Neumann, Steve Bromage, and Jamie Kingman Rice, and cannot thank them enough for their help.

Amy Chin Guen, who was entrusted with telling Toy Len Goon's life history, provided a wealth of information from her "living room archive." Her one-bedroom condo was overflowing with family photos, documents, and items that she and her husband, Edward, saved and supplemented by additional family history materials that they collected. I spent many days learning about family history from her. I regret that I am not able to include everything she shared in this book. Her daughter Terry Guen scanned many of the materials, making them readily accessible while preserving the archive.

Doris Wong, with the help of Linda and Doug Fifield, produced a book of memories encompassing family documents, photos, newspaper clippings, and a catalogue of her Mother of the Year awards that is an invaluable repository of family memories.

Nathaniel Wiltzen, archivist at the National Archives at Boston, located and copied Dogan Goon's file and shared the A-file number from the wrapper of Dogan's records that led to me finding Toy Len Goon's file using a USCIS Genealogy Program search. Thank you, Al Cheng, for connecting me with Marisa Louie, who helped guide me in this search. Desiree Butterfield-Nagy, at the Raymond H. Fogler Library, University of Maine Orono, generously provided me with electronic copies of materials related to Toy Len Goon's selection as Mother of the Year.

I was fortunate to receive a National Endowment for the Humanities Fellowship in 2020, which gave me time off from my usual faculty duties to complete a draft of this book manuscript. Funding from the Michigan State University Asian Studies Center's Delia Koo Endowment for Faculty paid for translations of Chinese-language materials associated with her award. Genevieve Leung connected me to Liyi Jack Tien and collaborated with him on many of the translations. I am forever grateful to her for offering to translate the 1992 interview I did with my grandmother using her expertise in Hoisanwa and linguistics, which revealed important aspects of Toy Len's story as told in her own words. The MSU Department of Anthropology provided funding for the citation conversion process, which was patiently and expertly done by Eric Baylis.

I have discussed this project with many colleagues over the years. Thank you to Allison Berg, Bunny McBride, Cathy Schlund-Vials, Harald Prins, Judy Wu, Madeline Hsu, Martin Manalansan, Naoko Wake, and Terese Monberg, with whom I discussed the project at various stages. Madeline wrote one of my NEH letters of recommendation and Susan Brownell wrote the other. Susan generously read through my manuscript draft before I submitted it to the press, as she did for my previous two books. My amazing writing group members, Anna Pegler-Gordon, Kirsten Fermaglich, and Mindy Morgan, gave me valuable feedback and support throughout the process. My Asian American studies colleagues at MSU have been a consistent source of support and encouragement, and the Diversity Research Network and Womxn of Color Initiative at MSU provided me with support from fellow scholars of color.

I had multiple opportunities to present this work at conferences, including the "Counter Cultures" conference at Toronto Metropolitan University, a Fulbright conference in Hong Kong, and conferences of the Organization of American Historians, the American Anthropological Association, the Maine Historical Society, and the Association for Asian American Studies. I would especially like to thank Nancy Riley for inviting me to present my research at Bowdoin College.

I thank my tennis friends, who helped provide an outlet for stress relief, and my walking/running buddies Echo Hansen, Laura Dyras, and Dan Talhelm (and Shirley) for their unwavering support and encouragement.

My parents, Janet and Thomas Louie, have waited a long time for me to tell this story. Thank you for your patience. My cousin Nise and my brother Alex and his family have provided much support from a distance over the years. Special thanks to Adán for cooking great meals and watching our son while I was busy doing research, and Toto, for accompanying me to interviews and being patient as I worked on the project outside regular working hours. I look forward to seeing you continue to tell powerful stories through your own writing.

NOTES

INTRODUCTION

1 Paramount newsreel fragment, Maine Historical Society, 1952.
2 Yeh, "A Saga of Democracy"; Ellen Wu, *The Color of Success*, 4.
3 Ellen Wu, *The Color of Success*; Dhingra, *Life Behind the Lobby.*
4 Massey, *Space, Place, and Gender*; Henry Yu, *Thinking Orientals*; Siu and Tchen, *The Chinese Laundryman.*
5 Geertz, "Thick Description," 3–30.
6 Miles, *Ties That Bind*, 3.
7 Miles, *Ties That Bind*, 5.
8 Miles, *Ties That Bind*, 5.
9 Miles, *Ties That Bind*, 5.
10 Louie, *Chineseness Across Borders*; Louie, *How Chinese Are You?*
11 Louie, *Chineseness Across Borders*, 12.
12 I visited and did research on my paternal grandfather's village. Though the program did not stipulate that we had to visit paternal villages, Chinese kinship follows the paternal line, and my father's side of the family was in touch with relatives still living in China, who accompanied me on the visit. My choice also reflects the ways that, with important exceptions, stories of female Chinese emigrant perspectives were often viewed as secondary to those of male migrants, who were more numerous due to migration patterns and laws restricting the entry of women.
13 The Chinese Exclusion Laws were in effect from 1882 to 1943.
14 Genevieve Leung is a linguist at the University of San Francisco who specializes in Hoisanwa and helped me with numerous translations.
15 I am using the abbreviations *C*, *M*, and *H* in parentheses to indicate the style of romanization. Romanization based on Cantonese language pronunciation is indicated by *C*. Mandarin romanization is indicated by *M*, while Hoisan (the local dialect of the region) is indicated by *H*.
16 Amy Chin Guen, interview by Andrea Louie, Boston, July 4, 2021.
17 Amy Chin Guen, "The Toy Len Goon Story," 2.
18 Amy Chin Guen, "The Toy Len Goon Story," 3.
19 I have engaged in subsequent conversations with her, the most recent being in May 2024, when she was one hundred years old.
20 Amy told me that she went back and forth between the English and Chinese versions as she crafted the narrative, as she had come to feel comfortable writing in

both languages. The handwritten Chinese version contained untranslated direct quotes from the notes she took during her conversations with Toy Len Goon. At the suggestion of her daughter Terry, I had the Chinese version translated with a focus on the direct quotes from Toy Len Goon. The translator worked with Genevieve Leung. Amy notes that she continued to revise only the English version.

21 I conducted interviews with my aunts and uncles prior to the pandemic, though I was not able to interview all of them because some had already passed away.

22 I did not systematically interview everyone from Toy Len Goon's great grandchildren's generation, as that would have resulted in large amounts of interview data that would not fit easily within the flow of this book. However, I may conduct these interviews as part of a separate project in the future.

23 Ellen Wu, *The Color of Success*, 6.

24 Ellen Wu, *The Color of Success*, 6.

25 The Chinese Alien Wives of American Citizens Act of 1946 enabled Chinese women to migrate to the United States on non-quota visas as the spouses of US citizens, followed by an amendment that removed racial restrictions for Asian women, allowing them to migrate through the 1945 War Brides Act and the 1946 Fiancées Act. Yeh, "A Saga of Democracy," 445.

26 Yeh, "A Saga of Democracy," 445.

27 Yeh, "A Saga of Democracy," 445.

28 Ellen Wu, *The Color of Success*.

29 Ellen Wu, *The Color of Success*, 51–52; Hsu, *The Good Immigrants*.

30 Ngai, *Impossible Subjects*, 13.

31 Yeh, "A Saga of Democracy," 435.

32 Yeh, "A Saga of Democracy," 437.

33 Yeh, "A Saga of Democracy," 437.

34 Yeh, "A Saga of Democracy," 435.

35 Klein, *Cold War Orientalism*; Yeh, "A Saga of Democracy."

36 Yeh, "A Saga of Democracy."

37 American Mothers, "About Us."

38 Yeh, "A Saga of Democracy," 439.

39 Yeh, "A Saga of Democracy," 439–40.

40 Yeh, "A Saga of Democracy," 440.

41 American Mothers, "1952 National Mother of the Year."

42 American Mothers, "About Us."

43 Yeh, "A Saga of Democracy," 441.

44 Yeh, "A Saga of Democracy," 440.

45 Hsu, *The Good Immigrants*; Yeh, "A Saga of Democracy"; Ellen Wu, "America's Chinese."

46 Judy Tzu-Chun Wu, *Dr. Mom Chung*; Hsu, *The Good Immigrants*; Ellen Wu, *The Color of Success*; Yeh, "A Saga of Democracy."

47 Lee and Zhou, *Asian American Achievement Paradox*.

48 Lee and Zhou, *Asian American Achievement Paradox*.

49 Ninh, "The Model Minority"; Lee and Zhou, *Asian American Achievement Paradox.*
50 Fong, *Paradise Redefined.*
51 Hsu, *The Good Immigrants*; Lee and Zhou, *Asian American Achievement Paradox.*
52 Ninh, *Passing for Perfect.*

CHAPTER 1. CHINESE MIGRANTS AND THE STATE

1 I deliberately refer here to this region as Toisan, as that is what Cantonese-, Toisanese-, and English-speaking Chinese Americans call it.
2 Hsu, *Dreaming of Gold.*
3 Even in the wake of the Open Policy and Economic Reform in 1978, Toisan has continued to send its young people to urban areas or abroad. Mckeown, "Transnational Chinese Families"; Hsu, *Dreaming of Gold*; Woon, "Social Change and Continuity."
4 Louie, *Chineseness Across Borders*, 12.
5 Huang, *The Spiral Road*; Potter and Potter, *China's Peasants.*
6 Hsu, *The Good Immigrants*, 21.
7 Hsu, *The Good Immigrants*, 21.
8 Hsu, *The Good Immigrants*, 21.
9 Amy Chin Guen, interview by Andrea Louie, Boston, July 4, 2021.
10 Amy Chin Guen, interview by Andrea Louie, Boston, July 4, 2021.
11 According to Mae Ngai, "The Chinese have the dubious distinction of being the only group to be excluded from immigration to the United States explicitly by name. The Chinese Exclusion laws, which barred all Chinese laborers from entry and prohibited Chinese from acquiring naturalized citizenship, generated the nation's first illegal aliens as well as the first alien citizens." Ngai, *Impossible Subjects*, 202.
12 Salyer, *Laws Harsh as Tigers*, 39.
13 Thank you to Nathaniel Wiltzen, archivist at the National Archives in Boston, for his help in locating and copying Dogan Goon's file, and suggesting that I submit an inquiry to the USCIS Genealogy Program to locate my grandmother's file, which was referenced on the wrapper to my grandfather's file but was listed beginning with an *A*, indicating that it was an alien registration file. Thanks also to Marissa Louie Lee for her additional guidance on finding my grandmother's A-file, and to Al Cheng, who put us in touch.
14 Toy Len Goon, interview by Andrea Louie, Janet Louie, and Doris Wong, 1992.
15 Genevieve Leung, who did the translation, pointed out to me how quickly Toy Len Goon changed the subject as a means of taking control of the conversation.
16 Amy Chin Guen, "The Toy Len Goon Story," 8.
17 Amy Chin Guen, "The Toy Len Goon Story," 8.
18 Amy Chin Guen, "The Toy Len Goon Story," 8.
19 Amy Chin Guen, personal communication with Andrea Louie, Boston, May 22, 2024.
20 Fifield et al., "The Goon Family Story."

21 As Mae Ngai notes, a complex bureaucratic system developed around Chinese exclusion, but Chinese immigrants contested their cases in court: "Between 1891 and 1905 the United States district and circuit courts in San Francisco heard over 2500 cases brought by Chinese petitioners and ruled favorably in over 60 percent of them." Ngai, *Impossible Subjects*, 204.
22 US Department of Labor Immigration Service, "In re Goon Do Gun."
23 US Department of Labor Immigration Service, "In re Goon Do Gun," 2.
24 US Department of Labor Immigration Service, "In re Goon Do Gun."
25 US Department of Labor Immigration Service, "In re Goon Do Gun," 3.
26 Pegler-Gordon, *In Sight of America*, 7–8.
27 Salyer, *Laws Harsh as Tigers*.
28 *Portland Evening Express*, August 17, 1917.
29 Wilson, letter to Skeffington.
30 Pegler-Gordon, *In Sight of America*, 2.
31 Salyer, *Laws Harsh as Tigers*, 59.
32 United States v. Goon Do Gun, 8.
33 Salyer, *Laws Harsh as Tigers*, 133.
34 Salyer, *Laws Harsh as Tigers*, 132–33.
35 United States v. Goon Do Gun, 8.
36 United States v. Goon Do Gun, 9.
37 United States v. Goon Do Gun, 10–11.
38 United States v. Goon Do Gun, 13.
39 United States v. Goon Do Gun, 22.
40 United States v. Goon Do Gun, 22.
41 United States v. Goon Do Gun, 23.
42 United States v. Goon Do Gun, 27.
43 Erika Lee, *At America's Gates*; Ngai, *Impossible Subjects*; Pegler-Gordon, *In Sight of America*.
44 Salyer, *Laws Harsh as Tigers*, 4.
45 The photograph, the transcription of Dogan's interview with Inspector McCabe, and the transcript of the hearing itself also provide a powerful picture of a Chinese immigrant's tenuous standing in the United States. Seeing documents associated with my grandfather's case, I can imagine him, young and apprehensive as he appeared in his photographs, attempting to respond to his interrogators in halting English, and wondering which answers might be used against him. Erika Lee, *At America's Gates*; Salyer, *Laws Harsh as Tigers*.
46 Do Gun Goon, Immigration Service No. 2513/126, from file 2500/3557, Record Group 85, National Archives, Waltham, MA.
47 Do Gun Goon, Immigration Service No. 2513/126.
48 He likely has said Forest Avenue, as that was the address of his laundry, but it was heard by the transcriber as First Avenue.
49 Do Gun Goon, Immigration Service No. 2513/126.
50 Ngai, *Impossible Subjects*, 205.

51 Ngai, *Impossible Subjects*, 205.
52 Ngai, *Impossible Subjects*, 205–6.
53 Amy Chin Guen, "The Toy Len Goon Story," 8.
54 Do Gun Goon, Immigration Service No. 2513/126.
55 Do Gun Goon, Immigration Service No. 2513/126.
56 Salyer, *Laws Harsh as Tigers*, 37.
57 Salyer, *Laws Harsh as Tigers*, 37.
58 US Census Bureau, 1920 United States Census.
59 Additional materials from the Maine Historical Society's collection were sent to me by Gary Libby. I also made in-person visits to the MHS, and visited Amy Guen numerous times to interview her or to take a look at additional materials she had come across while sorting through the numerous boxes occupying the living room of her one-bedroom condominium.
60 Due to Exclusion, many immigrants came into the United States as paper sons, using citizenship papers purchased from other families. Therefore, the testimonials given during interrogations did not reflect details associated with their own family's history, but rather those of their paper identities. Prior to landing, Chinese immigrants would memorize coaching booklets containing details associated with their paper name, based on what previous migrants had reported. Lai, Lim, and Yung, *Island*; Lee and Yung, *Angel Island*. See also Louie, *Chineseness Across Borders*.
61 Libby interviewed in Corby, "Mother's Mother."
62 Fifield et al., "The Goon Family Story."
63 Amy Chin Guen, "The Toy Len Goon Story."
64 Amy Chin Guen, interview by Andrea Louie, Boston, July 4, 2021.
65 Ngai, *Impossible Subjects*.
66 "Ambition and Pride."
67 Salyer, *Laws Harsh as Tigers*, 41; Lai, "Historical Development."

CHAPTER 2. TOY LEN GOON'S MIGRATION STORY

1 Amy Chin Guen, "The Toy Len Goon Story."
2 "Toy Len's father was Chin Wah Foon 陳華歡 and his married name was Chin Mun Wing 陳文榮. Mun was a name designated as the 23rd generation. He died in July 1920. Toy Len's mother was Ng Leong Ho 伍良好. She came from Yuan Shan Village 园山 村, next to Sing Moo Market Place 成務墟, Toisan [C] County. She died in July 1923 at the age of 88. She was 6 years younger than her husband." Amy Chin Guen, "The Toy Len Goon Story," 3.
3 Toy Len Goon, interview by Andrea Louie, Janet Louie, and Doris Wong, 1992.
4 According to Genevieve Leung, the Chinese version of the Toy Len Goon life story written by Amy Guen says that because the family was poor, her mother sent her to the neighboring village to 養女 ("raise the daughter"), but for the time period, it means to sell her daughter. However, in an interview, Amy emphasized that Toy Len's mother did not want to sell her.

Though her situation sounds similar to the practice of *tong yang xi*, or "daughter-in-law raised from childhood," in which a young girl is either given or sold to another family with the intent that she will later marry their son, Amy emphasized that Toy Len's situation was different. Wolf, "Adopt a Daughter-in-Law."

5 Amy Chin Guen, personal communication with Andrea Louie, Boston, May 22, 2024; Amy Chin Guen, "The Toy Len Goon Story."

6 Amy Chin Guen, "The Toy Len Goon Story," 6.

7 Field, "Mud Silk."

8 Watson, "Chinese Kinship Reconsidered"; Wolf, "Adopt a Daughter-in-Law."

9 Amy Chin Guen, interview by Andrea Louie, Boston, July 3, 2018.

10 Amy Chin Guen, interview by Andrea Louie, Boston, July 4, 2021.

11 Amy Chin Guen, "The Toy Len Goon Story," 6.

12 Amy Chin Guen, "The Toy Len Goon Story," 6.

13 Amy Chin Guen, "The Toy Len Goon Story," 6.

14 Amy Chin Guen, "The Toy Len Goon Story," 6.

15 Amy Chin Guen, "The Toy Len Goon Story," 9.

16 According to Genevieve Leung, the Chinese version said, 一個好主婦比多量黃金價值高，你有公民權，不應浪費這難得取家人來的機會. Guen, "The Toy Len Goon Story," 7.

17 Amy Guen notes in her biography of Toy Len Goon, "To confirm the fact that Sing Bon should take credit for helping Dogan, his son, Gam Ming Yuen 阮金銘, whom we later met in 1983, repeated what his father had told him back in the 1920s. Sing Bon had told Ed and me in 1952 that helping Dogan was the best thing he ever did in his life. He took pride in Toy Len's achievement as American Mother of the Year." Amy Chin Guen, "The Toy Len Goon Story," 7–8.

18 Tsien, *Asian Americans*, episode 3, "Good Americans."

19 Passenger manifest, *Empress of Asia*, November 28, 1921, Series RG 76-C, Roll T-14871, Library and Archives of Canada, Ottawa.

20 Toy Len Goon, interview by Andrea Louie, Janet Louie, and Doris Wong, 1992.

21 I was able to track down her file with the help of advice from Nathaniel Wiltzen from the National Archives, who had located my grandfather's file based on a certificate of identity number I had provided. He found an empty folder with an A-file reference number for my grandmother, and suggested that I submit a search request to USCIS. Marisa Louie Lee, a former "In Search of Roots" participant to whom I had been referred by Al Cheng, "In Search of Roots" program leader, told me that her file should have been transferred to the National Archives as it was one hundred years after her birth. Because she became a citizen in 1968, the transfer of her file was likely delayed. Her assumption was accurate. I submitted the claim in October 2020 and received a CD with my grandmother's immigration file in March 2021. Immigration file A4821428.

22 Upon seeing this document, Amy Guen said, "My family knew him" (referring to the translator, Moy Don Shing).

23 Immigration file A4821428, Toy Len Goon.
24 Amy Chin Guen, interview by Andrea Louie, Boston, July 4, 2021.
25 Amy Chin Guen, "The Toy Len Goon Story," 8.
26 Amy Chin Guen, interview by Andrea Louie, Boston, July 4, 2021.
27 That machine, a White Rotary stamped with the date 1913 inscribed, was donated to the Maine Historical Society in 2021. The sets of clothing she had brought with her would remain untouched, wrapped in paper in a box, until they were sent to the Maine Historical Society for assessment. Amy Chin Guen, interview by Andrea Louie, Boston, July 4, 2021.
28 Amy Chin Guen, "The Toy Len Goon Story," 10.
29 Amy Chin Guen, interview by Andrea Louie, Boston, March 7, 2019.
30 Amy Chin Guen, "The Toy Len Goon Story," 18.
31 Amy Chin Guen, "The Toy Len Goon Story," 12.
32 Amy Chin Guen, "The Toy Len Goon Story," 18.
33 Toy Len Goon, interview by Andrea Louie, Janet Louie, and Doris Wong, 1992.
34 I will discuss the interview and translation issues further in a later chapter.
35 Doris Wong, interview by Andrea Louie, Boston, July 2, 2018.
36 Amy Chin Guen, "The Toy Len Goon Story," 13.
37 Janet Louie, interview by Andrea Louie, Boston, August 12, 2019.
38 Arthur Len, interview by Andrea Louie, Elk Grove, CA, July 6, 2019.
39 Janet Louie, interview by Andrea Louie, Boston, August 12, 2019.
40 Doris Wong, interview by Andrea Louie, Boston, July 2, 2018.
41 Amy Chin Guen, interview by Andrea Louie, Boston, July 2, 2018.
42 Amy Chin Guen, interview by Andrea Louie, Boston, July 2, 2018.
43 Amy Chin Guen, "The Toy Len Goon Story," 15.
44 Amy Chin Guen, "The Toy Len Goon Story,"15.
45 Josephine and Tony Moy, interview by Andrea Louie, Wakefield, MA, July 1, 2018.
46 Josephine and Tony Moy, interview by Andrea Louie, Wakefield, MA, July 1, 2018.
47 Amy Guen said that Clara Soule had told her that Dogan's amputation was due to an infection in his leg acquired during his army training. There was no specific cause listed in his VA records.
48 Amy Chin Guen, "The Toy Len Goon Story," 14.
49 Toy Len Goon, interview by Andrea Louie, Janet Louie, and Doris Wong, 1992.
50 Amy Chin Guen, "The Toy Len Goon Story," 14.
51 Doris remembers Dogan giving her mother something from his pocket before he went to the hospital.
52 Amy Chin Guen, "The Toy Len Goon Story," 10.
53 Amy Chin Guen, "The Toy Len Goon Story," 11.
54 Certificate of Death, Form C, XC02825743, stamped April 11, 1955.
55 Doris Wong, interview by Andrea Louie, Boston, July 2, 2018.
56 Certificate of Death, Form C, XC02825743.
57 Amy Chin Guen, "The Toy Len Goon Story," 11.

58 US Veterans Administration, Memorandum Form 3229a. Copy courtesy of Terry Guen.
59 US Veterans Administration, Memorandum, Hum Foon Wahdo, 2.
60 US Veterans Administration, Memorandum, Hum Foon Wahdo.
61 US Veterans Administration, Memorandum Form 3229a.
62 Dogan Goon, Veterans Administration solicitor document, 3.
63 Ebrey, introduction, 8.
64 Kulp, *Country Life in South China*; Ebrey, introduction, 4.
65 Amy Chin Guen, "The Toy Len Goon Story," 5.
66 The memo notes that the file contained Form 526, filed by Dogan on April 14, 1939. It also included public records verifying the births of seven children to Dogan and Toy Len (between August 19, 1923, and September 29, 1936). In addition, the file notes that "in a letter dated July 24, 1939, over the signature of the Deputy Commissioner, Immigration and Naturalization Service, US Department of Labor, Washington, it is stated that the records of that service show 'Goon DO GUN or GOON YOU HANG was married to Chin Toy Len or Chin She on C.R. 10-6-15 (July 19, 1921). She entered at Boston December 17, 1921.'"
67 Dogan Goon, Veterans Administration solicitor document, 4.
68 According to searches for Blanchard H. Brown and James H. Pinkham on Ancestry.com, both men were residents of Portland. https://ancestors.familysearch.org.
69 Josephine and Tony Moy, interview by Andrea Louie, Wakefield, MA, July 1, 2018.
70 Josephine and Tony Moy, interview by Andrea Louie, Wakefield, MA, July 1, 2018.
71 Janet Louie, interview by Andrea Louie, Boston, August 12, 2019.
72 Janet was born in 1936 and Dogan passed away in 1941. Janet Louie, interview by Andrea Louie, Boston, August 12, 2019.
73 Arthur Len, interview by Andrea Louie, Elk Grove, CA, July 6, 2019.
74 Doris Wong, interview by Andrea Louie, Boston, July 2, 2018.
75 Josephine and Tony Moy, interview by Andrea Louie, Wakefield, MA, July 1, 2018.
76 Doris Wong, interview by Andrea Louie, Boston, July 2, 2018.
77 Josephine and Tony Moy, interview by Andrea Louie, Wakefield, MA, July 1, 2018.
78 Amy Chin Guen, "The Toy Len Goon Story," 15.
79 Amy Chin Guen, interview by Andrea Louie, Boston, July 4, 2021.
80 Doris Wong, interview by Andrea Louie, Boston, July 2, 2018.
81 Amy Chin Guen, interview by Andrea Louie, Boston, July 3, 2018.
82 Doris Wong, email correspondence with Andrea Louie, May 22, 2011.
83 Amy Chin Guen, "The Toy Len Goon Story," 11.
84 Amy Chin Guen, "The Toy Len Goon Story," 11.
85 Amy Chin Guen, "The Toy Len Goon Story," 11.
86 Yung, *Unbound Feet*, 193.
87 Josephine and Tony Moy, interview by Andrea Louie, Wakefield, MA, July 1, 2018.
88 Doris Wong, email correspondence with Andrea Louie, May 22, 2011.
89 Doris Wong, email correspondence with Andrea Louie, May 22, 2011.
90 Amy Chin Guen, interview by Andrea Louie, Boston, July 3, 2018.

91 Amy Chin Guen, interview by Andrea Louie, Boston, July 3, 2018.
92 Amy Chin Guen, interview by Andrea Louie, Boston, July 3, 2018.
93 Her Americanization work and role in the Mother of the Year nomination will be discussed further in a later chapter.
94 Miller, "Twenty Nationalities."
95 Amy Chin Guen, interview by Andrea Louie, Boston, July 3, 2018.
96 Amy Chin Guen, interview by Andrea Louie, Boston, July 3, 2018.
97 Josephine and Tony Moy, interview by Andrea Louie, Wakefield, MA, July 1, 2018.
98 Arthur Len, interview by Andrea Louie, Elk Grove, CA, July 6, 2019.
99 Arthur Len, interview by Andrea Louie, Elk Grove, CA, July 6, 2019.
100 Josephine Moy, interview by Andrea Louie, Wakefield, MA, July 1, 2018.
101 Josephine Moy, interview by Andrea Louie, Wakefield, MA, July 1, 2018.
102 Josephine and Tony Moy, interview by Andrea Louie, Wakefield, MA, July 1, 2018.
103 Arthur Len, interview by Andrea Louie, Elk Grove, CA, July 6, 2019.
104 Doris Wong, interview by Andrea Louie, Boston, July 2, 2018.

CHAPTER 3. KINSHIP TIES ACROSS BORDERS

1 Toy Len Goon, interview by Andrea Louie, Janet Louie, and Doris Wong, 1992.
2 In the context of the Philippines, Rhacel Parreñas has discussed how migrant mothers would send back goods for their children in addition to remittances in lieu of being able to physically return frequently, due to cost and the terms of their contracts abroad. Parreñas, *Servants of Globalization*, 58.
3 Cheng, "Out of Chinatown."
4 Hong, *Opening the Gates*; Hsu, *The Good Immigrants.*
5 Hong, *Opening the Gates*, 3.
6 Hsu, *The Good Immigrants*, 16.
7 Mckeown, "Transnational Chinese Families"; Hsu, *Dreaming of Gold*; Renqiu Yu, *To Save China.*
8 Levitt and Schiller, "Conceptualizing Simultaneity."
9 Hsu, *Dreaming of Gold.*
10 Freedman, *Chinese Lineage and Society*; Huang, *The Spiral Road*; Potter and Potter, *China's Peasants*; Watson, *Emigration and the Chinese Lineage.*
11 Tu, *The Living Tree*; Louie, *Chineseness Across Borders.*
12 Freedman, *Chinese Lineage and Society*; Huang, *The Spiral Road*; Potter and Potter, *China's Peasants*; Watson, *Emigration and the Chinese Lineage.*
13 Potter and Potter, *China's Peasants*, 9.
14 Louie, *Chineseness Across Borders*; Fong, *Paradise Redefined.*
15 Hsu, *Dreaming of Gold*; Watson, *Emigration and the Chinese Lineage.*
16 Ties between the Chinese diaspora and China have resumed, fueled by newer generations of post-1965 immigrants, the diaspora's interest in connecting to its roots and with their kin in China, and newer forms of communication such as email and social media. Beginning in the 1980s, Deng Xiaoping instituted a new economic strategy that appealed to overseas Chinese filial sentiments to lure them

and their capital back to build the homeland, facilitating these connections. Smart and Hsu, "The Chinese Diaspora"; Louie, *Chineseness Across Borders*.

17 Ngai, *Impossible Subjects*, 172.

18 Brooks, *Between Mao and McCarthy*.

19 Amy Chin Guen, "The Toy Len Goon Story."

20 Watson, "Chinese Kinship Reconsidered."

21 Amy Chin Guen, "The Toy Len Goon Story," 11.

22 Amy Chin Guen, "The Toy Len Goon Story," 11.

23 Amy Guen writes, "According to the tradition of the 23rd generation of the Goon family, the name would be 'bon.' Carroll was named Quong Bon 光本. 'Bon' stands for 'root,' and Quong is 'glory,' so his name is Glorious Root. Richard was named Ming Bon 明本, Bright Root. Edward was named Jeng Bon 正本, Proper Root. Albert was named Ai Bon 大本, Large Root. Arthur was named Hem Bon 添本, To Increase Root." Amy Chin Guen, "The Toy Len Goon Story," 15.

24 Watson, *Emigration and the Chinese Lineage*.

25 Lai, "Chinese Organizations in America."

26 Lai, "Historical Development."

27 Libby, "Marriage and Family Life," 81.

28 Amy Chin Guen, interview by Andrea Louie, Boston, July 3, 2018.

29 Amy Chin Guen, "The Toy Len Goon Story," 21.

30 Amy Chin Guen, "The Toy Len Goon Story," 28.

31 Amy Chin Guen, "The Toy Len Goon Story," 28.

32 Amy Chin Guen, "The Toy Len Goon Story," 29.

33 Amy Chin Guen, "The Toy Len Goon Story," 30.

34 Amy Chin Guen, "The Toy Len Goon Story," 30.

35 Amy Chin Guen, "The Toy Len Goon Story," 20.

36 Amy Chin Guen, "The Toy Len Goon Story," 20.

37 Amy Chin Guen, "The Toy Len Goon Story," 31–32.

38 These public events will be further discussed in chapter 6.

39 Amy Chin Guen, "The Toy Len Goon Story."

40 Amy Chin Guen, interview by Andrea Louie, Boston, July 3, 2018.

41 Amy Chin Guen, "The Toy Len Goon Story," 4.

42 Amy Chin Guen, "The Toy Len Goon Story," 4.

43 Amy Chin Guen, "The Toy Len Goon Story," 27.

44 Traditionally, only boys were educated, and many boys living in rural villages did not receive full primary and secondary education. After Chairman Mao took power in 1949, he implemented literacy programs in the countryside and made schooling available for both boys and girls, but Toy Kuen, who was born in 1898, would have already been in her fifties and would not have benefited from this educational opportunity.

45 Amy Chin Guen, interview by Andrea Louie, Boston, July 4, 2021.

46 Wolf and Huang, *Marriage and Adoption in China*.

47 Amy Chin Guen, interview by Andrea Louie, Boston, July 4, 2021.

48 Amy Chin Guen, “The Toy Len Goon Story,” 20–21.
49 Amy Chin Guen, “The Toy Len Goon Story,” 28.
50 Amy Chin Guen, “The Toy Len Goon Story,” 28.
51 Johnson, *China's Hidden Children*; Long Bow Group, *Small Happiness*; Potter and Potter, *China's Peasants.*
52 Huang, *The Spiral Road*; Louie, *Chineseness Across Borders*; Potter and Potter, *China's Peasants.*
53 In contrast, my paternal grandfather held a one-month party for me and my cousin Bruce, who is six months older than I.
54 She had started to go to a Chinese church in her later years and was baptized by Reverend Tan, who gave services in Cantonese. Amy Chin Guen, “The Toy Len Goon Story,” 20.
55 Amy Chin Guen, “The Toy Len Goon Story,” 20.
56 Amy Chin Guen, interview by Andrea Louie, Boston, July 4, 2021.
57 Amy Chin Guen, “The Toy Len Goon Story,” 8.
58 Amy Chin Guen, “The Toy Len Goon Story,” 8.

CHAPTER 4. COUNTER CULTURES

1 Tchen, introduction to Siu and Tchen, *The Chinese Laundryman*, xxiii.
2 Renqiu Yu, *To Save China.*
3 Tchen, introduction to Siu and Tchen, *The Chinese Laundryman*, xxxii.
4 Siu and Tchen, *The Chinese Laundryman*, 16.
5 Henry Yu, *Thinking Orientals*; Gupta and Ferguson, “Beyond ‘Culture.’”
6 Massey, *Space, Place, and Gender*, 155, 171.
7 Siu and Tchen, *The Chinese Laundryman*, 60.
8 Lo, “Chinese Laundries in Massachusetts,” 49.
9 Counter Cultures Network, “What Is the Counter Cultures Network?”
10 Lee-Loy, “Counter Culture Network.”
11 Siu and Tchen, *The Chinese Laundryman.*
12 Henry Yu, *Thinking Orientals*, 40.
13 Siu and Tchen, *The Chinese Laundryman*, 295.
14 Hsu, *The Good Immigrants*; Mckeown, “Transnational Chinese Families.”
15 Siu and Tchen, *The Chinese Laundryman*, 207.
16 Tien et al., “Laundry Rock.”
17 Tien et al., “Laundry Rock.”
18 Libby, “Historical Notes,” 47.
19 Libby, “Historical Notes,” 47.
20 Libby, “Historical Notes,” 47.
21 Libby, “Historical Notes,” 47.
22 Libby, “Historical Notes,” 48.
23 Amy Chin Guen, “The Toy Len Goon Story,” 27–28.
24 Ellen Wu, *The Color of Success.*
25 Robert G. Lee, *Orientals*; Ellen Wu, *The Color of Success.*

26 Henry Yu, *Thinking Orientals*, 7–8.
27 Henry Yu, *Thinking Orientals*, 45.
28 Henry Yu, *Thinking Orientals*, 47.
29 Henry Yu, *Thinking Orientals*, 54.
30 Said, *Orientalism*.
31 Henry Yu, *Thinking Orientals*, 71.
32 Gupta and Ferguson, "Beyond 'Culture'"; Massey, *Space, Place, and Gender*.
33 Goffman, *Presentation of Self*; Dhingra, *Life Behind the Lobby*.
34 Josephine Moy, email correspondence with Andrea Louie, May 22, 2011 .
35 Doris Wong, email correspondence with Andrea Louie, May 22, 2011.
36 Edward Guen, interview by Gary Libby and Fenggang Yang, August 21,2001, Maine Historical Society, Portland, 1. See also "Interview of Edward and Amy [Chin] Guen," Maine Historical Society collection 2080, Chinese Americans of Maine Collection 1875–present, Box 2, Folder 6 (August 1, 2001); and "Interview with Edward Guen" (August 24, 2001), Maine Historical Society, audiotapes 7–8, Folder 8.
37 Josephine and Tony Moy, interview by Andrea Louie, Wakefield, MA, July 1, 2018.
38 Josephine and Tony Moy, interview by Andrea Louie, Wakefield, MA, July 1, 2018.
39 Massey, *Space, Place, and Gender*, 120.
40 Massey, *Space, Place, and Gender*, 121.
41 Massey, *Space, Place, and Gender*, 149.
42 Massey, *Space, Place, and Gender*, 149.
43 Massey, *Space, Place, and Gender*, 179.
44 Massey, *Space, Place, and Gender*, 180.
45 Massey, *Space, Place, and Gender*, 204.
46 Massey, *Space, Place, and Gender*, 197.
47 Doris Wong, email correspondence with Andrea Louie, May 22, 2011.
48 Amy Chin Guen, interview by Andrea Louie, Boston, July 3, 2018.
49 Light and Gold, *Ethnic Economies*.
50 Dhingra, *Life Behind the Lobby*.
51 Dhingra, *Life Behind the Lobby*.
52 Dhingra, *Life Behind the Lobby*, 12.
53 Dhingra, *Life Behind the Lobby*, 125.
54 Dhingra, *Life Behind the Lobby*, 131.
55 Doris Wong, email correspondence with Andrea Louie, May 22, 2011.
56 Richard Chin from the "Laundry Rock" presentation, mentioned earlier, said that he was essentially raised by a Black woman. Tien et al., "Laundry Rock."
57 Based on Shauna Lo's oral history interviews of people who grew up in Chinese laundries in Boston, in the 1940s and 1950s it became common practice for Chinese laundries to send the dirty clothing out to be washed. Helen Schlitche's family had similar experiences in Charlestown, MA. Helen Schlitche, Zoom interview by Andrea Louie, May 20, 2022.
58 Arthur Len, interview by Andrea Louie, Elk Grove, CA, July 6, 2019.

59 Dhingra, *Life Behind the Lobby*, 124–25.
60 Doris Wong, email correspondence with Andrea Louie, May 22, 2011.
61 Amy Chin Guen, "The Toy Len Goon Story," 17.
62 Amy Chin Guen, "The Toy Len Goon Story," 17.
63 Amy Chin Guen, "The Toy Len Goon Story," 17.
64 Yeh, "A Saga of Democracy," 450.
65 Louie, *Chineseness Across Borders*; Louie, *How Chinese Are You?*
66 Hall, "Old and New Identities"; Lowe, "Heterogeneity, Hybridity, Multiplicity."
67 Henry Yu, *Thinking Orientals*.
68 Henry Yu, *Thinking Orientals*.
69 Massey, *Space, Place, and Gender*.
70 Cheng, "Out of Chinatown," 1068.
71 Cheng, "Out of Chinatown," 1069.

CHAPTER 5. MOTHER OF THE YEAR AWARD

1 Clara Soule, Mother of the Year nomination letter, family document collection, Amy Chin Guen, Boston.
2 Bethune, "The Trend of Thinking."
3 Toy Len Goon, interview by Andrea Louie, Janet Louie, and Doris Wong, 1992.
4 Hsu, *The Good Immigrants*; Ellen Wu, *The Color of Success*.
5 Ellen Wu, *The Color of Success*, 52.
6 Ellen Wu, *The Color of Success*, 53.
7 Ellen Wu, *The Color of Success*, 55.
8 "Chinese Family Joins Appeal."
9 He ended up not being able to go because of his eczema.
10 Ellen Wu, *The Color of Success*, 4.
11 "China-Born Woman."
12 "Mrs. Goon Overwhelmed."
13 "Mrs. Goon Overwhelmed."
14 "Mrs. Goon Overwhelmed."
15 "Mrs. Goon Overwhelmed."
16 Hsu, *The Good Immigrants*, 6.
17 Hsu, *The Good Immigrants*, 17.
18 Ellen Wu, "America's Chinese," 396.
19 Hsu, *The Good Immigrants*, 4.
20 Ellen Wu, *The Color of Success*, 4.
21 Hsu, *The Good Immigrants*, 17.
22 Hsu, *The Good Immigrants*, 17.
23 Robert G. Lee, *Orientals*, 256.
24 Robert G. Lee, *Orientals*, 257.
25 Meyerowitz, *Not June Cleaver*, 3.
26 Meyerowitz, *Not June Cleaver*, 4.
27 Meyerowitz, *Not June Cleaver*, 2.

28 Meyerowitz, *Not June Cleaver*, 2.
29 Meyerowitz, *Not June Cleaver*, 2.
30 "Immigrant Named Mother of the Year."
31 Craig, "We're Proud of Our Mother."
32 "We're Proud of Our Mother," editorial, *Boston Herald*.
33 Pomeroy, "How to Prepare Lobster Dish."
34 Ngai, *Impossible Subjects*, 203.
35 Judy Tzu-Chun Wu, *Dr. Mom Chung*; Yung, *Unbound Feet*.
36 Judy Tzu-Chun Wu, *Dr. Mom Chung*, 122.
37 Judy Tzu-Chun Wu, *Dr. Mom Chung*, 198.
38 Judy Tzu-Chun Wu, *Dr. Mom Chung*; Yeh, "A Saga of Democracy."
39 Judy Tzu-Chun Wu, *Dr. Mom Chung*, 101, 122.
40 Judy Tzu-Chun Wu, *Dr. Mom Chung*, 153–54.
41 Yeh, "A Saga of Democracy," 3.
42 Ngai, *Impossible Subjects*, 203.
43 Judy Tzu-Chun Wu, *Dr. Mom Chung*, 3.
44 Judy Tzu-Chun Wu, *Dr. Mom Chung*, 2.
45 Yeh, "A Saga of Democracy," 452.
46 Yeh, "A Saga of Democracy," 452.
47 Tien et al., "Laundry Rock."
48 Tien et al., "Laundry Rock."
49 Helen Schlitche, Zoom interview by Andrea Louie, May 20, 2022.
50 Libby, "Marriage and Family Life," 48.
51 Libby, "Marriage and Family Life," 49.
52 "The Chinese in Maine sometimes committed their own crimes, most related to gambling or opium smoking. Police would conduct raids in an effort to catch the Chinese in the act of gambling, but the Chinese were often able to evade capture. In 1892, the police raided a laundry owned by Ching Hoe, located in the United States Hotel, three times in an effort to arrest the men suspected of regularly gambling there. Federal agents were often brought in to deal with suspected opium, often placing the laundries under surveillance before conducting raids." Libby, "Marriage and Family Life," 49–50.
53 Ellen Wu, *The Color of Success*, 4.
54 Yeh, "A Saga of Democracy," 454.
55 Yeh, "A Saga of Democracy," 455.
56 Yeh, "A Saga of Democracy," 455–56.
57 Yeh, "A Saga of Democracy," 455–56.
58 Yeh, "A Saga of Democracy," 455–56.
59 Yeh, "A Saga of Democracy," 456.
60 Ellen Wu, *The Color of Success*, 4.
61 Ellen Wu, *The Color of Success*, 4.
62 Doris Wong, email correspondence with Andrea Louie, May 22, 2011.
63 Miller, "Twenty Nationalities."

64 Miller, "Twenty Nationalities."
65 Miller, "Twenty Nationalities."
66 Miller, "Twenty Nationalities."
67 Miller, "Twenty Nationalities."
68 Soule, Americanization pageant program.
69 Soule, Americanization pageant program.
70 Soule, Americanization pageant program.
71 Miller, "Twenty Nationalities."
72 Miller, "Twenty Nationalities."
73 Miller, "Twenty Nationalities."
74 Ellen Wu, *The Color of Success*; Yeh, "A Saga of Democracy."
75 Amy Chin Guen, interview by Andrea Louie, Boston, July 3, 2018.
76 "Gov. Payne Joins Portland Groups to Honor American Mother of the Year," *Portland Press Herald*, May 6, 1952.
77 "Mrs. Goon Overwhelmed."
78 "Portland Service Clubs."
79 "'Welcome' Sign."
80 "Former G-Man."
81 "Teachers Fete No. 1 Mother," *Portland Evening Express*, June 5, 1952.
82 Janet Louie, interview by Andrea Louie, Boston, August 12, 2019.
83 Josephine and Tony Moy, interview by Andrea Louie, Wakefield, MA, July 1, 2018.
84 Doris Wong, interview by Andrea Louie, Boston, July 2, 2018.
85 Janet Louie, interview by Andrea Louie, Boston, August 12, 2019.
86 Arthur Len, interview by Andrea Louie, Elk Grove, CA, July 6, 2019.
87 Doris Wong, interview by Andrea Louie, Boston, July 2, 2018.
88 *Chinese-American Weekly*, May 22, 1952, 15–17, translated by Jack Tien and Genevieve Leung.
89 Janet Louie, interview by Andrea Louie, Boston, August 12, 2019.
90 "May Craig," *Women Come to the Front* exhibit, Library of Congress, n.d. Accessed October 29, 2024. www.loc.gov/exhibits.
91 "May Craig, Feisty Capital Writer, Dies," *New York Times*, July 16, 1975.
92 "May Craig," *Women Come to the Front* exhibit.
93 Klein, *Cold War Orientalism*, 11.
94 Klein, *Cold War Orientalism*, 11
95 Craig, "Mrs. Goon in Washington."
96 Ellen Wu, *The Color of Success*, 123.
97 Ellen Wu, *The Color of Success*, 123.
98 Ellen Wu, "America's Chinese," 400.
99 Cheng, *Citizens of Asian America*, 1.
100 Cheng, *Citizens of Asian America*, 2.
101 Cheng, *Citizens of Asian America*, 2.
102 Cheng, *Citizens of Asian America*, 3.
103 Cheng, *Citizens of Asian America*, 10.

104 Cheng, *Citizens of Asian America*, 12.
105 Ellen Wu, *The Color of Success*, 7.
106 Ellen Wu, *The Color of Success*, 8.
107 Ellen Wu, *The Color of Success*, 4.
108 Ellen Wu, *The Color of Success*, 8.
109 Ellen Wu, *The Color of Success*, 9.
110 Siu, *Memories of a Future Home*; Ong, *Flexible Citizenship*.
111 Cheng, *Citizens of Asian America*; Ellen Wu, *The Color of Success*; Hsu, *The Good Immigrants*; Wong, *Americans First*.
112 Louie, *How Chinese Are You?*, 154.
113 Ellen Wu, *The Color of Success*.
114 Ellen Wu, "America's Chinese."
115 Klein, *Cold War Orientalism*, 27.

CHAPTER 6. "ONE LIFETIME IS LIKE OTHER PEOPLE'S WORKING FOUR"

1 Genevieve notes, "I actually think her codeswitching is really interesting here. She switches the verb and the negation into English but keeps the noun (lifetime) and sentence's final particles (ho, waa) in Hoisan."
2 Toy Len Goon, interview by Andrea Louie, Janet Louie, and Doris Wong, 1992.
3 Hong Hau is Dogan's village.
4 The translation by Janet was brief and partial: "She said she worked hard all her life before and after she was married and before and after my father died because he didn't help much." Toy Len Goon, interview by Andrea Louie, Janet Louie, and Doris Wong, 1992.
5 Craig, "Mrs. Goon in Washington."
6 Toy Len Goon, interview by Andrea Louie, Janet Louie, and Doris Wong, 1992.
7 Her comment about working the equivalent of four lives is discussed elsewhere in more depth.
8 Toy Len Goon, interview by Andrea Louie, Janet Louie, and Doris Wong, 1992.
9 Toy Len Goon, interview by Andrea Louie, Janet Louie, and Doris Wong, 1992.
10 Yung, *Unbound Feet*, 4.
11 Yung, *Unbound Feet*, 4.
12 Yung, *Unbound Feet*, 4.
13 Yung, *Unbound Feet*, 46.
14 Yung, *Unbound Feet*, 46.
15 Toy Len Goon, interview by Andrea Louie, Janet Louie, and Doris Wong, 1992.
16 Toy Len Goon, interview by Andrea Louie, Janet Louie, and Doris Wong, 1992.
17 Toy Len Goon, interview by Andrea Louie, Janet Louie, and Doris Wong, 1992.
18 "Chinese Launderer 1952 Ideal Mother."
19 Craig, "Mrs. Goon in Washington."
20 Edward Guen, interview by Gary Libby, August 24, 2001.
21 Amy Chin Guen, interview by Andrea Louie, Boston, June 26, 2017.

22 Janet Louie, interview by Andrea Louie, Boston, August 12, 2019.
23 Tsien, *Asian Americans*, episode 3, "Good Americans."
24 *Chinese-American Weekly*, May 22, 1952, 15–17, translated by Jack Tien and Genevieve Leung.
25 "Chinese Laundry Woman."
26 Kertzer, *Ritual, Politics, and Power*.
27 Craig, "Mrs. Goon in Washington."
28 Deng Hui Fang, letter to Toy Len Goon, May 16, 1952. Private collection of Amy Guen.
29 Craig, "Mother of Year Meets First Lady."
30 Janet Louie, interview by Andrea Louie, Boston, August 12, 2019.
31 Janet Louie, interview by Andrea Louie, Boston, August 12, 2019.
32 "Japs Offer Surrender."
33 Craig, "Chinese US Officials Honor Mrs. Goon."
34 Janet Louie, interview by Andrea Louie, Boston, August 12, 2019.
35 Yeh, "A Saga of Democracy," 438.
36 Yeh, "A Saga of Democracy," 458.
37 Spallholz, letter to Toy Len Goon.
38 Renqiu Yu, *To Save China*.
39 Josephine and Tony Moy, interview by Andrea Louie, Wakefield, MA, July 1, 2018.
40 Ellen Wu, *The Color of Success*; Yeh, "A Saga of Democracy."
41 New York Historical Society Museum and Library, "Toy Len Goon"; Kanes, "Toy Len Goon."
42 New York Historical Society Museum and Library, "Toy Len Goon."
43 New York Historical Society Museum and Library, "Toy Len Goon."
44 Poling and Poling, *Mothers of Men*.
45 Field, "Mud Silk," 236.
46 Field, "Mud Silk," 236.
47 Field, "Mud Silk," 236.
48 Amy Chin Guen, interview by Andrea Louie, Boston, July 3, 2021.
49 Amy Chin Guen, interview by Andrea Louie, Boston, July 3, 2021.
50 Field, "Mud Silk," 255.
51 Kennedy, *Maine's Remarkable Women*, 103.
52 Doris Wong, interview by Andrea Louie, Boston, July 2, 2018.
53 Amy Chin Guen, interview by Andrea Louie, Boston, 2017.
54 Doris Wong, interview by Andrea Louie, Boston, July 2, 2018.

CHAPTER 7. DIRTY LAUNDRY (OR KEEPING CLEAN LAUNDRY CLEAN)

1 I contacted all of Toy Len Goon's surviving grandchildren (twenty-three in all) and interviewed eighteen, as some were not available or interested in being interviewed, and some thought that they had nothing new to add.
2 Chua, *Battle Hymn of the Tiger Mother*.

3 Lee and Zhou, *Asian American Achievement Paradox*, xv.
4 Lee and Zhou, *Asian American Achievement Paradox*, 1.
5 Lee and Zhou, *Asian American Achievement Paradox*, 1.
6 Lee and Zhou, *Asian American Achievement Paradox*, 3.
7 Lee and Zhou, *Asian American Achievement Paradox*, xvi.
8 Lee and Zhou, *Asian American Achievement Paradox*, xvi.
9 Roseanne Len, email correspondence with Andrea Louie, April 13, 2021.
10 Lee and Zhou, *Asian American Achievement Paradox*, 18.
11 Toy Len Goon, interview by Andrea Louie, Janet Louie, and Doris Wong, 1992.
12 Rosanne Len, correspondence with Andrea Louie, April 13, 2021.
13 Toy Len Goon, interview by Andrea Louie, Janet Louie, and Doris Wong, 1992.
14 According to Genevieve Leung, "This is a really interesting use of reported speech here. It could be read as TLG only reporting the speech of Carroll, but I think it's more complex than this. TLG is actually reporting the speech of Carroll, herself, and of others. You can tell this because the pronouns are different (and are used in the same sentence/utterance) to refer to different referents). Also her use of "ko" ('like this/that')." Genevieve Leung, correspondence with Andrea Louie, September 19, 2021.
15 Ninh, *Passing for Perfect*, 7–10.
16 Ellen Wu, *The Color of Success*, 123–24, 191.
17 Hsu, *The Good Immigrants*.
18 Petersen, "Success Story"; Brand, "Education."
19 Chin, *Stuck*; Dhingra, *Hyper Education*; Warikoo, *Race at the Top*.
20 Chin, *Stuck*, 14.
21 Far from being encouraged to enter the C-suites, I had to look up this term when I first came upon it recently.
22 Chung, *Saving Face*, 13.
23 Chung, *Saving Face*, 14.
24 Chung, *Saving Face*, 15.
25 Chung, *Saving Face*, 14.
26 Chung, *Saving Face*, 47.
27 Chung, *Saving Face*, 55.
28 Chung, *Saving Face*, 53.
29 Ninh, "The Model Minority," 169.
30 Ninh, *Passing for Perfect*, 93–136.
31 Multiple family members, including some of Carroll's children, some of my cousins, and his granddaughter, told me that he and Marguerite had to be driven to Colorado to be legally married because interracial marriage was against the law in Utah at the time. His granddaughter Maggie shared with me that she sensed he still had a "feeling of shame" about it, an impression she got when she spent some time with him in his apartment in his retirement complex in Danvers, Massachusetts, where he had moved after Marguerite passed away to be closer to his sisters. Even though he was in his nineties at the time, she could tell that he still

felt ashamed of the incident as he shared it with her, thinking that it was his fault, and not the consequence of the racist laws. His son Jonathan recalled hearing a story from his father about wanting to join a fraternity at Syracuse University but not being allowed to because he was Chinese. Instead, the fraternity offered him a job, which he took to help support himself. Carroll Hart Guen, Zoom interview by Andrea Louie, May 27, 2021; Kathy Grant, Zoom interview with Andrea Louie, May 19, 2021.

32 Carroll Hart Guen, Zoom interview by Andrea Louie, May 27, 2021.
33 Carroll Hart Guen, Zoom interview by Andrea Louie, May 27, 2021.
34 Carroll Hart Guen, Zoom interview by Andrea Louie, May 27, 2021.
35 Kathy Grant, Zoom interview by Andrea Louie, May 19, 2021.
36 Connie Psaros, Zoom interview by Andrea Louie, April 24, 2021.
37 Connie Psaros, Zoom interview by Andrea Louie, April 24, 2021.
38 Connie Psaros, Zoom interview by Andrea Louie, April 24, 2021.
39 Tim Guen, Zoom interview by Andrea Louie, April 22, 2021.
40 Terry Guen, Zoom interview by Andrea Louie, April 4, 2021.
41 Janine Pipitone, Zoom interview by Andrea Louie, April 6, 2021.
42 Janine Pipitone, Zoom interview by Andrea Louie, April 6, 2021.
43 Janine Pipitone, Zoom interview by Andrea Louie, April 6, 2021.
44 Janine Pipitone, Zoom interview by Andrea Louie, April 6, 2021.
45 Janine Pipitone, Zoom interview by Andrea Louie, April 6, 2021.
46 Janine Pipitone, Zoom interview by Andrea Louie, April 6, 2021.
47 Marie Hill, Zoom interview by Andrea Louie, May 1, 2021.
48 Tim Guen, Zoom interview by Andrea Louie, April 22, 2021.
49 Tim Guen, Zoom interview by Andrea Louie, April 22, 2021.
50 Tim Guen, "Re-branding a Culture."
51 Tim Guen, Zoom interview by Andrea Louie, April 22, 2021.
52 Tim Guen, Zoom interview by Andrea Louie, April 22, 2021.
53 Terry Guen, Zoom interview by Andrea Louie, April 4, 2021.
54 Terry Guen, Zoom interview by Andrea Louie, April 4, 2021.
55 Michael Yuen, Zoom interview by Andrea Louie, May 21, 2021.
56 Leo Guen, Zoom interview by Andrea Louie, April 5, 2021.
57 Leo Guen, Zoom interview by Andrea Louie, April 5, 2021.
58 Leo Guen, Zoom interview by Andrea Louie, April 5, 2021.
59 Leo Guen, Zoom interview by Andrea Louie, April 5, 2021.
60 Leo Guen, Zoom interview by Andrea Louie, April 5, 2021.
61 He retired in 2024 as vice president at JP Morgan.
62 Leo Guen, Zoom interview by Andrea Louie, April 5, 2021.
63 Leo Guen, Zoom interview by Andrea Louie, April 5, 2021.
64 Leo Guen, Zoom interview by Andrea Louie, April 5, 2021.
65 Leo Guen, Zoom interview by Andrea Louie, April 5, 2021.
66 Richard Len, Zoom interview by Andrea Louie, May 5, 2021.
67 Richard Len, Zoom interview by Andrea Louie, May 5, 2021.

68 Richard Len, Zoom interview by Andrea Louie, May 5, 2021.
69 Richard Len, Zoom interview by Andrea Louie, May 5, 2021.
70 Rosanne Len, Zoom interview by Andrea Louie, April 14, 2021.
71 Rosanne Len, email correspondence, April 13, 2021.
72 Rosanne Len, email correspondence, April 13, 2021.
73 Rosanne Len, Zoom interview by Andrea Louie, April 14, 2021.
74 Rosanne Len, Zoom interview by Andrea Louie, April 14, 2021.
75 Rosanne Len, Zoom interview by Andrea Louie, April 14, 2021.
76 Rosanne Len, Zoom interview by Andrea Louie, April 14, 2021.
77 Rosanne Len, Zoom interview by Andrea Louie, April 14, 2021.
78 Linda Fifield, Zoom interview by Andrea Louie, April 13, 2021.
79 Linda Fifield, Zoom interview by Andrea Louie, April 13, 2021.
80 Linda Fifield, Zoom interview by Andrea Louie, April 13, 2021.
81 Amy Chin Guen, interview by Andrea Louie, Boston, July 3, 2021.
82 "Por" is what Toy Len Goon's daughter's children called her, as opposed to Ngin, which is what her son's children called her.
83 Linda Fifield, Zoom interview by Andrea Louie, April 13, 2021.
84 Marie Hill, Zoom interview by Andrea Louie, May 1, 2021.
85 Stephen Len, phone interview by Andrea Louie, May 9, 2021.
86 Stephen Len, phone interview by Andrea Louie, May 9, 2021.
87 Kasey Chatterji-Len, Zoom interview by Andrea Louie, June 1, 2021.
88 Terry Guen, Zoom interview by Andrea Louie, April 4, 2021.
89 Nancy Len Hunt, Zoom interview by Andrea Louie, April 27, 2021.
90 Nancy Len Hunt, Zoom interview by Andrea Louie, April 27, 2021.
91 Nancy Len Hunt, Zoom interview by Andrea Louie, April 27, 2021.
92 Nancy Len Hunt, Zoom interview by Andrea Louie, April 27, 2021.
93 Nancy Len Hunt, Zoom interview by Andrea Louie, April 27, 2021.
94 This is the focus of researchers such as Warikoo and Dhingra, discussed earlier.
95 Lee and Zhou, *Asian American Achievement Paradox*; Chin, *Stuck*.
96 Nancy Len Hunt, Zoom interview by Andrea Louie, April 27, 2021.
97 They are among the younger group of cousins, so I found this comparison to be very interesting. I do not remember being compared to them.
98 Pamela Wang, Zoom interview by Andrea Louie, May 10, 2021.
99 Pamela Wang, Zoom interview by Andrea Louie, May 10, 2021.
100 Pamela Wang, Zoom interview by Andrea Louie, May 10, 2021.
101 Pamela Wang, Zoom interview by Andrea Louie, May 10, 2021.
102 Pamela Wang, Zoom interview by Andrea Louie, May 10, 2021.
103 Pamela Wang, Zoom interview by Andrea Louie, May 10, 2021.
104 Pamela Wang, Zoom interview by Andrea Louie, May 10, 2021.
105 Lee and Zhou, *Asian American Achievement Paradox*.
106 Lee and Zhou, *Asian American Achievement Paradox*.
107 Pamela Wang, Zoom interview by Andrea Louie, May 10, 2021.
108 Pamela Wang, Zoom interview by Andrea Louie, May 10, 2021.

109 Pamela Wang, Zoom interview by Andrea Louie, May 10, 2021.
110 Pamela Wang, Zoom interview by Andrea Louie, May 10, 2021.
111 Stephen Len, phone interview by Andrea Louie, May 9, 2021.
112 Stephen Len, phone interview by Andrea Louie, May 9, 2021.
113 Stephen Len, phone interview by Andrea Louie, May 9, 2021.

CONCLUSION

1 Murphy, "Celebrated Chinese American Mom."
2 Andrea Louie, Doris Wong, and Gary Libby, email correspondence, July 25, 2021.
3 Andrea Louie and Gary Libby, personal communication, October 2, 2021.
4 Roseanne Len, email correspondence with Andrea Louie, April 13, 2021.
5 Janine Pipitone, Zoom interview by Andrea Louie, April 6, 2021.
6 Janine Pipitone, Zoom interview by Andrea Louie, April 6, 2021.
7 Janine Pipitone, Zoom interview by Andrea Louie, April 6, 2021.
8 Janine Pipitone, Zoom interview by Andrea Louie, April 6, 2021.
9 Nancy Len Hunt, Zoom interview by Andrea Louie, April 27, 2021.
10 Pamela Wang, Zoom interview by Andrea Louie, May 30, 2021.
11 Pamela Wang, Zoom interview by Andrea Louie, May 30, 2021.
12 Pamela Wang, Zoom interview by Andrea Louie, May 30, 2021.
13 Stephen Len, phone interview by Andrea Louie, May 9, 2021.
14 Stephen Len, phone interview by Andrea Louie, May 9, 2021.
15 Stephen Len, phone interview by Andrea Louie, May 9, 2021.
16 Stephen Len, phone interview by Andrea Louie, May 9, 2021.
17 Stephen Len, phone interview by Andrea Louie, May 9, 2021.
18 Stephen Len, phone interview by Andrea Louie, May 9, 2021.
19 Janine Pipitone, Zoom interview by Andrea Louie, April 6, 2021.
20 Roseanne Len, email correspondence with Andrea Louie, April 13, 2021.
21 Linda Fifield, Zoom interview by Andrea Louie, April 13, 2021.
22 Ilene Ball, Zoom interview by Andrea Louie, April 30, 2021.
23 Pamela Wang, Zoom interview by Andrea Louie, May 30, 2021.
24 Leo Guen, Zoom interview by Andrea Louie, April 5, 2021.
25 Siu and Tchen, *The Chinese Laundryman*.

BIBLIOGRAPHY

"Ambition and Pride Keynotes of Character Local Chinese Family: Professional Careers Planned for Chinese Father of Eight." *Portland Press Herald*, May 26, 1940.

American Mothers. "1952 National Mother of the Year." May 30, 2024. www.americanmothers.org.

American Mothers. "About Us." Accessed October 27, 2024. www.americanmothers.org.

Bethune, Mary McLeod. "The Trend of Thinking Is Forward but Positive Action Must Support It." *New York Age*, May 24, 1952.

Brand, David. "Education: The New Whiz Kids." *Time*, August 31, 1987. https://time.com.

Brooks, Charlotte. *Between Mao and McCarthy: Chinese American Politics in the Cold War Years*. University of Chicago Press, 2015.

Burnett, Jeff. Map of Guangdong Province. Map information based upon: "Third-level Administrative Divisions, China, 2015," created by Robert J. Hijmans. University of California, Berkeley, Museum of Vertebrate Zoology, 2015. https://purl.stanford.edu.

Chan, Sucheng. "Against All Odds: Chinese Female Migration and Family Formation on American Soil During the Early 20th Century." In *Chinese American Transnationalism: The Flow of People, Resources, and Ideas Between China and America during the Exclusion Era*, edited by Sucheng Chan. Temple University Press, 2006.

Cheng, Cindy I-Fen. *Citizens of Asian America: Democracy and Race During the Cold War*. New York University Press, 2013.

Cheng, Cindy I-Fen. "Out of Chinatown and into the Suburbs: Chinese Americans and the Politics of Cultural Citizenship in Early Cold War America." *American Quarterly* 58, no. 3 (2006): 1067–90. https://doi.org/10.1353/aq.2007.0003.

Chin, Margaret M. *Stuck: Why Asian Americans Don't Reach the Top of the Corporate Ladder*. New York University Press, 2020.

"China-Born Woman Named 'American Mother of 1952.'" *Dallas Morning News*, May 5, 1952.

"Chinese Family Joins Appeal for Success of Chest Drive." *Portland Evening Express*, October 10, 1944.

"Chinese Launderer 1952 Ideal Mother: Portland Widow Worked, Raised 8." *Portland Press Herald*, May 4, 1952.

"Chinese Laundry Woman Maine's Mother of the Year." *New York Times*, April 8, 1952.

Chua, Amy. *The Battle Hymn of the Tiger Mother*. Penguin, 2011.

Chung, Angie. *Saving Face: The Emotional Costs of the Asian Immigrant Family Myth*. Rutgers University Press, 2016.

Clifford, James. "Introduction: Partial Truths." In *Writing Culture: The Poetics and Politics of Ethnography*, edited by James Clifford and George E. Marcus. 25th anniversary ed. University of California Press, 2010.

Corby, Rhiannon. "Mother's Mother: The Story of an American Mother of the Year." Web documentary. Salt Story Archive, 2014. www.saltstoryarchive.com.

Counter Cultures Network. "What Is the Counter Cultures Network?" 2013. http://countercultures.net.

Craig, May. "Chinese US Officials Honor Mrs. Goon at Capitol Luncheon." *New York Times*, May 14, 1952.

Craig, May. "Mother of Year Meets First Lady: Mrs. Goon Children Tour White House." *Portland Press Herald*, May 13, 1952.

Craig, May. "Mrs. Goon in Washington." *Portland Press Herald*, May 20, 1952.

Craig, May. "We're Proud of Our Mother." *Portland Press Herald*, May 10, 1952.

"Declaration of the Chinese Hand Laundry Alliance." In *Chinese American Voices: From the Gold Rush to the Present*, edited by Judy Yung, Gordon H. Chang, and Him Mark Lai. University of California Press, 2006.

Deng Hui Fang. Letter to Toy Len Goon. May 16, 1952. Private collection of Amy Guen.

Dhingra, Pawan. *Hyper Education: Why Good Schools, Good Grades, and Good Behavior Are Not Enough*. New York University Press, 2020.

Dhingra, Pawan. *Life Behind the Lobby: Indian American Motel Owners and the American Dream*. Stanford University Press, 2012.

Ebrey, Patricia Buckley. Introduction to *Marriage and Inequality in Chinese Society*, edited by Rubie S. Watson and Patricia Buckley Ebrey. University of California Press, 1991.

Field, Jacqueline. "Mud Silk and the Chinese Laundress: From the South China Silk Industry to Mud Silk Suits in Maine." *Textile History* 45, no. 2 (2014): 234–60. https://doi.org/10.1179/0040496914Z.00000000054.

Fifield, Doug, Linda Fifield, Amy Guen, Edward Guen, and Doris Wong. "The Goon Family Story." In *Book of Memories: The Family of Dogan and Toy Len Goon*. Privately published, 2003.

Fitzgerald, Stephen. *China and the Overseas Chinese: A Study of Peking's Changing Policy: 1949–1970*. Cambridge University Press, 1980.

Fong, Vanessa. *Paradise Redefined: Transnational Chinese Students and the Quest for Flexible Citizenship in the Developed World*. Stanford University Press, 2011. https://doi.org/10.1515/9780804781756.

"Former G-Man Regrets Missing Mother of the Year on Arrival in Portland for Lecture Series." *Portland Press Herald*, May 9, 1952.

Freedman, Maurice. *Chinese Lineage and Society: Fukien and Kwangtung*. Athlone Press; Humanities Press, 1971.

Geertz, Clifford. "Thick Description: Toward an Interpretive Theory of Culture." In *The Interpretation of Cultures: Selected Essays*. Basic Books, 1973.

Goffman, Erving. *The Presentation of Self in Everyday Life*. Doubleday, 1990.

"Goon Do Gun, Chinaman, Was Charged with Being Illegally in This Country." *Portland Evening Express*, August 1917.

Goon, Toy Len. Interview by Andrea Louie, Janet Louie, and Doris Wong. Translated by Genevieve Leung. Swampscott, MA, 1992.

Guen, Amy Chin. "The Toy Len Goon Story." Unpublished, 2019.

Guen, Tim. "Re-branding a Culture." LinkedIn, February 12, 2021. www.linkedin.com.

Gupta, Akhil, and James Ferguson. "Beyond 'Culture': Space, Identity, and the Politics of Difference." In *Culture, Power, Place: Explorations in Critical Anthropology*, edited by Akhil Gupta and James Ferguson. Duke University Press, 1997. https://doi.org/10.2307/j.ctv11vc7nf.

Hall, Stuart. "Old and New Identities, Old and New Ethnicities." In *Culture, Globalization and the World-System: Contemporary Conditions for the Representation of Identity*, edited by Anthony D. King. Department of Art and Art History, State University of New York at Binghamton, 1991.

Hom, Marlon K. *Songs of Gold Mountain: Cantonese Rhymes from San Francisco Chinatown*. University of California Press, 1987.

Hong, Jane H. *Opening the Gates to Asia: A Transpacific History of How America Repealed Asian Exclusion*. University of North Carolina Press, 2019.

Hsu, Madeline Y. "The Cold War." In *The Oxford Handbook of Asian American History*, edited by David Yoo and Eichiro Azuma. Oxford University Press, 2016. https://doi.org/10.1525/phr.2012.81.3.432.

Hsu, Madeline Y. *Dreaming of Gold, Dreaming of Home: Transnationalism and Migration Between the United States and South China, 1882–1943*. Stanford University Press, 2000.

Hsu, Madeline Y. *The Good Immigrants: How the Yellow Peril Became the Model Minority*. Princeton University Press, 2015.

Hsu, Madeline Y. "Qiaokan and the Transnational Community of Taishan County, Guangdong, 1882–1943." *China Review* 4, no. 1 (2004): 123–44.

Huang, Shu-min. *The Spiral Road: Change in a Chinese Village Through the Eyes of a Communist Party Leader*. Westview, 1989.

"Immigrant Named Mother of the Year; Born in China." Press clipping, May 5, 1952. Maine Historical Society. www.mainememory.net.

"Japs Offer Surrender if Hirohito Spared." Maine Historical Society, Collection 2080, "Chinese Americans in Maine," Box 4: Genealogies and Genealogical Information.

Johnson, Kay Ann. *China's Hidden Children: Abandonment, Adoption, and the Human Costs of the One-Child Policy*. University of Chicago Press, 2016.

Kanes, Candace. "Toy Len Goon: Mother of the Year." Maine Memory Network, n.d. Accessed November 1, 2024. www.mainememory.net.

Kennedy, Kate. *Maine's Remarkable Women: Daughters, Wives, Sisters, and Mothers Who Shaped History*. Globe Pequot, 2016.

Kertzer, David Israel. *Ritual, Politics, and Power*. Yale University Press, 1988.

Klein, Christina. *Cold War Orientalism: Asia in the Middlebrow Imagination, 1945–1961.* University of California Press, 2003.

Kulp, Daniel Harrison. *Country Life in South China: The Sociology of Familism.* Bureau of Publications, Teachers College, Columbia University, 1925.

Lai, Him Mark. "Chinese Organizations in America Based on Locality of Origin and/or Dialect-Group Affiliation, 1940s–1990s." *Chinese America: History and Perspectives,* January 1995, 19–92. https://himmarklai.org.

Lai, Him Mark. "Historical Development of the Chinese Consolidated Benevolent Association/Huiguan System." *Chinese America: History and Perspectives* 1 (1987): 13.

Lai, Him Mark, Genny Lim, and Judy Yung. *Island: Poetry and History of Chinese Immigrants on Angel Island, 1910–1940.* University of Washington Press, 1991.

Lee, Erika. *At America's Gates: Chinese Immigration During the Exclusion Era, 1882–1943.* University of North Carolina Press, 2003.

Lee, Erika, and Judy Yung. *Angel Island: Immigrant Gateway to America.* Oxford University Press, 2010.

Lee, Jennifer, and Min Zhou. *The Asian American Achievement Paradox.* Russell Sage, 2015.

Lee, Robert G. *Orientals: Asian Americans in Popular Culture.* Temple University Press, 1999.

Lee-Loy, Anne-Marie. "Counter Culture Network: Behind the Chinese Shopkeeping Diaspora." Conference lecture, Ryerson University, July 2011.

Levitt, Peggy, and Nina Schiller. "Conceptualizing Simultaneity: A Transnational Social Field Perspective on Society." *International Migration Review* 38, no. 3 (2004): 1002–39. https://doi.org/10.1111/j.1747-7379.2004.tb00227.x.

Lew-Williams, Beth. "Paper Lives of Chinese Migrants and the History of the Undocumented." *Modern American History* 4, no. 2 (2021): 109–30. https://doi.org/10.1017/mah.2021.9.

Libby, Gary W. "Historical Notes on Some of Maine's Chinese Hand-Laundries and Laundrymen." *Chinese America: History and Perspectives* (2016): 47–57.

Libby, Gary W. "Marriage and Family Life Among Maine's Earliest Chinese Residents." *Chinese America: History and Perspectives* (2017): 81. Gale Academic OneFile, https://link.gale.com.

Light, Ivan Hubert, and Steven J. Gold. *Ethnic Economies.* Academic, 2000.

Lo, Shauna. "Chinese Laundries in Massachusetts: An Oral History Project." *Institute for Asian American Studies Publications* 49 (2023). https://scholarworks.umb.edu.

Long Bow Group. *Small Happiness: Women of a Chinese Village.* Produced and directed by Carma Hinton and Richard Gordon. New York: New Day Films; dist. by Modern Educational Video Network, 1992.

Louie, Andrea. *Chineseness Across Borders: Renegotiating Chinese Identities in China and the United States.* Duke University Press, 2004.

Louie, Andrea. *How Chinese Are You? Adopted Chinese Youth and Their Families Negotiate Identity and Culture.* New York University Press, 2015.

Lowe, Lisa. "Heterogeneity, Hybridity, Multiplicity: Marking Asian American Differences." *Diaspora: A Journal of Transnational Studies* 1, no. 1 (1991): 24–44. https://doi.org/10.1353/dsp.1991.0014.

Maine Historical Society. "The Peopling of Maine." N.d. Accessed October 6, 2024. www.mainememory.net.

Malkki, Liisa. "National Geographic: The Rooting of Peoples and the Territorialization of National Identity Among Scholars and Refugees." *Cultural Anthropology* 1, no. 7 (1992): 24–44.

Massey, Doreen. *Space, Place, and Gender.* University of Minnesota Press, 1994. http://www.jstor.org/stable/10.5749/j.cttttw2z.

May, Elaine Tyler. *Homeward Bound: American Families in the Cold War Era.* Basic Books, 1988.

Mckeown, Adam. "Transnational Chinese Families and Chinese Exclusion, 1875–1943." *Journal of American Ethnic History* 18, no. 2 (1999): 73–110.

Meyerowitz, Joanne. *Not June Cleaver: Women and Gender in Postwar America, 1945–1960.* Temple University Press, 1994.

Miles, Tiya. *Ties That Bind: The Story of an Afro-Cherokee Family in Slavery and Freedom.* University of California Press, 2016.

Miller, Rachel. "Twenty Nationalities, but All Americans." Maine Memory Network, n.d. Accessed November 8, 2024. www.mainememory.net.

"Mrs. Goon Overwhelmed, Happy as She Prepares for American Mother Ceremonies in New York City." *Portland Press Herald*, May 6, 1952.

Murphy, Edward D. "Celebrated Chinese American Mom to Be Honored Posthumously in Portland." *Portland Press Herald*, September 30, 2021. www.pressherald.com.

New York Historical Society Museum and Library. "Toy Len Goon." In *Chinese American: Exclusion/Inclusion* exhibit, September 26, 2014–April 19, 2015. https://chineseamerican.nyhistory.org.

Ngai, Mae M. *Impossible Subjects: Illegal Aliens and the Making of Modern America.* Princeton University Press, 2004.

Ninh, erin Khuê. "The Model Minority: Asian American Immigrant Families and Intimate Harm." *Kalfou* 1, no. 2 (2014): 168–73.

Ninh, erin Khuê. *Passing for Perfect: College Impostors and Other Model Minorities.* Temple University Press, 2021.

Ohnuki-Tierney, Emiko. "'Native' Anthropologists." *American Ethnologist* 11, no. 3 (1984): 584–86.

Omi, Michael, and Howard Winant. *Racial Formation in the United States.* 3rd ed. Routledge/Taylor & Francis Group, 2015.

Ong, Aihwa. *Flexible Citizenship: The Cultural Logics of Transnationality.* Duke University Press, 1999.

Parreñas, Rhacel Salazar. *Servants of Globalization: Migration and Domestic Work.* 2nd ed. Stanford University Press, 2015.

Pegler-Gordon, Anna. *In Sight of America: Photography and the Development of US Immigration Policy*. University of California Press, 2009.

Petersen, William. "Success Story, Japanese American Style." *New York Times*, January 9, 1966.

Poling, Daniel, and Lillian Poling. *Mothers of Men: A Twenty-Five Year History of the American Mothers of the Year, 1935–1959*. 2nd ed. V. K. Polk, 1967.

Pomeroy, Jeannette. "How to Prepare Lobster Dish Using Recipe of No. 1 Mother." *Portland Evening Express*, May 6, 1952.

"Portland Service Clubs, Merchants Ready Party for Mrs. Goon Sunday." *Portland Press Herald*, June 3, 1952.

Potter, Sulamith Heins, and Jack Potter. *China's Peasants: The Anthropology of a Revolution*. Cambridge University Press, 1990.

Said, Edward W. *Orientalism*. Penguin Classics, 2003.

Salyer, Lucy E. *Laws Harsh as Tigers: Chinese Immigrants and the Shaping of Modern Immigration Law*. University of North Carolina Press, 1995.

Shah, Nayan. *Contagious Divides: Epidemics and Race in San Francisco's Chinatown*. University of California Press, 2001. https://doi.org/10.2307/j.ctv1gwqmp3.

Shibusawa, Naoko. *America's Geisha Alley: Reimagining the Japanese Enemy*. Harvard University Press, 2010.

Siu, Lok C. D. *Memories of a Future Home: Diasporic Citizenship of Chinese in Panama*. Stanford University Press, 2005.

Siu, Paul C. P., and Jack Kuo Wei Tchen. *The Chinese Laundryman: A Study of Social Isolation*. New York University Press, 1988.

Smart, Alan, and Jinn-Yuh Hsu. "The Chinese Diaspora, Foreign Investment and Economic Development in China." *Review of International Affairs* 3, no. 4 (2004): 544–66.

Soule, Clara. Americanization pageant program. Portland, ME, 1927. Accessed October 28, 2024. www.mainememory.net.

Spallholz, Walter L. Letter to Toy Len Goon. May 6, 1952. From "The Goon Family Story" in *Book of Memories*, 2003.

Tien, Wen-hao, Shauna Lo, Eugenio Menegon, Richard Chin, Raymond Chin, and Walter Wong. "Laundry Rock: Histories of Laundries of Boston's Chinatown." Zoom panel at the Pao Arts Center, Boston, March 13, 2021.

To, Wing-Kai, and Chinese Historical Society of New England. *Chinese in Boston, 1870–1965*. Arcadia, 2008.

Tsien, Jean, executive producer. *Asian Americans*. Episode 3, "Good Americans." Featuring Daniel Dae Kim. Aired May 20, 2020. PBS.

Tu, Weiming. *The Living Tree: The Changing Meaning of Being Chinese Today*. Stanford University Press, 1994.

United States v. Goon Do Gun. Hon. Arthur Chapman presiding. October 26, 1917. National Archives and Records Administration, Waltham, MA. Immigration file 2500/3557.

US Census Bureau. 1920 United States Census. Portland Ward 8, Cumberland, Maine, T625_640, page 19B, Enumeration District 54. Record Group 29.

US Department of Labor Immigration Service. "In re Goon Do Gun Alleged unlawful resident interview, statement by Goon Do Gun." 1917. Goon Do Gun Immigration Service No. 2513/126. From file 2500/3557, Waltham, MA. Record Group 85.

US Veterans Administration. Memorandum Form 3229a. From the Solicitor to Major Clark, Assistant Administrator, Subject Goon, Dogan C-2, 825, 743, October 27, 1939.

US Veterans Administration. Memorandum. Hum Foon Wahdo, C02, 028, 511 (35 Sol. 194), November 17, 1937.

Warikoo, Natasha Kumar. *Race at the Top: Asian Americans and Whites in Pursuit of the American Dream in Suburban Schools*. University of Chicago Press, 2022.

Watson, James L. "Chinese Kinship Reconsidered: Anthropological Perspectives on Historical Research." *China Quarterly* 92 (1982): 589–622. https://doi.org/10.1017/S0305741000000965.

Watson, James L. *Emigration and the Chinese Lineage: The Mans in Hong Kong and London*. University of California Press, 1975.

"'Welcome' Sign Is Hung Out for Mrs. Goon Party." *Portland Herald Express*, June 6, 1952.

"We're Proud of Our Mother." Editorial. *Boston Herald*, May 26, 1952.

Wilson, John S. Letter to Henry J. Skeffington. August 22, 1917. File 2513–126C, Department of Justice, Office of the United States Marshal, District of Maine, Portland, ME.

Wolf, Arthur P. "Adopt a Daughter-in-Law, Marry a Sister: A Chinese Solution to the Problem of the Incest Taboo." *American Anthropologist*, n.s., 70, no. 5 (1968): 864–74.

Wolf, Arthur P., and Chieh-shan Huang. *Marriage and Adoption in China, 1845–1945*. Stanford University Press, 1980.

Wong, K. Scott. *Americans First: Chinese Americans and the Second World War*. Harvard University Press, 2005.

Woon, Yuen-fong. "Social Change and Continuity in South China: Overseas Chinese and the Guan Lineage of Kaiping County, 1949–87." *China Quarterly* 118 (1989): 324–44.

Wu, Ellen. "America's Chinese: Anti-Communism, Citizenship, and Cultural Diplomacy During the Cold War." *Pacific Historical Review* 77, no. 3 (2008): 391–422.

Wu, Ellen. *The Color of Success: Asian Americans and the Origins of the Model Minority*. Princeton University Press, 2015.

Wu, Judy Tzu-Chun. *Dr. Mom Chung of the Fair-Haired Bastards: The Life of a Wartime Celebrity*. University of California Press, 2005.

Yeh, Chiou-Ling. "A Saga of Democracy: Toy Len Goon, American Mother of the Year, and the Cultural Cold War." *Pacific Historical Review* 81, no. 3 (2012): 432–61.

Yu, Henry. *Thinking Orientals: Migration, Contact, and Exoticism in Modern America*. Oxford University Press, 2001.

Yu, Renqiu. *To Save China, to Save Ourselves: The Chinese Hand Laundry Alliance of New York*. Temple University Press, 1992.
Yung, Judy. *Unbound Feet: A Social History of Chinese Women in San Francisco*. University of California Press, 1995.
Zhao, Xiaojian. *Remaking Chinese America: Immigration, Family, and Community, 1940–1965*. Rutgers University Press, 2002.

INDEX

Italicized page references indicate Figures

ABOUT THE AUTHOR

Andrea Louie is Professor of Anthropology at Michigan State University, where she founded the Asian Pacific American Studies Program. She is the author of *Chineseness Across Borders: Renegotiating Chinese Identities in China and the United States* and *How Chinese Are You? Adopted Chinese Youth and Their Families Negotiate Identity and Culture.*